W9-CIM-055

Federal Estate and Gift Taxes

Studies of Government Finance

TITLES PUBLISHED

Federal Fiscal Policy in the Postwar Recessions, by Wilfred Lewis, Jr.

Federal Tax Treatment of State and Local Securities, by David J. Ott and Allan H. Meltzer.

Federal Tax Treatment of Income from Oil and Gas, by Stephen L. McDonald.

Federal Tax Treatment of the Family, by Harold M. Groves.

The Role of Direct and Indirect Taxes in the Federal Revenue System, John F. Due, Editor. A Report of the National Bureau of Economic Research and the Brookings Institution (Princeton University Press).

The Individual Income Tax, by Richard Goode.

Federal Tax Treatment of Foreign Income, by Lawrence B. Krause and Kenneth W. Dam.

Measuring Benefits of Government Investments, Robert Dorfman, Editor.

Federal Budget Policy, by David J. Ott and Attiat F. Ott.

Financing State and Local Governments, by James A. Maxwell.

Essays in Fiscal Federalism, Richard A. Musgrave, Editor.

Economics of the Property Tax, by Dick Netzer.

A Capital Budget Statement for the U.S. Government, by Maynard S. Comiez.

Foreign Tax Policies and Economic Growth, E. Gordon Keith, Editor. A Report of the National Bureau of Economic Research and the Brookings Institution (Columbia University Press).

Defense Purchases and Regional Growth, by Roger E. Bolton.

Federal Budget Projections, by Gerhard Colm and Peter Wagner. A Report of the National Planning Association and the Brookings Institution.

Corporate Dividend Policy, by John A. Brittain.

Federal Estate and Gift Taxes, by Carl S. Shoup.

Federal Estate and Gift Taxes

CARL S. SHOUP

A background paper prepared for a conference of experts held April 21-22, 1965, together with a summary of the conference discussion

Studies of Government Finance

THE BROOKINGS INSTITUTION

WASHINGTON, D.C.

THE BROOKINGS INSTITUTION
1775 Massachusetts Avenue, N. W., Washington, D. C.

Published May 1966

Library of Congress Catalogue Card Number 66-20016

THE BROOKINGS INSTITUTION is an independent organization devoted to nonpartisan research, education, and publication in economics, government, foreign policy, and the social sciences generally. Its principal purposes are to aid in the development of sound public policies and to promote public understanding of issues of national importance.

The Institution was founded December 8, 1927, to merge the activities of the Institute for Government Research, founded in 1916, the Institute of Economics, founded in 1922, and the Robert Brookings Graduate School of Economics and Government, founded in 1924.

The general administration of the Institution is the responsibility of a self-perpetuating Board of Trustees. The trustees are likewise charged with maintaining the independence of the staff and fostering the most favorable conditions for creative research and education. The immediate direction of the policies, program, and staff of the Institution is vested in the President, assisted by the division directors and an advisory council, chosen from the professional staff of the Institution.

In publishing a study, the Institution presents it as a competent treatment of a subject worthy of public consideration. The interpretations and conclusions in such publications are those of the author or authors and do not purport to represent the views of the other staff members, officers, or trustees of the Brookings Institution.

Foreword

FEDERAL ESTATE AND GIFT TAXES in the United States have remained substantially unchanged since 1948. Although their yield has increased in recent years, they provide only about 2.5 percent of federal cash receipts. These taxes are nevertheless important components of the nation's progressive tax system. To clarify the issues in estate and gift taxation, a conference was held at the Brookings Institution on April 21 and 22, 1965, where a group of experts reviewed the major controversial issues, analyzed the provisions of the present law, and clarified differences of opinion on this part of the tax system.

This volume contains the background study and a summary of the conference of experts, both prepared by Carl S. Shoup of Columbia University. The appendix materials were prepared under the auspices of the Brookings Institution by his associates and students in a research project on estate and gift taxation at Columbia University.

In addition to this volume, the following contributions also grew out of the work of the Columbia University project: (1) *Estate and Gift Taxation: A Comparative Study* (Australia, Canada, Great Britain, and the United States), by G. S. A. Wheatcroft and associates at the London School of Economics and Political Science (London: Street and Maxwell, 1965), parts of which appeared earlier in the *British Tax Review;* (2) *Trusts and Estate Taxation,* by Gerald R. Jantscher, to be published in 1966 by Brookings; and (3) a master's thesis on "The Marital Deduction," by Robert Freedman (Columbia University, 1963).

Richard M. Bird, associated with the project from July 1963 to September 1964, assisted in the formulation of much of the research program and in the preparation of the manuscript. The author is also indebted to W. Douglas Kilbourn, Jr., for information and suggestions. Helpful comments on earlier drafts of the text and appendixes were received from Boris I. Bittker, Richard M. Bird, Seymour Fiekowsky, C. Lowell Harriss, Gerald R. Jantscher, Joseph A. Pechman, Alan N. Polasky, Richard C. Pugh, and William Vickrey. Robert Goldfarb, Gerald Jantscher, Dale S. Mayer, Donald McLeod, Krishan Saini, Jeffrey Schaefer, and Stuart Sieger provided research assistance. Members of the reading committee, consisting of James Casner, Robert Lampman, and Stanley S. Surrey, also made numerous helpful suggestions.

Virginia C. Haaga edited the manuscript and prepared the index. Jane Levandowsky and Marcia Casais served as secretaries to the project. Typing and other services were rendered by John S. Erthein, Peter G. Sack, and Carla Stea.

The conference was part of a special program of research and education on taxation and public expenditures, supervised by the National Committee on Government Finance and financed by a special grant from the Ford Foundation.

The views expressed in this book are those of the authors and are not presented as the views of the National Committee on Government Finance or its Advisory Committee, or the staff members, officers, or trustees of the Brookings Institution, or the Ford Foundation.

Robert D. Calkins
President

January 1966
Washington, D.C.

Studies of Government Finance

Studies of Government Finance is a special program of research and education in taxation and government expenditures at the federal, state, and local levels. These studies are under the supervision of the National Committee on Government Finance appointed by the trustees of the Brookings Institution, and are supported by a special grant from the Ford Foundation.

MEMBERS OF THE ADVISORY COMMITTEE

Contents

Text Tables

Appendix Tables

CHAPTER I

Introduction

FEDERAL ESTATE AND gift taxes pose complex legal, economic, and social problems, although they yield only about $3 billion a year, some 2 percent of federal tax receipts. This yield is not much more than the revenue from the 8-cent-a-package tax on cigarettes. An analogy may be drawn to the progressive-rate portion of the personal income tax, which has been supplying only about 7 percent of total federal tax revenues.[1] A wealth of analysis has been lavished on administrative and economic problems of the income tax that could be disregarded if it were not for the progressive rates.

The problems to be considered date from 1916, the year the present federal estate tax was imposed, but they became acute only in the 1930's, when rates were raised well above even the temporary peak during World War I, and when the gift tax was reenacted, this time to stay, in contrast to its brief appearance in the years 1924-26.[2] The earlier ventures of the federal government into

[1] The total individual income tax base for 1961 was $181.8 billion, and the total individual income tax before credits was $42.7 billion (U.S. Treasury Department, Internal Revenue Service, *Statistics of Income, 1961,* Individual Income Tax Returns, p. 11). At a flat 20 percent rate the tax would have been $36.4 billion. The balance, $6.3 billion, is 15 percent of the total individual income tax.

[2] For a perceptive summary of the history of the federal estate and gift taxes, see Louis Eisenstein, "The Rise and Decline of the Estate Tax," in U.S. Congress,

TABLE I–1. Federal Estate Tax Rate Schedule, 1942 to Date

Amount of taxable estate (In dollars)[a]				Tax on amount at lower boundary of bracket[b] (In dollars)	Bracket rate (In percent)
	0	to	5,000	0	3
Over:	5,000	to	10,000	150	7
	10,000	to	20,000	500	11
	20,000	to	30,000	1,600	14
	30,000	to	40,000	3,000	18
	40,000	to	50,000	4,800	22
	50,000	to	60,000	7,000	25
	60,000	to	100,000	9,500	28
	100,000	to	250,000	20,700	30
	250,000	to	500,000	65,700	32
	500,000	to	750,000	145,700	35
	750,000	to	1,000,000	233,200	37
	1,000,000	to	1,250,000	325,700	39
	1,250,000	to	1,500,000	423,200	42
	1,500,000	to	2,000,000	528,200	45
	2,000,000	to	2,500,000	753,200	49
	2,500,000	to	3,000,000	998,200	53
	3,000,000	to	3,500,000	1,263,200	56
	3,500,000	to	4,000,000	1,543,200	59
	4,000,000	to	5,000,000	1,838,200	63
	5,000,000	to	6,000,000	2,468,200	67
	6,000,000	to	7,000,000	3,138,200	70
	7,000,000	to	8,000,000	3,838,200	73
	8,000,000	to	10,000,000	4,568,200	76
	10,000,000			6,088,200	77

Source: Internal Revenue Code of 1954, as amended.
[a] Total gross estate less deductions and an exemption of $60,000.
[b] Without allowance for credit for gift tax, for death taxes paid to the states, for foreign death taxes, or for taxes on transfers from prior decedents.

death taxation (1797-1802, 1862-1870, and 1898-1902) apparently had little influence on the form of the 1916 tax.

The World War I rates were modest compared with the present schedule, which reaches 77 percent (see Table I-1). The World

Joint Committee on the Economic Report, *Federal Tax Policy for Economic Growth and Stability* (Nov. 9, 1955), pp. 820-31. For a historical tabulation of rate schedules, exemptions, etc., see U.S. Internal Revenue Service, *Statistics of Income, 1949*, Part 1, pp. 456 ff. See also Harvard University, International Program in Taxation, *World Tax Series: Taxation in the United States* (Commerce Clearing House, 1963), pp. 182-84, and William J. Shultz, *The Taxation of Inheritance* (Houghton Mifflin, 1926).

War I schedule went from 2 percent on the first $50,000 of taxable estate to 25 percent on the portion in excess of $10 million. But even these rates were high compared with the initial rates in the 1916 law, which ranged from 1 percent on the first $50,000 to 10 percent on the part in excess of $5 million. The exemption, however, was comparable in dollars to today's exemption: $50,000 as against the present $60,000. In real terms, after deflating for the rise in prices since 1916, comparability disappears, both for the rate-scale brackets and for the exemption.[3]

In the 1920's the estate tax barely escaped being eliminated from the federal system and left to the states, which for the most part had levied light death taxes of one sort or another for some decades. The states were placated by the introduction of a credit against the federal tax. The credit was first limited to 25 percent of the federal tax (1924); in 1926 the limit was raised to 80 percent. In the 1930's, the estate tax rates were raised along with income tax rates. The top bracket rate, which had been reduced to 20 percent by the 1926 law, was raised to 45 percent in 1932, 60 percent in 1934, and 70 percent (on the portion over $50 million) in 1935. The exemption was reduced from $100,000 (1926) to $50,000 (1932), then to $40,000 (1935). The credit for state taxes was kept at the same absolute levels by retaining the formula of the Revenue Act of 1926, that is, a maximum credit equal to 80 percent of the tax as computed under the 1926 Act rates.

World War II brought little change in the estate tax, except in community property states.[4] The contrast with the income tax is striking. A "defense tax" (10 percent of the tax after application of credits) was imposed on estates of individuals who died within the period June 26, 1940 through September 20, 1941. In 1941 a rate scale was adopted that is still in effect. To be sure, it is not the same in real terms because of the rise in prices. For all estates except those that were already well above the 77 percent dividing line in 1941, the effective rate on an estate unchanged in real terms (that is, after adjustment by a price index) is higher now than it was in 1941. On the other hand, estates containing non-

[3] See Chap. VI, below.

[4] The short-lived (1942-48) attempt to disregard community property precepts is discussed in the section on "Interspousal Transfers" in Chapter IV below.

TABLE I-2. Federal Tax Receipts: Total, Estate Tax, and Gift Tax, 1917–64
(Dollar amounts in millions)

Fiscal year	*Total federal tax receipts*[a]	*Estate tax*	*Gift tax*	*Estate plus gift tax*	*Estate plus gift tax as a percentage of total federal tax receipts*
1917	$1,035.3	$6.1		$6.1	0.6
1918	3,366.0	47.5		47.5	1.4
1919	4,499.7	82.0		82.0	1.8
1920	5,727.9	103.6		103.6	1.8
1921	4,905.0	154.0		154.0	3.1
1922	3,569.7	139.4		139.4	3.9
1923	3,186.4	126.7		126.7	4.0
1924	3,340.8	103.0		103.0	3.1
1925	3,136.7	101.4	$7.5	108.9	3.5
1926	3,417.1	116.0	3.2	119.2	3.5
1927	3,474.9	100.3		100.3	2.9
1928	3,364.0	60.1		60.1	1.8
1929	3,540.3	61.9		61.9	1.7
1930	3,626.3	64.8		64.8	1.8
1931	2,808.1	48.1		48.1	1.7
1932	1,888.8	47.4		47.4	2.5
1933	1,855.2	29.7	4.6	34.3	1.8
1934	2,954.1	104.0	9.2	113.2	3.8
1935	3,619.0	140.4	71.7	212.1	5.9
1936	3,899.7	218.8	160.1	378.9	9.7
1937	5,083.5	281.6	23.9	305.5	6.0
1938	6,033.6	382.2	34.7	416.9	6.9
1939	5,480.1	332.3	28.4	360.7	6.6
1940	5,651.7	330.9	29.2	360.1	6.4
1941	7,753.5	355.2	51.9	407.1	5.3
1942	12,382.1	340.3	92.2	432.5	3.5
1943	22,468.3	414.5	33.0	447.5	2.0
1944	42,116.2	473.5	37.7	511.2	1.2
1945	44,256.8	596.1	46.9	643.0	1.5
1946	40,745.8	629.9	47.2	677.1	1.7
1947	39,873.5	708.8	70.5	779.3	2.0
1948	39,998.9	822.4	77.0	899.4	2.2
1949	37,849.3	735.8	60.8	796.6	2.1
1950	37,716.6	657.4	48.8	706.2	1.9
1951	49,631.1	638.5	91.2	729.7	1.5
1952	63,892.6	750.6	82.6	833.2	1.3
1953	67,666.6	784.6	106.7	891.3	1.3

TABLE I-2 (continued)

Fiscal year	Total federal tax receipts[a]	Estate tax	Gift tax	Estate plus gift tax	Estate plus gift tax as a percentage of total federal tax receipts
1954	67,484.4	863.3	71.8	935.1	1.4
1955	63,469.1	848.5[b]	87.8	936.3	1.5
1956	72,130.0	1,053.9[b]	117.4	1,171.3	1.6
1957	77,009.1	1,253.1	124.9	1,378.0	1.8
1958	76,345.3	1,277.1	133.9	1,411.0	1.8
1959	75,813.0	1,235.8	117.2	1,353.0	1.8
1960	87,853.0	1,439.3	187.1	1,626.4	1.9
1961	89,432.8	1,745.5	170.9	1,916.4	2.1
1962	94,346.4	1,796.2	239.0	2,035.2	2.2
1963	100,594.5	1,971.6	215.8	2,187.4	2.2
1964	106,396.4	2,111.0	305.3	2,416.3	2.3

Source: *Annual Report of the Secretary of the Treasury on the State of the Finances*, various years.

[a] Includes customs duties and trust fund taxes; tax refunds subtracted.

[b] Advance payments of estate and gift taxes were reported in combined amount only and were included in estate tax. The total amount of such advance payments for 1956 and 1955 was $19.4 million and $16.1 million, respectively.

community property are now better off under this rate scale than in 1941 to the extent of the marital deduction introduced in 1948. The $40,000 exemption was raised to $60,000 in 1942, but only because at the same time a special life insurance exclusion of $40,000 was eliminated. In general, the stability of the nominal rate scale and the exemption level of the estate tax over two and a half decades is without parallel in any significant federal, state, or local tax in the same period, except indeed for the companion tax on lifetime gifts.

The gift tax, introduced in 1932, with rates three-fourths those of the estate tax, has also remained unaltered since 1942 as to rate scale, lifetime exemption ($30,000), and the annual exclusion per donee ($3,000). As with the estate tax, the treatment accorded married couples for noncommunity property has been altered in their favor.

The relative revenue position of the federal estate and gift taxes has been increasing modestly in the past decade, but is still below that of the 1920's and well below that of the 1930's. (See Table I-2.)

Meanwhile the states, through their inheritance and estate taxes, have been taking advantage of the federal credit.[5] In many instances the state taxes exceed that credit, even on large estates. Only Nevada refrains from a death tax. Twelve states impose gift taxes that have minor revenue significance. In fiscal 1963 the states obtained 2.4 percent of their tax revenues from death and gift taxes. (See Table I-3.) No local unit imposes a death tax or a gift tax. (New York City's abortive tax of the early 1930's has not been copied.)

In other countries the experience has been much the same. The estate tax, or its counterpart levied on heirs, the inheritance tax, is found in virtually every revenue system and almost universally supplies little revenue. Even in the United Kingdom, the estate tax (there is no gift tax) provides only 4.2 percent of national tax revenues.[6] But as in the United States, the tax ranks with the income tax in the complexity of the problems it raises.[7]

For the reader's convenience, certain historical tables are grouped at the end of this chapter, showing composition of estate for selected years (Table I-4), size distribution of number of estates (Table I-5), and value of gross estate (Table I-6).

The next five chapters deal with important structural problems in death and gift taxation.

Attention is first given to the question whether the gift tax should be integrated with the tax at death and, if so, whether integration should be in terms of all transfers made by a given transferor or all transfers received by a given donee (accessions tax).

Chapter III analyzes the use of trusts to skip transfer taxation for one or more generations. Chapters II and III both use data gathered by the Internal Revenue Service for the U.S. Treasury Department's special study of estate tax returns filed in 1957 and 1959.

[5] See Chap. VII below.

[6] In 1963-64 total tax revenue (including customs and excise revenue and motor vehicle duties) of the central government was £6.658 billion, of which £316 million, or 4.7 percent, came from the estate duty. *Report of the Commissioners of H.M. Inland Revenue for the Year Ended 31st March 1964* (London: HMSO, February 1965), pp. 4 and 5.

[7] See, for example, G. S. A. Wheatcroft, ed., *Estate and Gift Taxation, A Comparative Study* (London: Sweet and Maxwell, 1965).

TABLE I–3. State Tax Receipts: Total and Death and Gift Taxes, 1940–63
(Dollar amounts in millions)

Fiscal year	Total state tax receipts[a]	Death and gift taxes	Death and gift tax receipts as a percentage of total state tax receipts
1940	$4,157	$113	2.7
1941	4,507	118	2.6
1942	4,979	110	2.2
1943	5,094	109	2.1
1944	5,384	114	2.1
1945	5,561	132	2.4
1946	5,968	146	2.4
1947	6,690	164	2.5
1948	7,791	180	2.3
1949	8,349	176	2.1
1950	9,106	168	1.8
1951	10,416	196	1.9
1952	11,454	211	1.8
1953	12,103	222	1.8
1954	12,555	247	2.0
1955	12,922	249	1.9
1956	14,875	310	2.1
1957	16,250	338	2.1
1958	16,630	351	2.1
1959	17,675	347	2.0
1960	20,352	420	2.1
1961	21,568	501	2.3
1962	23,373	516	2.2
1963	25,288	595	2.4

Source: U. S. Bureau of the Census, *Compendium of State Government Finances in 1944, 1948, 1949, 1950, 1955–59, 1963.*
[a] Includes unemployment compensation insurance tax collections.

Certain other structural problems are covered in Chapter IV, including the treatment of interspousal transfers, transfers to children, transfers to charitable organizations, and the liquidity problem that might be encountered if the income tax law recognized capital gains and losses accrued at death and at gift.

Specific exemptions and tax rate schedules are discussed in Chapter V. Chapter VI deals with the relation of the federal transfer taxes to those of the states.

A broad view of some of the major economic effects of the death and gift taxes is given in Chapter VII. In Chapter VIII, the chief aims of transfer taxation are suggested and a tax structure proposed to implement these aims. For such a tax structure and, alternatively, for the existing tax structure if it is to be retained, recommendations are made covering each of the technical issues covered in Chapters II through VI.

Chapter IX contains a summary of the discussion at the conference of experts held at the Brookings Institution, April 21-22, 1965.

A series of appendixes provides certain technical information and analyses for those interested in exploring these problems more intensively.

TABLE I–4. Composition of Gross Estate of Resident Decedents,[a] 1922, 1929, and 1933, and of All Decedents, Selected Years, 1937–60

(Dollar amounts in millions)

Assumed[b] year of death	Real Estate		Bonds		Mortgages and Notes		Cash[c]		Stocks		Insurance		Other		Total[e]	
	Value	Per-cent	Value	Per-cent	Value	Per-cent	Value	Per-cent	Value	Per-cent	Value	Per-cent	Value	Per-cent	Value	Per-cent
1922	615.7	24.7	373.1	15.0	c	c	321.9	12.9	780.7	31.3	77.3	3.1	326.3	13.1	2,495.0	100.0
1929	563.9	13.7	583.4	14.2	c	c	396.0	9.6	1,959.9	47.7	128.6	3.1	476.8	11.6	4,108.6	100.0
1933	378.5	16.9	502.2	22.4	c	c	323.1	14.4	784.2	34.9	143.8	6.4	112.3	5.0	2,244.1	100.0
1937	464.4	14.8	610.5	19.4	c	c	429.7	13.7	1,273.7	40.6	164.0[d]	5.2	199.0	6.3	3,141.3	100.0
1944	520.0	15.2	621.6	18.1	123.3	3.6	330.2	9.6	1,357.1	39.5	238.0[d]	6.9	244.3	7.1	3,434.6	100.0
1949	1,007.6	20.5	653.7	13.3	191.5	3.9	524.3	10.7	1,772.4	36.1	356.6	7.3	408.5	8.3	4,914.6	100.0
1954	1,557.5	20.9	739.6	9.9	274.4	3.7	747.2	10.0	3,073.2	41.2	468.3	6.3	602.3	8.1	7,462.4	100.0
1958	2,509.2	21.5	1,015.1	8.7	414.9	3.6	1,152.0	9.9	4,984.9	42.8	651.9	5.6	920.1	7.9	11,648.1	100.0
1960	2,857.3	19.5	1,304.5	8.9	522.3	3.6	1,396.3	9.5	6,766.4	46.3	755.2	5.2	1,020.2	7.0	14,622.1	100.0

Source: U. S. Treasury Department, Internal Revenue Service, *Statistics of Income*, various years.

[a] Data were not available for these years for nonresident decedents for whom estate tax returns were filed.

[b] The year of death is assumed to be that immediately preceding the year of filing.

[c] For the years 1922–37, mortgages and notes are included in the cash column since data for those years could not be broken down.

[d] The 1937 and 1944 insurance figures represent gross insurance rather than taxable insurance; hence the figures in the total column in this table are greater than those reported by the Internal Revenue Service.

[e] Details may not add to totals due to rounding.

TABLE I–5. Number of Estate Tax Returns by Size of Net Estate, 1922, 1929, 1933 and by Size of Gross Estate, Selected Years, 1937–60

Size of Net Estate (thousands of dollars)	1922		1929		1933[a]	
	Number	Percent	Number	Percent	Number	Percent
0– 200			8,053	77.6	9,376	90.6
0– 250	12,970	91.7				
200– 400			1,025	9.9	450	4.3
250– 450	567	4.0				
400– 1,000			819	7.9	360	3.5
450– 1,000	414	2.9				
1,000– 5,000	188	1.3	441	4.3	161	1.6
5,000–10,000	10	0.1	29	0.2	4	0.0
10,000 and over	1	0.0	15	0.1	2	0.0
Total[b]	14,150	100.0	10,382	100.0	10,353	100.0

Size of Gross Estate (thousands of dollars)	1937		1944		1949		1954		1958		1960	
	Number	Percent	Number	Percent	Number	Percent	Number	Percent	Number	Percent	Number	Percent
0– 200	12,986	81.5	12,345	77.8	20,345	78.8	28,409	77.8	42,980	77.2	48,868	75.7
200– 500	2,046	12.8	2,482	15.6	4,065	15.8	6,021	16.5	9,322	16.7	11,420	17.7
500– 1,000	524	3.3	671	4.2	961	3.7	1,392	3.8	2,242	4.0	2,747	4.3
1,000– 5,000	337	2.1	344	2.2	420	1.6	670	1.8	1,056	1.9	1,399	2.2
5,000–10,000	28	0.2	26	0.2	19	0.1	37	0.1	57	0.1	65	0.1
10,000 and over	11	0.1	10	0.1	4	—[c]	11	—[c]	28	0.1	39	0.1
Total[b]	15,932	100.0	15,878	100.0	25,814	100.0	36,540	100.0	55,685	100.0	64,538	100.0

Source: U. S. Treasury Department, Internal Revenue Service, *Statistics of Income*, various years.
[a] For 1933, information is available for resident decedents only.
[b] Details may not add to totals due to rounding.
[c] Less than 0.05 percent.

TABLE I–6. Value of Gross Estate by Size of Net Estate, 1922, 1929, and 1933 and by Size of Gross Estate, Selected Years, 1937–60

(Value amounts in millions of dollars)

Size of Net Estate (thousands of dollars)	1922		1929		1933[a]	
	Value	Percent	Value	Percent	Value	Percent
0– 200			1,338.0	32.1	1,211.4	54.0
0– 250	1,374.7	54.5				
200– 400			486.2	11.7	220.3	9.8
250– 450	266.0	10.5				
400– 1,000			734.2	17.6	318.3	14.2
450– 1,000	341.2	13.5				
1,000– 5,000	429.0	17.0	1,074.9	25.8	414.5	18.5
5,000–10,000	83.5	3.3	267.5	6.4	44.3	2.0
10,000 and over	28.6	1.1	264.8	6.4	35.4	1.6
Total[b]	2,523.0	100.0	4,165.6	100.0	2,244.2	100.0

Size of Gross Estate (thousands of dollars)	1937		1944		1949		1954		1958		1960	
	Value	Percent	Value	Percent	Value	Percent	Value	Percent	Value	Percent	Value	Percent
0– 200	1,065.3	35.0	1,275.0	37.1	2,120.7	43.2	3,010.0	40.3	4,594.5	39.4	5,259.5	36.0
200– 500	592.7	19.5	742.8	21.6	1,194.0	24.3	1,786.5	23.9	2,762.0	23.7	3,399.0	23.2
500– 1,000	350.9	11.5	458.6	13.4	657.8	13.4	941.6	12.6	1,530.2	13.1	1,864.0	12.8
1,000– 5,000	618.8	20.3	614.3	17.9	752.0	15.3	1,205.3	16.2	1,890.8	16.2	2,559.8	17.5
5,000–10,000	175.4	5.8	183.4	5.3	133.8	2.7	246.5	3.3	383.5	3.3	442.9	3.0
10,000 and over	243.9	8.0	159.5	4.7	56.3	1.1	272.6	3.7	487.0	4.2	1,096.8	7.5
Total[b]	3,047.0	100.0	3,433.6	100.0	4,914.6	100.0	7,462.5	100.0	11,648.0	100.0	14,622.0	100.0

Source: U. S. Treasury Department, Internal Revenue Service, *Statistics of Income*, various years.
[a] For 1933, information is available for resident decedents only.
[b] Details may not add to totals due to rounding.

CHAPTER II

Gifts Inter Vivos

GIFTS INTER VIVOS, that is, gifts from one living person to another, are not subject as such to an estate tax or an inheritance tax. But if gifts were left completely untaxed, even when they are made in contemplation of death, escape from death duties would be far too easy. Accordingly property given in contemplation of death usually has to be included in the donor's estate.[1] A further step is to impose a gift tax on lifetime gifts generally. The tax may be graduated by size of gift or by cumulative amount of gifts given by the donor in question over a stated period of years or over his lifetime. A final stage in this evolution would be integration of the gift tax and the death tax into one transfer tax. The rate applicable to the donor's transfers at death would depend on the amount he had given during life and the size of his estate.[2]

[1] As in the United Kingdom, which imposes no gift tax as such.

[2] Integrated death and gift taxation on the donor is not unknown, but is apparently rare. Under Italy's estate tax, "In order to thwart attempts to minimize the burden of the progressive rates by making gifts before death, the computation of the estate tax . . . requires inclusion . . . in the decedent's estate of all gifts and donations made by the decedent to his heirs or legatees on or after 12 May 1942, that is, the date on which the estate tax was first introduced in Italy. The taxes which would be due on these gifts and donations . . . are credited against the amount of the estate tax." (Harvard University, International Program in Taxation, *World Tax Series: Taxation in Italy* [Commerce Clearing House, 1964], p. 256).

These taxes are all levied on the donor or on his estate. A parallel set of taxes can be devised to be paid by donees, the rates to be graduated according to the amount received by a donee, either at any one transfer, or over his lifetime,[3] or over some shorter

---

With respect to gifts, this tax has been called the "tax on the aggregate value of gifts." The gift tax itself is cumulative. "Against the tax payable on each successive gift, a credit is given for the tax which would be payable at current rates on the value of all previous gifts." (*Ibid.*, pp. 259-60.) In Colombia, the taxable estate of the decedent includes all gifts made by him during his lifetime. However, no credit is allowed for gift tax paid. (See *World Tax Series: Taxation in Colombia* [Commerce Clearing House, 1964], pp. 150-52.) Accordingly a severe, perhaps insoluble, collection problem seems inherent in the case of a decedent who has made large gifts during his lifetime, but information supplied to the present writer indicates that in practice no such problem has arisen in Colombia. Perhaps many gifts go unreported. Gifts and estates are said to be greatly undervalued, and estate tax rates are low.

[3] As in Japan from 1950 to 1953. In 1953 this accessions tax was divided into an inheritance tax and a gift tax. (Saburo Shiomi, *Japan's Finance and Taxation, 1940-1956* [Columbia University Press, 1957], pp. 85-86, 99.) "In 1958 a revision was made to calculate the tax on the basis of the statutory shares under the Civil Code of the estates." (Ministry of Finance, *Outline of Japanese Tax, 1961,* Tokyo, 1961.) The reasons for considering the accessions tax superior to other forms of transfer taxation were given in *Report on Japanese Taxation by the Shoup Mission* (General Headquarters, Supreme Commander for the Allied Powers, Tokyo, 1949), Vol. 2, pp. 143-55. Italy imposes an inheritance tax in addition to its estate tax. ". . . for purposes of determining the applicable rate brackets, the value of inter vivos gifts made by the decedent to the heirs and legatees must be added to the value of inheritance shares and legacies received by the respective beneficiaries . . . The law allows as a credit against the inheritance tax the taxes which would be due on those gifts and donations if passing at death under the laws currently in force." (*World Tax Series: Taxation in Italy,* p. 217.) "Since, presumably, the previous gifts have been subjected cumulatively to the tax on gifts . . . the net result is the taxing of the cumulative total of the inheritance plus previous gifts [from the same donor] at the current rate applicable to it, refunding [crediting] taxes payable at the current [*sic*] rates on the value of the previous gifts." (*Ibid.*, p. 237.) With respect to gifts, this tax has been called the "tax on gifts" to distinguish it from the "tax on the aggregate value of gifts" mentioned in note 2 above. (*Ibid.*, p. 259.) The cumulating rule for gifts is the same as that given in note 2. Colombia also levies both an inheritance tax and an estate tax. In an heir's taxable inheritance there are included all gifts received by him during his life from the particular decedent who left him the inheritance. In computing the tax base, the heir may deduct the gift taxes paid on such gifts but may not credit the gift taxes against the inheritance tax. (*World Tax Series: Taxation in Colombia,* pp. 150-52; compare Milton C. Taylor and Associates, *Fiscal Survey of Colombia* [Johns Hopkins Press, 1965], Chap. 5, "Death and Gift Taxes.") Since in neither Italy nor Colombia does the donee cumulate all gifts and inheritances from all donors, neither tax is a complete cumulated accessions tax.

period.[4] Conceivably, the amount of tax could vary as between lifetime gifts and inheritances.[5] However, such a distinction is not likely to be drawn in a donee tax unless each transfer is treated separately.

Since the chief concern of this study is with immediate policy issues in the United States for federal taxation of transfers during life and at death, this chapter concentrates on the donor tax and states the case for and against integration of the present lifetime cumulated gift tax with the separate estate tax.

The Case for Integration[6]

Integration of the present federal estate and gift taxes can be supported on several grounds:

1. It would prevent escape from the more severe rates of the estate tax that is now open to anyone through inter vivos giving. It would be closer to a neutral tax, not influencing the distribution of transfers between those inter vivos and those at death. The same amount of revenue could be raised by a rate scale somewhat lower than that of the present estate tax.

[4] Germany levies a donee tax on gifts and inheritances under a limited cumulation formula. Successive acquisitions by a given donee from a given donor over a period of ten years, whether by gift or inheritance, are cumulated for the exemptions and progressive rate scales, which vary with the relation of donee to donor. (*World Tax Series: Taxation in the Federal Republic of Germany,* Commerce Clearing House, 1963), pp. 179-80, 188-89. Presumably the German ten-year periods start with the first gift received by the donee from a given donor.

[5] Compare the inheritance tax in Colombia, which cumulates transfers from any one donor to any one donee. See note 2 above.

[6] For a detailed proposal for integration, and supporting arguments, see U. S. Treasury Department, Advisory Committee, and Office of Tax Legislative Counsel, *Federal Estate and Gift Taxes, A Proposal for Integration and Correlation with the Income Tax* (U. S. Government Printing Office, 1947). The reader is also invited to test his predilections in this field against the ingenious, carefully worked out, proposal by Harold M. Groves and Wallace I. Edwards in "A New Model for an Integrated [Donor] Transfer Tax," *National Tax Journal* (December 1953). Under the Groves-Edwards plan, husband, wife, and minor children form a "family unit" within which transfers can be made freely without tax. "When each child reaches majority, he leaves the FU and a transfer tax settlement is made on his behalf by the FU" (p. 354). Expiry of a life estate would give rise to a tax on the corpus at a rate determined by aggregation with the cumulated transfers from the FU whence the property was settled, even though no member of that FU was then living (p. 357).

2. It would permit some simplification by reducing, if not eliminating, the need to include certain kinds of lifetime gifts in the donor's estate. At present, such gifts must be included in the estate even though they have been considered completed gifts for gift tax purposes; a credit is given for gift tax paid. The kinds of gifts at issue are (a) those made in contemplation of death and (b) gifts of property or interests in property to which the donor has retained a "string" or interest[7] of some sort.

3. Integration would permit a better adjustment to encourage lifetime giving in lieu of waiting until death.

Integration as a means of preventing avoidance of the estate tax may seem unimportant in view of the surprisingly small amount of inter vivos giving that takes place, even under the present bargain federal rates. The federal bargain is substantial.[8] The gift tax rates are only three-fourths those of the estate tax, and they are applied to the net gift exclusive of tax,[9] not, as is the estate tax, to the entire transfer including tax; the donor obtains a $30,000 lifetime exemption for lifetime gifts, while not losing the $60,000 exemption at death; each year the transferor can give up to $3,000 tax free to any one donee, and a married couple, $6,000 (even though the gift is in fact made wholly by one or the other spouse); in the early stages of inter vivos giving, property moves off the top of the potential estate, to the lower levels of cumulated gifts, hence to lower-level bracket rates.[10]

Aside from the loss of interest when the tax is paid earlier, the only definite tax disadvantages of inter vivos giving are those that arise from (1) the treatment of capital gains and losses under the personal income tax, (2) the potential marital deduction at death that is lost in an amount equal to one-half the gift tax paid, and (3) the fact that nonspousal gifts do not increase the marital de-

[7] Hereinafter "string" is to be interpreted as including also any interest even if unaccompanied by control.

[8] The twelve state gift taxes offer similar bargains. Advisory Commission on Intergovernmental Relations, *Coordination of State and Federal Inheritance, Estate and Gift Taxes* (U. S. Government Printing Office, 1961), pp. 81-82, 114.

[9] Even if the property donated inter vivos is swept into the donor's estate, the amount already paid as gift tax remains outside the taxable estate.

[10] Income from the transferred property may become subject to lower income tax rates than it was in the hands of the donor.

duction. There are a number of contingent disadvantages of lifetime giving: higher income tax rates on the transferee; possible future decreases in tax rates; a decrease in the future value of the property transferred; extra transfer taxation if the donee dies leaving the property to the surviving donor or returns the property.

The treatment of capital gains and losses requires some explanation. When the value of a capital asset at the time of transfer by gift exceeds its cost to the transferor (or other basis in his hands), a subsequent sale leads to a larger capital gain under the income tax, or to a smaller capital loss, or changes a capital loss into a capital gain, compared with what happens if the transfer is made at death. The increase in gain or decrease in loss amounts to the excess of the transfer value over the basis value. The disadvantages in these three cases when the transfer is inter vivos are partly offset by the fact that, if the value of the capital asset at the time of transfer is *below* its cost or other basis, there is at the time of sale by transferee either (1) no gain or loss if the transfer has been inter vivos, contrasted with a gain if the transfer has been at death (this is the result when the sale price is below cost but above transfer value); or (2) a gain on the inter vivos transfer that is smaller by the difference between transfer value and cost (this is the result when the sale price is above cost); or (3) if the sale price lies below both transfer value and cost, the same loss is recognized for transfers inter vivos and by bequest.

As to the interest lost on the earlier-paid gift tax, there is a partial offset in that the aim of the donor, transfer of the property, is achieved that much sooner. He may, for example, succeed in placing the income from the property in a lower income tax bracket.

Integration of death and gift taxes, if it is to be complete, requires the following provisions:

1. The tax paid on lifetime gifts must be based on an amount equal to the net gift plus the tax. The formula for computing the tax on a specified amount of net gift is as follows: if the donor wants to transmit a net gift g, at a tax rate r applicable to a gross transfer t (that is, the gift before deducting tax), that gross transfer t must be such that $t = g/1 - r$. Since g and r are known, the value of t can be found. The only complication, abstracting from state gift taxes, arises from graduation of the rate scale. If the value of t turns out to be such that, cumulated with all previous

gross gifts, it reaches into a higher bracket or brackets, the procedure would be modified as follows: find the value of t that can be fitted into the existing applicable bracket and solve for g; take the remainder of the desired g and solve for t, using the next bracket rate; if this t exceeds the width of that bracket, use the bracket width to solve for the second part of g, and proceed as before.

2. There must be a single rate scale.

3. There must be a single exemption, not one exemption for inter vivos gifts and another for transfers at death.

4. An annual exclusion per donee for each donor, which presumably should remain in any circumstances, would need to be much smaller than the present $3,000 (effectively, $6,000 for a married couple), perhaps no more than $500.

5. The basis for computing capital gain and capital loss would have to be the same under an inter vivos transfer as under a transfer at death. Presumably this means that upon any transfer, inter vivos or at death, either (a) the basis to the transferor would have to be taken over by the transferee, or (b) accrued gain or loss would be recognized upon the transfer. A third possibility, (c) to establish a new basis by gift equal to the market value at the time of the gift in addition to those cases where it now obtains (in certain accrued-loss transfers) is inadmissible; it would open a broad highway for avoidance of capital gains taxation. A wealthy parent could give his children securities or real estate that had appreciated in value, rather than cash.

In the following discussion "integration" refers to an integrated gift-estate tax constructed in accordance with the five requirements just noted. A type of integration that would favor lifetime gifts, for example, through a lower rate scale, is practicable and will be noted later. But it reduces simplification, for it requires retention of certain complex provisions of the present law regarding incomplete transfers and gifts in contemplation of death.

Data on Lifetime Giving

Not only is the yield of the gift tax very small relative to that of the estate tax (see Table I-2 above), but the number of returns and the dollar value of gifts each year are likewise very small. And we know from special statistical studies made by the Treasury Department that there are few individuals who transfer enough during their lifetimes to even approach the dividing line between inter vivos gifts and transfers at death that would minimize the combined gift tax and estate tax. In these special studies, each decedent's taxable lifetime giving record was ascertained as accurately as possible by a search of his gift tax returns back to 1932. Although much of that record was probably not uncovered for many decedents, the evidence is strong that close approaches to tax minimization were few indeed.

Three such special studies were made. The first covered those decedents whose estate tax returns were filed in 1945; the second, 1951 returns; the third, 1957 and 1959 returns. These studies will henceforth be described as "the '1945' or '1951' or '1957, 1959' special studies." The 1945 study covered all returns filed in that year. The 1951 study covered all returns showing a net estate, before deduction of the $60,000 exemption, of $300,000 or more. The 1957 and 1959 study included (1) all returns of *gross* estates of $1,000,000 or more; (2) a random sample of one out of six returns in the gross estate range of $300,000 to $1,000,000; (3) a random sample of one out of one hundred returns showing a gross estate of less than $300,000.

The following paragraphs concentrate on the data that are most significant for a decision on the integration issue, namely, data on lifetime giving by wealthy decedents who filed returns in 1957 and 1959. "Wealthy" here means those with a gross estate of $1,000,000 or more. They are referred to hereinafter as "millionaires." Data on the smaller estates will be found in Appendix C. Some comparisons with the findings of the earlier special studies of 1945 and 1951 returns are given in Appendix F. They show that the percentage of decedents reporting lifetime gifts has declined from one study year to the other, and that the percentage of the total value of transfers in the form of gifts has declined even more sharply.

Of the 2,256 millionaire decedents in 1957 and 1959 combined, only a few more than half made any taxable gifts at all during their lifetime. More precisely, 54 percent of these decedents made taxable gifts in the period from 1932 to their death, according to the records of the special study, admittedly somewhat incomplete.[11] Even if this percentage is adjusted upward substantially to allow for decedents who did in fact give something but are not reported as having done so, the result is astonishing. These are persons who, as it turned out, transferred property at death subject to marginal tax rates from, say, 35 percent up to 77 percent.[12]

Nor is it much less surprising even when one recalls that nontaxable gifts under the $3,000 exclusion, and nontaxable gifts to charities, etc., are not counted here.

In the very highest wealth categories, inter vivos giving is indeed nearly universal. The data for those with gross estates of $1,000,000 or over are broken down into groups, not by size of gross estate, but by size of total transfers during life and at death, including all gift taxes and estate and inheritance taxes paid, but less claims against the estate, and expenses of administering the estate. This concept is referred to here as "gross transfers." A subcategory is "gross transfers at death," which includes lifetime gifts that have had to be included in the estate (gifts in contemplation of death, and lifetime transfers where the donor retained some interest or control, as explained below).

The reason for subdividing the returns by this gross transfer criterion rather than by the same criterion used to distinguish the 100 percent sample from less complete sample groups (size of gross estate) concerns certain technical problems in handling the returns. Here we simply emphasize the importance of keeping these two concepts, gross estate and gross transfers, separate when analyzing the findings of the 1957 and 1959 special study. A "gross estate" of more than $1,000,000 might fall in a "gross transfer" group of much less than $1,000,000. Claims against the gross estate might be large and inter vivos gifts small. The reverse phenomenon is also possible. A gross estate of less than $1,000,000 might fall in a gross transfer group of more than $1,000,000, owing to a large total of inter vivos gifts and a small amount of claims against

[11] Of the 2,256 decedents, 1,219 were found to have made noncharitable gifts during life. See Appendix C, Table C-2.

[12] The rates cannot be deduced exactly, since they apply to *taxable* estate, not gross estate.

TABLE II–1. Millionaires Reporting No Inter Vivos Gifts, Gross Transfers Under $3,000,000, 1957 and 1959

Size of gross transfers (In thousands of dollars)	*Total number of decedents*	*Percentage of decedents reporting no inter vivos gifts*
Under $900	99	71
$900–$1,000	137	74
$1,000–$1,250	523	52
$1,250–$1,500	381	45
$1,500–$1,750	236	40
$1,750–$2,000	181	31
$2,000–$3,000	317	33

Source: Unpublished data supplied by U. S. Treasury Department.

the estate. The latter type of case is, of course, not included in data concerning returns with gross estate of $1,000,000 or more, as in the present analysis; the term "millionaire decedent" is reserved for those whose gross estate was $1,000,000 or more.

Of the 52 millionaire decedents[13] showing gross transfers of $10,000,000 or more, 50 made[14] lifetime gifts; 48 made noncharitable gifts. One cannot help wondering what must have been the familial and social circumstances of the two who, leaving a net estate[15] of $10,000,000 or more, reported no inter vivos gifts.

There were 115 millionaire decedents with gross transfers of $5,000,000 to $10,000,000, and 91 of these reported inter vivos gifts; 90 of the 91 made noncharitable gifts.

For the middle class millionaire decedents, those with gross transfers of $3,000,000 to $5,000,000, the results are even harder to understand. Of the 215 millionaire decedents in this category, 51 made no gifts at all, and 62 made no noncharitable gifts. Even when recalling that the data on gifts are incomplete, the percentage of nongift returns, 24 percent, is difficult to explain.

The low-group millionaire decedents, those with gross transfers below $3,000,000, were still less inclined to give during life.

[13] All data are for the 1957 and 1959 returns combined unless otherwise noted.

[14] For economy in exposition, the more precise expression, "filed estate tax returns which, when matched against available gift tax returns, revealed" is replaced here and henceforth by the term "made."

[15] In these two cases, "gross transfers" is equivalent to net estate in the sense of gross estate less claims (and expenses), given that inter vivos transfers were zero.

(See Table II-1.) The data for this group are perhaps the most surprising of all. Consider the millionaire decedents with gross transfers of $1,000,000 to $1,250,000. How could it be that more than half of them made no lifetime gifts? The percentage is so large that even allowing for possible gross under-reporting, especially for 1957,[16] there is still a startling picture of wealthy individuals clinging to their possessions throughout life.

When the amounts given during life, rather than the number of decedents making gifts, are considered, the mystery deepens. The wealthy millionaire decedents, those with gross transfers of $10,000,000 or more, reported total gross transfers of $1,112 million ($938 million at death). The inter vivos gifts of this group, split about evenly in amount between charitable and noncharitable gifts, came to only 14 percent of total transfers, including tax. When one thinks of the substantial tax saving that probably remained to this group, the percentage, even if revised upward substantially to allow for nonreporting, indicates how strong must be the nontax considerations. And in the group with gross transfers of $1 million to $1.25 million, only 3 percent of the gross transfers were lifetime gifts.

Why So Little Lifetime Giving?

The data on lifetime giving stimulate conjectures about the nontax considerations that have induced disregard of tax savings that were readily available.

1. The most important seems to be uncertainty. For example, uncertainty as to how long one will live leads to the possibility that better occasions for giving will be available in the future. Uncertainty exists with respect to medical expenses, including self-indulging luxury travel for health reasons. Actuarial tables on life expectancy are of little use to any one individual, who wants to be sure that he will not find himself short of funds at some time before death. The uncertainty factor may not explain the conduct of those with gross transfers of more than $10 million, but it goes a long way toward explaining, for example, why only about half of those with $1 million to $1.25 million gross transfers report gifts,

[16] See Appendix F.

and why only 3 percent of all that group's transfers are lifetime transfers.

2. Next most important is perhaps the desire to maintain some degree of control over the actions of others. This desire is directed at two groups: (a) one's potential beneficiaries, especially children, and nephews and nieces, and (b) anyone else the individual wishes to control.

Members of the former group, while it may not be expected or desired that they answer to every whim of their wealthy aged relative, are likely to be more considerate, or at least less discourteous, as long as some weighty transfer decisions remain unresolved. And they may let their choice of activity, of residence, and even of spouse be directed to some degree. Moreover, if enough money is transferred during life, the transferor will not only lose some of his power, he will also give others the means of power over him. Tax lawyers in Great Britain report that this fear is more likely to characterize the newly rich, who do not have the psychic support of a long family history of wealth well maintained and harmonious relations established between generations, and who may even actively distrust their children. In sum, the rich probably do believe that money is power; and while inter vivos transfer of money is often agreeable to the donor, no one who has tasted power yields it without reluctance. Sections 2036(a) (2) and 2038 of the Internal Revenue Code, to be discussed below, are testimony to this effect.

The others whom the wealthy individual may want to control are depersonalized to him. He will say he wants to control events, not persons. And if he has, say, $10 million at the age of 70 and is in good health and acute of mind, why should he, except under the most compelling circumstances, strip himself of potential opportunities to influence events (the outcome of a presidential election, the development of a promising invention, the market fluctuations of a stock)?

In this category too is the desire to remain active after formal retirement; management of one's wealth is a productive activity that can be carried on into old age.

3. Next in importance is probably a reluctance to contemplate

one's own death, coupled sometimes with the gradual onset of senility. The first factor postpones until tomorrow the decision on giving, and the second makes it less likely that tomorrow will be the day of decision. Anyone in good health and spirits has a normal resistance to acting as if he were to die soon. Why not wait now and give later? In one recent year three partners in a prominent New York City law firm doing much of its business in taxes died, all in their 50's, all intestate, the result of a heart attack, an airplane crash, a traffic accident, respectively. "Warm weather will" forms for wealthy clients are kept in the desk drawer of one prominent tax adviser, to hand to the old gentleman as he strides into the office just before departing on that summer excursion to Europe with his wife, the Rolls Royce waiting at the curb with engine running. The client has just remembered, on the way to the airfield, that he did not, after all, make—or revise—the will to set up trusts. If he has failed to erect even this simple safeguard against the tax net, how can he be expected to have followed a tax-directed plan of lifetime giving? Many other instances of postponement can be cited, some almost unbelievable to those who do not have both great wealth and high spirits.

4. Fourth in explaining the lack of inter vivos giving is a consideration more to the donor's credit than are the other motives attributed to him. He may not want to spoil his children or grandchildren. Money, like alcohol, must be taken in moderation. This consideration must weigh heavily with wealthier millionaires.

5. Another reason is based on a somewhat irrational dislike for consuming one's capital. A wealthy executive who has been receiving an "earned" income in the hundreds of thousands of dollars a year (including stock options and profit shares) finds his income upon retirement reduced by an amount that forces him to rethink his whole standard of living. This is so, even if he has accumulated some millions of dollars, which yield an investment income of some tens of thousands of dollars. If he were willing to cut his capital somewhat after retirement, he could of course prevent the decline in his annual available cash flow. But often he will irrationally follow the rule of capital preservation without considering all the consequences. One of the results is a resistance to lifetime giv-

ing, no matter how attractive the opportunity. Meanwhile he probably fails to consider adequately the "accruing" liabilities against his capital in the form of the approaching death tax.

The remaining explanations offered here for scanty lifetime giving are probably of a lower order of importance:

6. Lifetime giving has a competitor that giving at death does not: consumption spending by the otherwise donor. At death the only choice is to whom to leave it.

7. The individual often overlooks the possibility that the value of his real estate and security holdings may greatly increase in the future, as they have in the past, thus raising the effective marginal rate of the tax.

8. He may be ignorant of the provisions of the tax law.

9. He may expect that tax rates will be lower in future years.[17]

[17] One wonders which, if any, of the forces listed above explain the following (to choose only a few of the news clippings the writer has filed away over the years): "Approximately $50,000,000 of the $64,000,000 estate left by Howard Gould, last surviving son of Jay Gould, railroad builder, will go for estate taxes," of which the federal tax was to be about $38 million after credits and the New York State tax, about $12 million. (*New York Times,* March 11, 1960.) "The amount of the [Howard Gould] residuary estate has not yet been determined. Twenty-three grand-nephews, grandnieces, and five great-grandnephews and great-grandnieces of Howard Gould will share in it." (*New York Times,* Oct. 20, 1960.)

"Federal tax liability on the estate of A. Atwater Kent, the radio manufacturer, amounted to $5,030,348 . . . For Federal tax purposes the net estate . . . was valued at $10,090,531 . . . . in the calculation of the Federal Tax, the estate received credit for California inheritance and estate taxes of $1,081,360." (*New York Times,* Dec. 3, 1952.)

"The [Internal] Revenue Bureau . . . put the net value [of Edsel Ford's estate] at $198,313,550.61, allowing a deduction of $106,339,024.65 for charitable bequests . . . The remaining tax claim of $50,446,284.58 against the . . . estate . . . has been settled for $8,810,724.27 (which payment is in addition to a $15,824,369.07 payment by Mrs. Ford in August, 1944 . . .). Another $3,600,000 was paid by the estate in taxes on gifts made by Edsel Ford before his death May 26, 1943, and brings his total estate and gift [tax?] payments to more than $28,200,000." (*New York Times,* Sept. 28, 1947.)

"Uncle Sam stands to become principal beneficiary of a $43,954,062 estate left by Mrs. Lillian Timken, widow of a co-founder of the Timken Roller Bearing Co. Sequestered among art treasures in her Fifth Avenue apartment until she died in 1959 at the age of 78, the wealthy recluse gave her paintings (among them a Goya, two Rembrandts, two Titians, and a Rubens) to three U. S. museums, intended her principal assets (stocks and bonds) for her heirs. But she failed to set up the proper trusts and other tax-reducing gimmicks, and so an appraisal filed in Manhattan Surrogate's Court indicates a bite of $28,175,009 to the Federal Government, $7,481,504 in state taxes." (*Time,* April 26, 1963.)

A tenth reason might be unexpected death at an early age, before lifetime transfers could be consummated. In practice, this possible reason was unimportant; there were very few such deaths among the higher classes of millionaire decedents (in 1957 and 1959).[18]

Since gifts inter vivos are so few, either the gift tax is safeguarding the estate revenue adequately, or the nontax impediments to giving are so strong that the gift tax is not greatly needed. In either case, what is to be gained by integrating the estate and gift taxes?

There are at least three replies to this question:

1. Congress has established an elaborate set of policing provisions, which are described below. It must have considered the threat of avoidance to be substantial or at least politically important.

2. Many if not all of these provisions could be eliminated, or emphasized less, under a completely integrated transfer tax.

3. The desired amount of encouragement to lifetime giving could be more closely approximated under an integrated tax.

These arguments will now be examined in some detail.

"The will was drawn up in 1939 before tax laws were eased to lessen the Government bite on estates. Lawyers drew up a later will, but Oklahoma Senator Robert S. Kerr, who died in 1963, never got around to signing it. So the widow and four children had to pay a whopping tax of $9.4 million (45 percent) on Kerr's more-than-$20.8 million estate . . ." (*Time,* April 10, 1964). For another instance of large estate tax, see Appendix G, Taxpayer 4.

[18] The ages at death of the two 1957 and 1959 decedents with gross transfers of $10,000,000 or more for whom no lifetime transfers of any kind were reported were 76 and 78. The two decedents in this gross transfer class who, although reporting no gifts to persons, did report contributions during life, were aged 76 and 80. In the gross transfer class $5,000,000 to under $10,000,000, no lifetime transfers were reported for 24 decedents. The ages of these 24 decedents were as follows (only one of each age except as indicated in parentheses): 54, 57, 59, 60 (2), 61, 63, 66, 68, 70, 79, 82, 83, 84 (3), 85, 87, 88, 90, 91, 92, 99 or over (2). In addition, there was an 82-year-old decedent in this $5,000,000-$10,000,000 gross transfer class who, although reporting no gifts to persons, did report contributions during life. In the gross transfer class $3,000,000 to under $5,000,000, no lifetime transfers were reported for 51 decedents. Of these decedents, 3 were in their fifties; 17 in their sixties; 11 in their seventies; 15 in their eighties; 4 in their nineties; one decedent's age was not stated.

Policing Gifts in Contemplation of Death and Incomplete Gifts[19]

The policing mechanism for gifts made in contemplation of death and incomplete gifts consists of provisions of the estate tax law (though not of the gift tax law) that bring into the taxable estate certain transfers that are in fact made during life. Some advantage to the taxpayer remains, however, since the gift tax paid is not included later in the estate. (See provision 1, page 16, above.)

The first of these provisions is Section 2035 of the Internal Revenue Code, which includes in the taxable estate all gifts made in contemplation of death. This concept covers a wider range than the concept of gifts *causa mortis,* those made in anticipation of, and conditional upon, death of the donor, and it is this wider range that has created difficulties. They have been only partly resolved by the law's rebuttable presumption that if death occurs within three years from the time of gift, the gift was made in contemplation of death, and the law's further irrebuttable presumption that if more than three years have passed, the gift was not in contemplation of death. The rebuttable presumption has in fact been successfully rebutted many times, and has also prevailed many times; an area of indefiniteness remains.[20] The British have removed all uncertainty by using the lapse-of-time test alone (five years, but with inclusion of increasingly smaller portions of the gift beyond a two-year period).

The second of these policing provisions is directed against "incomplete" transfers, whereby the decedent has during his lifetime attempted to have the best of both worlds by giving outright but retaining some sort of interest or control, some kind of "strings" to the property. The strings fall into three groups:

1. The donor tries to retain possession or enjoyment of the property or the right to income from the property for the remain-

[19] For a lucid, well organized statement of the law and regulations on treatment of such gifts under the estate tax, see James B. Lewis, *The Estate Tax* (Practising Law Institute, 1964), pp. 26-67.

[20] And an area of the laughable, if not farcical. For the Oliver Johnson case, see Philip M. Stern, *The Great Treasury Raid* (Random House, 1962), p. 262.

der of his life, or keeps the right to determine who shall have those interests. Section 2036 stipulates that such transfers, whether or not complete enough to make the gift tax applicable, or to shift income tax liability from donor to donee, cannot prevent the property from being included in the taxable estate of the donor. The language, to be effective, has had to be cast in terms more complex than the simple paraphrase above, "for the remainder of his life," suggests.

2. The transferor, *T*, keeps a reversionary interest in the property that he passes by inter vivos transfer, and possession of the property by another remainderman can be obtained only if the latter survives the transferor. A typical procedure has been to arrange for an income to the wife for life, the remainder to the husband-transferor if he is living, and, if he is not, the remainder to their children. If the husband dies before the wife, and if his contingent reversionary interest was substantial enough (more than 5 percent of the value of the property at the moment just *before* his death), his taxable estate must include the value of the children's remainder interest as that interest stands at date of his death (that is, just *after* his death) or at the alternate valuation date with adjustments to eliminate changes in value due merely to the lapse of time. In general terms, if the transferor, *T*, retains a substantial reversionary interest (the 5 percent rule) and if someone else's (for example, the children's) interest in the property is such that they can possess the property only by surviving *T*, then *T*'s taxable estate must include the value of their interest. Note the distinction between the value of the donor's reversionary interest (just *before* he dies), which is compared with the value of the entire property to ascertain whether it exceeds 5 percent of that value, and the value of the remainder interest of the other(s), just *after* *T* dies (or at the alternate valuation date), which is the amount that must be included in *T*'s taxable estate if the 5 percent limit has been exceeded.

3. Finally, the donor might be content with a string that would give him power to alter, amend, revoke, or terminate the trust or other instrument upon which the interest of the beneficiaries depended. Section 2038 requires that the estate of the donor include any interest the enjoyment of which is thus subject

to change by action of the donor. This provision, applicable in the original law, had to be strengthened twice (as of June 2, 1924, and June 23, 1936) before it became reasonably avoidance-proof.

Under an integrated estate-gift tax, little tax advantage would attach to gifts during life compared with transfers at death. Accordingly the provisions that sweep into the estate certain transfers during life (gifts in contemplation of death, incomplete transfers) would no longer be required. To be sure that the tax revenue is obtained before the property can be dissipated, the law would define all transfers that give the *donee* any interest whatsoever as immediately taxable transfers.

Encouragement of Lifetime Giving

The discussion up to this point has covered the first two of the grounds on which integration has been urged: to prevent tax avoidance and to allow simplification. But the third aim often advanced for integration runs somewhat counter to these two: namely, to allow a desired, but no more than desired, tax stimulus to lifetime gifts, at the expense of transfers at death. The most common proposal is to grant a rate reduction, from the otherwise cumulated scale of progressive rates, for gifts inter vivos, presumably with some upper limit on cumulated gifts, beyond which further gifts would put the donor back on the regular rate scale.

But this favored treatment would presumably not be afforded to gifts made in contemplation of death nor to gifts where the donor retains a string to the property. If it were not, either (a) much of the simplification that could be achieved by integration would be lost, as Sections 2035-38 would need to be retained, or (b) some tax avoidance would have to be tolerated.

To stimulate inter vivos giving substantially, the rate reduction would have to be on the order of 50 or 75 percent, judging from the small amount of taxable giving that takes place under the present system, where a rate reduction of 25 percent is coupled with several other tax advantages that would be lost under integration. The revenue decrease would be about proportional to the rate reduction, if the loss of interest on the earlier paid tax is disregarded. Total giving, during life and at death, would increase little if at all.

Integration would remove the inequity inherent in the present law with respect to donors who, for reasons having nothing to do with tax avoidance, are unable or unwilling to transfer property during life. This aim would not be achieved, however, if low rates were granted for gifts inter vivos.

The only disadvantage to integration, other than those already implied, seems to be the cost of transition to the new system—cost in terms of effort needed to master the new law, of possible misunderstanding of it, of changes needed in wills and insurance plans, and of certain complexities inherent in whatever special provisions might be needed during a transition period.

Cumulation by Donor or Donee; Inheritance Taxes

The decision whether a transfer tax is to be cumulated for each donor or for each donee will depend on the answers to the following questions:[21]

1. Do donors restrict their consumption somewhat, or work harder, in order to lessen the impairment of the donee's economic status threatened by the transfer tax? Insofar as they do, the burden of the tax rests on donors, not donees, and equity considerations for the progressive-rate schedule suggest that the cumulation be by donor. But, for reasons to be given later, it seems likely that the burden is more on donees than on donors. If the burden is in fact on the donee, cumulation should be by donee (accessions tax).

2. Administratively, are donees more or less likely than donors to comply with the tax law? Donors are probably fewer in number. Being usually older, richer, and more accustomed to keeping records, they are likely to be more responsible in fulfilling their tax obligations, although also more astute and more highly motivated in using tax avoidance techniques. The administrative aspect seems to be slightly in favor of cumulation by donor.

3. The economic consequences would presumably differ under

[21] See also Chap. VIII below.

the two methods of cumulation for an integrated transfer tax, but it is not evident in just what ways. Cumulation by donee would invite the transferor to give more widely, and to donees with less transferred wealth, but the response might not be very strong.

An ordinary inheritance tax is to an ordinary estate tax somewhat as an integrated donee tax is to an integrated donor tax, but not quite. To be sure, in both comparisons, it would be illogical to argue for a graduated rate on equity grounds for the donee tax if every donor reacts to the tax by sparing his prospective donee, through restricting his own consumption or increasing his work, so that the donee would receive just as much as if there were no tax. Progression on the donee makes no sense on equity grounds if the tax does not change his economic status.

But the donor should not be expected to assume the whole burden of the tax or even very much of it. Moreover, under the integrated donee tax any one donor would find it a puzzle to cut his consumption by just the right amount. He would face the virtually impossible task of estimating, well in advance (so that he could restrict his consumption over several years to meet the tax at death), where in the cumulated bracket schedule the donee would be at the time of transfer. Hence the burden of the accessions tax is less easily shouldered by the donor than that of the inheritance tax.

The integrated donee tax (accessions tax), like the donor taxes, would take little or no account of differences in the relationship of donee to donor. (Such differences could be built into the tax, however, if desired.) Accordingly a central issue in the debate over an inheritance tax versus an estate tax may be missing in a debate over an accessions tax versus an integrated donor tax. To be sure, the importance of the issue may be overstated for an inheritance tax, since a donor may defeat the legislator's intent. Consider, for example, an inheritance tax with a rate higher on nephews and nieces than on sons and daughters. A decedent, under this tax, may decide to leave more to a nephew and less to a son than he would have under an estate tax. This reaction is more likely than that the donor would assume the burden (by restricting consumption or working harder), especially for transfers at death. At death, the higher tax to pay, if the decedent leaves more to the nephew, can be a cost to the donor only in this sense: he has less total, net of tax, to dispose of if he gives more to the higher-taxed nephew, and less to the lower-taxed son in an effort to thwart the intent of the rate differences.[22] He does not have the option of refusing to transfer the property at all, as he does when contemplating a transfer inter vivos.

[22] Indifference curves may be drawn on a diagram having "transfer to son" on the *y*-axis and "transfer to nephew" on the *x*-axis. A straight line from one axis to the other forming an isosceles triangle with the axes (the origin being the apex) is the pre-tax price line. An estate tax, proportional or progressive, creates an after-tax price line parallel but nearer the origin. An inheritance tax produces a price line with a steeper slope than the estate tax price line if, as is usual, transfers to a son are taxed at a lower rate than are transfers to a nephew. The point of tangency under the inheritance tax may represent, for a certain transfer, a greater pre-tax bequest to the nephew than does the point of tangency under an estate tax with the same total yield, without requiring any unusual features in the system of indifference curves. The pre-tax bequest to the nephew is measured on a line parallel to the *x*-axis through the point of tangency, extended to the right of the point by an amount equal to the tax on the nephew.

CHAPTER III

Generation-Skipping Through Trusts

THAT PECULIARLY Anglo-Saxon legal device, the trust, and its complementary devices, the life estate and the power of appointment,[1] have opened avenues of tax avoidance under death and gift taxation that are unavailable in countries operating under the civil law system of the European continent.[2] For example, the father *A*, by his will, places certain property in a trust, the income to go to his son *B* for life; upon *B*'s death the trust is dissolved, and the property passes to *B*'s son *C*. *A*'s taxable estate includes that property, but upon *B*'s death the property does not go into *B*'s estate. It will not be taxed again until *C* disposes of it. Thus the tax is skipped by one generation, in the sense that *B*'s generation enjoys use of the property but never pays death tax on it. Note that an outright bequest from *A* to grandchild *C* does not, in this sense, skip one generation of tax; *B*, in this instance, never enjoys use of the property. Of course he may benefit indirectly in that he may thereby be relieved of an obligation to support his children.

[1] These two complementary devices can be employed without using the trust, with the same potential for tax avoidance, but such usage is not common.

[2] This is not to imply that still other legal systems may not use the trust or its equivalent. Moreover, the civil law countries have substitutes for the trust, and even in some cases instruments that approximate the Anglo-Saxon trust. See Harvard University, International Program in Taxation, *World Tax Series: Taxation in Italy* (Commerce Clearing House, 1964), pp. 218-22.

The Problem

The seriousness of even one-generation skipping should not be underestimated. To make the point as simply as possible, let us postulate that the estate tax base is a circulating fund of constant size and that generations skipped are of constant duration. Then, if all decedents leave all their property in trusts that skip only one generation, 50 percent of the estate tax base is lost. Generation *A* pays estate tax upon leaving property in trust, the income to generation *B*, and the remainder to generation *C*. When generation *C* dies, it leaves property in trust for one generation, and so on. Generations *A, C, E,* . . . pay estate tax; generations *B, D, F,* . . . do not.

If all decedents leave all their property in trusts that skip two generations instead of one generation, the estate tax base is one-third what it would be under no skipping, instead of one-half. The reduction in base, from what it would be under one-generation skipping, is from 50 to 33⅓ (with 100 as the base under no skipping). This is a decrease of one-sixth (16⅔ percent) of the base under no skipping. Three-generation skipping reduces the base from 33⅓ to 25, or by one-twelfth of the base under no skipping. Thus the big erosion occurs with one-generation skipping. Further skipping is proportionately much less serious.

The special characteristic of the trust, as contrasted with outright bequests, is that it allows the wishes of the settlor with respect to disposition of the property to be carried out by a party acting in a fiduciary capacity, who can be so selected that he has no interest adverse to the future interest holders. It therefore provides a mechanism whereby the property may be conserved while a generation enjoys the income from it.

As has just been indicated, the trust may skip two or three generations: the income to *B* for life, then to his son *C* for life, then to *C*'s son *D* for life, the remainder over to *E*, *A*'s great great grandson. No estate or gift tax will be levied between *A*'s and *E*'s dispositions of the property.

Of course, the trust instrument cannot be so simply drawn as this sketch might imply, if only because various contingencies must be provided for. And the skipping cannot go on forever, owing to the rule against perpetuities.[3] In most states this rule provides roughly that interests designated in the trust instrument must vest within a period not exceeding the length of lives in being when the instrument becomes effective plus 21 years.

A trust is not always necessary; a legal life interest in a parcel of real estate may be given to *B,* with the remainder to *C.* In this discussion, however, the term "trusts" is used loosely to include nontrust life interests.[4] Interests in life insurance policies will be separately analyzed in Chapter IV in the section on "Correlation of Transfer Taxes With the Income Tax."

The trust instrument need not specify who shall receive title to the property when the last life interest expires. This decision may be left to the income beneficiary by giving him a power to "appoint" the property, that is, to designate the person or persons to whom interests in the property shall pass.[5] The power may be general in the legal, nontax sense. That is, it may place no restrictions at all on the choice by the holder of the power. Or it may be "general" in the tax-law sense. That is, it may allow the holder of the power to appoint the property to himself, or to his creditors during life, or (alternatively or in addition) to appoint the property to his estate or to the creditors of his estate. It is then termed "general" by the tax law, even though it does not specifically give the holder complete freedom of choice. Henceforth the term "general" is used only in this tax law sense.

If the holder of the power cannot appoint the property to himself or to his estate, or to the creditors of either, the power is a "special" power of appointment in tax law terminology.

The holder of a general power is viewed for transfer tax purposes as if he owned the property, and upon his exercise of the

[3] See *World Tax Series: Taxation in the United States* (Commerce Clearing House, 1963), p. 188.

[4] But trusts where the life tenant and remainderman are the same person are excluded. And dual transactions such as the following are not included: cash sufficient to buy an annuity equal to the income of the corpus is given to *B;* the remaining portion is given to *C* in cash to be used by *C* to buy a single-premium insurance policy on *B*'s life.

[5] On powers of appointment, see American Law Institute, Federal Estate and Gift Tax Project, Study Draft No. 1, *Unified Transfer Tax* (1965), pp. xxi, and 21-25.

general power during his lifetime the property becomes subject to gift tax. If the holder of the general power exercises it in his will or dies without exercising it, so that other provisions of the power-creating instrument determine where the property goes, the property still must be included in his taxable estate. (Release of the power raises further problems not analyzed here.)

The power of appointment need not be in the hands of the income beneficiary; some other party or parties may be made the holder(s).

The trustees may be given a limited special power of appointment whereby they may invade the corpus, under certain standards, for the benefit of those designated. Moreover, if the beneficiary himself is given a noncumulative power to draw down $5,000 or 5 percent of the corpus, whichever is larger, in any one year, there is no transfer tax in any year in which he does not exercise this power at all (except for the year of his death), even though by so refraining he is truly giving something to the remaindermen. The policy question arises whether the law has not gone too far in allowing an income beneficiary access to the corpus without imposing a transfer tax on him when he or his trustees do not make use of such access.

The trustees may be given the responsibility of deciding to what persons and in what amounts the income shall be paid while the trust is in existence.

So flexible an instrument is bound to be used for tax avoidance, but it is also bound to be used for nontax purposes. The trust did not come into being centuries ago as a tax avoidance device. If it is assumed that these other aims are socially desirable, the problem of tax policy is certainly not to destroy the trust but to make it useless as an instrument of tax avoidance. A common form of "settled" property (to use the British term)[6] is a life interest to the widow with an appropriately tailored power of appointment. The alternative of outright bequest to the widow may be unacceptable to the husband; a second husband might get control

[6] "Settled property" means "any property subject to trusts or rights which prevent one person having complete ownership." G. S. A. Wheatcroft, "The Anti-Avoidance Provisions of the Law of Estate Duty in the United Kingdom," *National Tax Journal* (March 1957), p. 47.

of the property, or the widow might dissipate it at the expense of their children. But the decedent may not be able to foresee, when he makes the will, whether it would be best for all the children to share in the property after their mother's death, and he may not know what will be the optimum ratios of sharing among them. Such details can be left to the widow by giving her a special power of appointment, or even a general power if it is exercisable only by will, not by inter vivos gift. She cannot then squander the property or pass it over to a second husband during her lifetime.

Trusts that do not let a child obtain title to the property ever, title passing only to the grandchildren or an even later generation, may likewise be socially desirable if the child shows signs of being incompetent to handle the property himself. Trusts that do not trust even grandchildren who have not yet had an opportunity to demonstrate their adult competence seem rather officious, however. What can such trusts reflect other than a desire to perpetuate a family dynasty of wealth?

Findings of the 1957 and 1959 Special Study

To ascertain the duration, in terms of number of generations represented, of trusts or life tenancies, the Internal Revenue Service of the United States Treasury compiled a number of tables from information obtained in the special study of 1957 and 1959 returns. Further tables were compiled at Columbia University by Gerald R. Jantscher, from data on the punched cards for those returns. Comparative details on these two sets of tabulations are given in Appendix A.

From these tabulations, inferences have been drawn about the extent of generation-skipping in two studies: one by Professor Robert Anthoine, using the Treasury tabulations, the other by Dr. Jantscher, using the tabulations he made at Columbia University. The Anthoine study comprises Appendix B to this study; the Jantscher findings appear in his *Trusts and Estate Taxation.*[7] A comparison of the 1957 and 1959 results with those of the 1945 and 1951 special studies is made in Appendix E below by Dr. Seymour Fiekowsky.

[7] To be published by the Brookings Institution in 1966.

Some of the major findings of the 1957 and 1959 special study are summarized briefly below. Unless otherwise noted, the findings refer only to those returns with gross estate of $1,000,000 or more.[8] The first definition of generation-skipping to be given here is used in interpreting data that do not show the relation of the remainderman to the settlor. The second definition, more precise, is used when such data are available.[9]

The first definition states that one or more generations are skipped whenever any one of the income beneficiaries of a trust is of a generation later than that of the transferor. If any one of such beneficiaries is of a generation twice removed from that of the transferor, the trust is said to skip two generations, as when *A* leaves property in trust, with income to his childen and grandchildren (or income only to his grandchildren), and the remainder to his great grandchildren.[10] The skipping of three or more generations is similarly defined. No account, perforce, is taken of the relationship of the remainderman. Accordingly skipping is said to occur even when the remainderman is of the same generation as the life tenant (for example, one child is the income beneficiary, another is the remainderman). This definition, as well as the second definition to be given below, implies that there is no skipping when the income beneficiary is of the same generation as the transferor, or an earlier generation, even if a grandchild, or great grandchild (or indeed, a child) is the remainderman. Here the case

[8] A size classification unfortunately does not always carry the same real meaning in community property states and other states. Suppose that in a community property state a married couple starts with no property and the husband builds up a fortune of $1,000,000 through his earnings and investment of community property. Suppose the wife has no separate property of her own. If the husband dies first, his gross estate is $500,000, not $1,000,000 (half is deemed already to be the wife's). In a noncommunity property state, his gross estate would be $1,000,000. If the wife dies first, her gross estate is $500,000 in the community property state, zero in the noncommunity property state.

[9] At the request of the present writer the Internal Revenue Service employed the classification by "duration" of trusts or life tenancies, in taking information from the returns. The Service is therefore not responsible for whatever difficulties arise in translating this classification into one of "generation-skipping," a more ambiguous concept, less readily usable for basic tabular classification.

[10] If a child is the sole income beneficiary, but is given a special power to appoint the property in trust to his children (that is, the grandchildren of the transferor), the trust is here classified as skipping only one generation.

of income to spouse, remainder to grandchild, is not one of generation-skipping under either definition.

The second definition of generation-skipping excludes those cases where at least one of the remaindermen is of the same generation as one of the income beneficiaries. That common generation is not skipped under this definition; when the remainderman disposes of the property, the transfer tax will apply. Hence his generation has not avoided tax. The tax on his generation has simply been postponed while another member of that generation is enjoying an income interest. The data required to implement this second, more precise, definition of skipping include information on the relationship of the remainderman to the life tenants, grouped by size classes. This three-way classification was not available in the Treasury tables of the 1957 and 1959 special study. It became available in the course of the computations made at Columbia University with the aid of a computer. (See Appendix A.)

The two definitions are distinguished here by the terms "broader" (no account being taken of remaindermen) and "narrower." In discussing generation-skipping, the broader definition will be used unless the narrower one is specified.

Neither definition covers skipping accomplished by direct transfer. A gift or bequest outright to a grandchild is not counted in these data as skipping, since the data are focussed on the use of trusts or their legal equivalents. Moreover, it can be argued that these direct transfers are not skipping if the essence of skipping is the enjoyment of property by a generation that pays no transfer tax. A direct transfer to a grandchild allows the intermediate generation, the child's generation, no direct enjoyment of the property. The child's generation pays no transfer tax, but, the argument runs, this is as it should be.

This argument has its shortcomings, however, when skipping is to be defined in a way useful to implementing the aim of taxing property once every generation, as a crude substitute for an annual tax on net wealth. This aspect of the definition of skipping is considered in Chapter VIII.

Three other technical points must be mentioned briefly if even the summary data are to be understood.

1. The data do not indicate the date on which the will was

signed. A decedent whose estate filed a return in 1957 or 1959 may have signed the will many years earlier. The degree of skipping that was being embodied in wills being drawn up in 1957 and 1959 may have been considerably less or more than that revealed by the 1957 and 1959 returns.

2. Certain types of trusts were excluded in assembling the data from the 1957 and 1959 returns: those (a) where the life beneficiary and the remainderman are the same person; (b) where the life tenant is a surviving spouse and has such power over the corpus of the trust as to cause it to fall into his or her estate upon his or her death, so that the trust qualifies for the marital deduction (typically, this occurs where property is left in trust with income to the surviving spouse for life plus a general power of appointment in the hands of that spouse exercisable by will); (c) where a charity (broadly defined) is either the remainderman or life tenant; in such a case only the noncharitable interest in the trust is tabulated as trust property.

3. A bequest in trust may be to an already existing trust, one that might have been created by a gift inter vivos.

Distribution by Size Categories

Among millionaires, those with gross estates of $1,000,000 or more, use of the trust was substantial; slightly more than half of them created trusts. (See Table III-1.) And about two-thirds of the millionaires' trusts skipped one generation. (See Table III-2, lines 1, 3, 4, and 6.) In most of the cases the life beneficiaries did not include the spouse and did include members of but one generation, who in general were at least one generation below the transferor (line 3). Thus, about one-third of the millionaires represented in the 1957 and 1959 returns created trusts skipping one generation, and the skipping problem is correspondingly important. As was pointed out above, if all transferors skipped one generation, half of the tax base would disappear.

There was some skipping of two or more generations, but not much. As Table III-2 shows, about 10 percent of the trusts skipped two generations (lines 5 and 7)—for example, income to children and the remainder to grandchildren—and another 5 percent or less, more than two generations (lines 8, 9, and 10). Added to the roughly two-thirds that skipped one generation, these figures indicate that not far from four-fifths of the trusts skipped one or more generations.

The percentage of millionaire decedents who created trusts rises as gross transfers rise (see Table III-1). From two-thirds (1957) to four-fifths (1959) in the highest group ($10 million gross

TABLE III–1. Number and Percentage of Millionaire Decedents Creating Trusts, 1957 and 1959 Returns, by Size of Gross Transfers

Size of gross transfers (In millions of dollars)	1957			1959		
	Decedents[a]	Decedents creating trusts[b]	Percentage creating trusts[c]	Decedents[d]	Decedents creating trusts[e]	Percentage creating trusts[f]
Under 0.9	47	19	40	52	18	35
0.9–1.0	75	40	53	62	32	52
1.0–1.25	260	135	52	263	136	52
1.25–1.50	191	99	52	190	104	55
1.50–1.75	118	57	48	118	72	61
1.75–2.00	78	45	58	103	66	64
2.00–3.00	155	89	57	162	97	60
3.00–5.00	105	62	59	110	71	65
5.00–10.00	64	44	69	51	30	59
10.00 or more	26	17	65	26	20	77
Totals	1,119	607	54	1,137	646	57

[a] Appendix B, Table B-1, Col. 1.
[b] *Ibid.*, Table B-4, Col. 1.
[c] *Ibid.*, Table B-1, Col. 6.
[d] *Ibid.*, Table B-1, Col. 1.
[e] *Ibid.*, Table B-4, Col. 1.
[f] *Ibid.*, Table B-1, Col. 6.

transfers or more) used trusts, compared with slightly more than half of all millionaires.[11]

But did the millionaire decedents make very intensive use of trusts? The fact that most of them used trusts would not be significant for tax policy if only a small part of each estate went into trusts. But this was not the case. As Table III-3 shows, one-

[11] In the Jantscher study it is shown that the variation from one *adjusted-gross-estate* class to another in the proportion of decedents who bequeathed some property in trust is statistically significant. But the difference in proportion between husbands and wives is not statistically significant. This is true of all estates, not just those of millionaires.

TABLE III–2. Percentages of Trusts and of Trust Corpora Skipping Generations, by Types of Tenancies, Millionaires, 1957 and 1959

Line	Category of income beneficiaries	Number of genera-tions skipped	As a percentage of total number of trusts		As a percentage of total value of corpora of trusts	
			1957	1959	1957	1959
1	Term of years	1	2.5	4.0	1.0	3.4
2	1 generation, spouse sole life tenant	0	23.1	15.7	25.9	19.7
3	1 generation, other life tenant	1	56.7	59.3	49.4	49.8
4	1 generation plus term years, spouse life tenant	1	0.7	2.2	1.4	3.3
5	1 generation, plus term years, other life tenant	2	5.3	5.1	6.3	6.6
6	2 generations, spouse 1 life tenant	1	3.7	3.7	7.1	6.0
7	2 generations, other life tenants	2	4.6	6.3	5.5	5.7
8	2 generations plus term years	3	2.5	2.8	2.4	4.1
9	3 lives	3	0.7	0.5	0.9	0.8
10	3 generations, plus term years	4	0.2	0.3	0.2	0.6

Source: Appendix B, Table B-3.

TABLE III-3. In-Trust, Noncharitable Bequests as a Percentage of Disposable Estate, 1957 and 1959 Returns, Millionaires, by Size of Gross Transfers

Size of gross transfers (In millions of dollars)	1957	1959
Under 0.9	24	18
0.9–1.0	25	22
1.0–1.25	26	25
1.25–1.50	24	28
1.50–1.75	21	29
1.75–2.00	33	30
2.00–3.00	30	28
3.00–5.00	29	30
5.00–10.00	29	23
10.00 or more	17	16
All estates	26	25

Source: Appendix B, Table B-1, Col. 8.

fourth of the millionaires' *disposable* (after-tax) estate was put into noncharitable trusts.[12]

From other data, not reproduced here,[13] it is estimated that 19 percent of millionaires' disposable estates went into trusts that skipped one or more generations. Thus the intensive use of trusts in general, noted above, is in large part devoted to generation-skipping.[14]

[12] Eighteen percent of "gross transfers at death," which here means the same as "adjusted gross estate," went into noncharitable trusts. The percentages of total value of estate passed in trust are more irregular than are the percentages of decedents by size of gross transfers. The lowest percentage of value of estate passed in trust is in fact found in the highest transfer-value group, both as a percentage of disposable estate and as a percentage of adjusted gross estate. High tax rates help explain the adjusted gross estate percentage. Moreover, the high-transfer groups gave relatively more to charities, and this helps explain the low ratios of in-trust noncharitable bequests to disposable estate as well as to adjusted gross estate. If these in-trust noncharitable bequests are expressed as a percentage merely of all noncharitable bequests, the resulting percentages are rather generally high in the high-transfer groups. See Appendix B, Tables B-1 and B-2, cols. 7 and 9.

[13] *Ibid.*

[14] In terms of the proportion of trust value (trust corpora) that skipped one or more generations, the percentage does not rise regularly with the size of gross transfers of millionaires, as might perhaps have been anticipated. The 1957 millionaires in the under-$900,000 gross transfer group made 58 percent of their trust corpora value skip one generation; those in the $10,000,000-or-more group made 74 percent of it skip one generation; but in between, the percentages fluctuate considerably. (Appendix B, Table B-4, one-generation column.) In 1959 the gap is wider: 31 percent and 62 percent, respectively, but the in-between groups are more nearly uniform, near 60 percent (Appendix B, Table B-4, one-generation column). And for both years, the high percentage of one-generation skipping for the $10,000,000-and-over group is accompanied by a rate of two-generation skipping much lower than in most of the smaller gross transfer groups. Indeed, in 1957 the $10,000,000-or-more group left only 4.1 percent of trust corpora value in two-generation skipping trusts, and nothing at all in three- and four-generation skipping trusts. The Jantscher tabulations indicate that a *greater* proportion of the *smaller* adjusted gross estates that do use trusts makes *more* intensive use of the trust, and that such differences among adjusted-gross-estate classes are statistically significant for the husband subgroup. In each of the four lowest adjusted-gross-estate size classes, a greater proportion of trust-using husbands than in any larger size group put from 40 to 60 percent of their *disposable* estates in trust. In the next three higher size groups, a larger proportion put 20 to 40 percent of their disposable estates in trust. In the largest size group, nearly two-thirds of all trust-using husbands left less than 20 percent of their disposable estates in trust. The explanation of these findings probably is that wives are commonly the sole tenants of testamentary trusts created by the less wealthy husbands, and are often the only recipients of their husbands' outright bequests. The trust is probably used in these cases primarily to

If we turn to nonmillionaires, those with gross estates between $0 and $300,000 (the "small" estates), and between $300,000 and $1,000,000 (the "medium" estates), we find that the percentages concerning use of trusts, and generation-skipping, are lower, as might be expected.

The 1957 proportion of gross transfers at death minus death taxes (disposable estate) that was bequeathed in trust was only 9 percent (14 percent of the decedents) for the small estates, and 20 percent for the medium estates (37 percent of decedents), against 26 percent for the millionaires (54 percent of decedents). The 1959 proportions were about the same.[15]

As to generation-skipping, in 1957 returns the proportion of trust corpora value for the small estates skipping one generation[16] fell well behind that for millionaires; 31.5 percent and 59 percent, respectively. In skipping two generations, the small estates almost matched the millionaires—10 percent and 12 percent, respectively. The medium estates about matched the millionaires in one-generation skipping but were well behind them in two-generation skipping. The pattern is thus somewhat mixed. None of the small estates, however, skipped more than two generations; none of the medium estates, more than three. The 1959 data[17] show a steady increase, in all skip classes, from small to medium to millionaires; but the proportion of small-estate trust corpora value skipping one generation is larger even than in 1957: 44 percent against 31.5 percent. These are, to be sure, only percentages of total trust corpora value, not percentages of adjusted gross estate. We conclude that not many small estates use trusts, but when they do use them, they are fairly sophisticated as to skipping one generation.

Power to invade corpus, powers of appointment, and accumulating trusts all raise difficult issues for transfer taxation. What the 1957 and 1959 data revealed on these points is summarized briefly below.

---

protect the legacy and assure efficient management. Hence there is a tendency to place a large proportion, if any at all, of the disposable estate in trust, but not so large a proportion as to lose part of the marital deduction.

[15] Appendix B, Table B-2, cols. 6 and 8.

[16] *Ibid.*, Table B-6.

[17] *Ibid.*

Unlimited power to invade the corpus was given to the trustee in trusts representing only a small portion of total trust corpora value: 14 percent of the trust corpora value for 1957 millionaires and 18 percent for 1959 millionaires. On the other hand, the respective percentage for power limited by a standard was large: 52 percent for both years. The percentages for medium and small estate trusts were close to those for the millionaires.[18] These percentages apply to trusts created during life and at death, in contrast to all the data cited up to this point, which refer only to trusts in estates.

Powers of appointment in the hands of the life tenant were not used much in the millionaire estate returns,[19] and hence presumably little in the smaller estates. In 1957 the total value of trust corpora in millionaire estates was $455 million. The value subject to power of appointment in life tenant was $19 million (in 55 out of 1,119 trusts).

It will be recalled that for the special study tabulations, trusts that provided a general power of appointment to the life tenant were not included in the trust tables at all, since a general power makes the life tenant's estate include the corpus, and hence allows no generation-skipping. Thus it may be inferred that the power of appointment in the hands of the life tenant to which the $19 million was subject consisted entirely of special powers of appointment, which do not make the life tenant's estate include the corpus. For 1959 the respective data for millionaires are $30 million of trust corpora value out of a total of $448 million (in 101 trusts out of 1,334 trusts).

Mandatory direction to trustees to accumulate income was found in only two of the millionaire estates (both in 1959) and in none of the millionaire lifetime trusts.

Tenant-Remainderman Combinations

Trusts may be classified by tenant-remainderman combinations, in their relation to the settlor. By far the most common combination found in the special study of 1957 and 1959 returns

[18] *Ibid.*, Table B-10.
[19] *Ibid.*, Table B-9.

is: wife life tenant, children remaindermen. In gross estates of $300,000 or less, husbands placed 53 percent, by value, of their trusts in this wife-children combination. The percentage is slightly less in the $300,000-$1,000,000 group: 42. It drops sharply in the millionaire group to 22 percent, where trusts in which children are the life tenants, and grandchildren remaindermen represent 17 percent of total trust value.

There may be some temptation to discount the importance of the findings for the group under $300,000 because most decedents in this group do not use the trust at all. But there are so many decedents in this group that in the aggregate the trust users count heavily. Indeed, the total of property bequeathed in trust by the two lower-wealth groups (the nonmillionaires) covered by the 1957 and 1959 returns, was about equal to the total of property bequeathed in trust by millionaires. In addition there are the trusts created by those with estates too small for them to be included in the 1957 and 1959 data. Policy measures designed to restrict the use of trusts to avoid large estate taxes must consider the importance of trusts in the lower wealth groups.

Similar computations restricted to wives reveal, as might be expected, no such concentration of trusts in the spouse-children category; in general there is more dispersal among several combinations of tenant and remainderman.

What of widowers and widows who created trusts? These two groups acted almost exactly alike in the lowest wealth range. A little over half the property they put in trust was in the simple combination: children tenants, grandchildren remaindermen. They acted nearly alike in the millionaire group: about two-fifths of the trust property was in this combination. The proportion of property put in trust by widowers or widows with children as tenants in some form or other (sole, joint, successive), ranges from 52 to 80 percent. In the middle and upper wealth groups widowers and widows acted almost exactly alike.

Inter Vivos Gifts in Trust

The pattern of variation of inter vivos giving in trust is, in its broad outlines, similar to that of bequests in trust, but the extent to which trusts were used was generally much smaller. Jantscher's computations show that, among husbands with adjusted gross estates of less than $500,000, only 1.3 percent had made inter vivos gifts in trust. This percentage increases fairly regularly in every higher wealth range, reaching 40 percent in the above-$10 million group. A similar association is to be found in the other marital classes.

Comparison with 1945 and 1951 Data

The proportion of transferors using trusts, during life and at death, has declined appreciably. From about 74 percent in the 1945 and 1951 special studies it fell to 61 percent in the 1959 returns. There has also been some decline in intensity of use by those who do use trusts. These declines may well be traceable to the marital deduction enacted in 1948. (See Chapter IV.) Property that formerly had to be put in trust to avoid being taxed twice in one generation can now be passed outright, tax-free, within the limits of the marital deduction.[20]

Solutions to the Problems

If generation-skipping by trusts is prevalent enough to warrant remedial measures, what measures are available?

Four alternatives will be noted here.

One would be to tax the entire corpus upon expiration of the life interest. The British law uses this method, decreeing that the corpus is taxable upon expiry of the life interest, on the grounds that the property "passes" at death when death brings a change in beneficial interests in income. This provision can be defeated, however, by a discretionary trust, or in American legal slang, a spray trust, whereby the trustees are empowered to distribute the income of the trust among three or more beneficiaries concurrently in such proportions as they see fit, including even a zero proportion for all but one. They may vary the proportions from year to year. Upon the death of any one of three or more such potential beneficiaries, no one of the survivors has any more of an interest than he did before, since there has been no change in beneficial

[20] For details see Appendix E.

interests in income; no one of the "beneficiaries" has had an enforceable equitable interest. Thus a trust may include two or three generations of persons as such beneficiaries, and not until the last but one dies can there be deemed to be a passing of an interest. The trustees, meanwhile, pursuant to what they know to be the decedent's wishes, could be paying income only to the first generation, and so on. It appears that the discretionary trust is used in Britain extensively to defeat taxation of the corpus upon expiry of a life interest.[21]

This loophole might be plugged by taxing, upon the death of any one such beneficiary, that proportion of the corpus equal to the proportion of the income that has in fact been paid to that beneficiary over the years. Such a provision would not, to be sure, meet the British test for taxability mentioned above; and it has certain obvious administrative and enforcement disadvantages. Moreover, it shares with the British approach the vexing problem of how to fit taxation of the corpus under these conditions into the progressive rate scale.[22]

For the United States, the British record, discouraging though it is, does not reveal all the problems. If the spray trust loophole were closed, attempts would be made to open others that the British taxpayers have not needed to search for intensively. For a thorough and enlightening exploration of the problems to be expected in taxing effectively upon the expiry of a life interest, see the proposals of the American Law Institute's Federal Estate and Gift Tax Project,[23] where the type of tax that might be imposed

[21] Wheatcroft, "The Anti-Avoidance Provisions of the Law of Estate Duty in the United Kingdom," p. 52. Another loophole much used in Britain until 1958 was the purchase, by the life tenant, of the remainderman's interest for full value. "Hence, when the tenant-for-life is elderly and the value of the remainderman's interest is high, the balance remaining in the tenant-for-life's hands at the end of the transaction, which will pay duty on his death if he does not spend it, will be much less than the value of the fund, which would otherwise have paid duty." (*Ibid.*, p. 53.) What escaped taxation here was not the corpus of the settled property, but the cash that moved from life tenant to remainderman. This loophole was largely plugged by Section 28 of the Finance Act 1958, which charged duty on an imputed sum of money equivalent to the amount paid by the tenant-for-life for the remainder.

[22] *Ibid.*, pp. 47-48.

[23] *Unified Transfer Tax* (cited in note 5 above), p. xxxi, and Appendix II, "A Successions Tax," pp. 118-90.

is spelled out, and some seventy illustrative hypothetical cases are given to explain various aspects of the tax.

A second alternative would be to impose an additional tax at the time of transfer of the property to the trust, a tax that "would be in effect a payment in advance on the tax that would be assessed on *S*'s death [*S* is the life beneficiary] if *S* had been given the property outright."[24] In the American Law Institute's draft of the project for such a tax,[25] the rate of the tax is a fraction of the average rate "applicable to the included transfers for the taxable period in question, or for included transfers on the death of the transferor [an integrated gift-death tax is the basic proposal]."[26] In effect, the fraction varies with the length of tax postponement achieved by the trust.

A third possibility is that suggested by Professor Wheatcroft: a quinquennial tax on accumulating and discretionary trusts and for other trusts, taxation, at the death of the life tenant, of the proportion of the corpus represented by the actuarial (or actual) value of the life tenant's interest. The remaining part of the corpus would be taxed when the remainderman dies.[27]

A fourth alternative has been suggested to the author by Professor William Vickrey: "A property owner may at any time make a deposit with the Treasury and for each year that such dollars remain on deposit until the death of the taxpayer, a license is created to set up by will trusts that will tie up corresponding amounts for corresponding numbers of years (or the total number of dollar years may be rearranged by amount and term). Trusts set up within the limits of the license thus created will be taxed only at normal rates; trusts set up beyond this limit will be taxed at relatively prohibitive rates. In effect, a testator wishing to extend his power over his property beyond the grave would be allowed to do so only by relinquishing a corresponding amount of power over his property during his lifetime. The licensure created might be measured not by the actual lifetime of the taxpayer, but perhaps by his life

[24] *Ibid.*, p. xxxii.

[25] *Ibid.*, pp. 98-108.

[26] *Ibid.*, p. 106.

[27] See G. S. A. Wheatcroft, ed., *Estate and Gift Taxation, A Comparative Study* (London: Sweet and Maxwell, 1965), p. 134, and note 14 in Chapter IV below.

expectancy at the time the deposit was made (which would then have to be irrevocable), in order to enable appropriate trusts to be established in the case where the taxpayer dies unexpectedly young."

The remarks up to this point refer to a donor tax. Would a cumulative accessions tax on donees afford a complete answer to this problem of life-estate expiry? It would if (1) upon formation of the trust the value at that time of the remainderman's interest were taxed as an accession to him; (2) the income interest were valued and taxed, or, alternatively, the income flows were taxed as they were received; and (3) upon expiry of the trust the full value of the corpus were taxed as an accession to the remainderman.

An alternative would be to omit step (1) and compensate for the omission by imposing a special high rate of tax at stage (3). The aim would be to avoid tax pressure on a potential remainderman before he comes into possession of the property.

Both versions of this (1)-(2)-(3) tax are open to the objection that they are conceptually invalid, for they tax the remainderman twice on what he gets—once, early, at a discounted present value and again, later, when he comes into the property. Yet this double taxation in some form is essential if generation-skipping through the trust is to be averted. Otherwise, there will remain a tax penalty against property that is passed directly from parent to child to grandchild (for example) rather than reaching the grandchild as remainderman through a trust with the child as life beneficiary.

CHAPTER IV

Other Structural Problems

OTHER STRUCTURAL PROBLEMS also arise in connection with estate and gift taxes. This chapter considers those arising, for example, from transfers between spouses, to sons and daughters, and to charitable organizations. It also examines the problem of correlating transfer taxes with the income tax and that of taxing life insurance proceeds.

Interspousal Transfers[1]

The present treatment of interspousal transfers under the federal estate and gift taxes can be understood only in a historical context.

Community-property spouses held a notable advantage in certain instances under the federal estate tax until 1942. Community property that arises during marriage, normally through the earnings of either spouse, or from investment income from community property, is at once half the husband's, half the wife's; nothing has to "pass," either inter vivos or at death, to assure this result. Until 1942, a community-property couple with $1,000,000 accumulated

[1] For a statistical study of interspousal transfers in trust, see Gerald R. Jantscher, *Trusts and Estate Taxation,* to be published by the Brookings Institution in 1966.

from a decedent husband's earnings could have all this property remain in the hands of the widow, then pass at her death to the children, while paying estate tax once on $500,000, and once on: $1,000,000 less the first estate tax paid. A noncommunity-property couple would pay once on $1,000,000, and once on: $1,000,000 less the first estate tax paid. The penalty for living in a noncommunity-property state was, in this instance, the upper bracket rates on the top $500,000 (of $1,000,000). Alternatively, the community-property husband could leave one-half to the children, with an advantage equal to the tax on: the top $500,000 of $1,000,000 less the discounted estate tax on that amount.

In 1942 the law was changed in an effort to achieve roughly equal treatment by requiring that community property be treated approximately as if it were noncommunity property.

In 1948 this was reversed; noncommunity property was given the possibility of receiving much the same treatment as community property had received before 1942, and community property was restored to its pre-1942 status. A marital deduction was granted to noncommunity property, up to an amount equal to 50 percent of the gross estate less claims and expenses ("adjusted gross estate"). Apparently this reversal of policy was necessary to obtain the support of community-property state congressmen for an income-splitting provision that removed an important income tax advantage of the community-property states.

A similar[2] marital deduction is allowed under the gift tax.

Data from the Treasury's special study of 1957 and 1959 returns show that, as might be expected, the marital deduction is widely and intensively used. In the aggregate, it is not used to the full extent allowed by the law; but this is not surprising. If a married couple's property is divided evenly between them, or nearly so, tax minimization will be achieved by eschewing the marital deduction altogether in the normal case where the children are to inherit, sooner or later. If the husband and wife each have 10, and if the first to die leaves his 10 to the children, the total tax will be the first tax on 10 plus a later tax on 10. But if the first to die leaves 5 to the spouse, and 5 to the children, the tax bill will be:

[2] But not identical. One-half of a gift to a spouse is exempt (not "up to one-half of all gifts by the donor").

tax on 5 at first death, tax on 15 at second death.[3] Progressivity of the rates may easily outweigh the time-discount factor. This result may occur even under moderately unequal division. Thus, if the husband has 12 and is the first to die, and the wife has 8, the tax will be (if there is no transfer to spouse) a tax on 12 plus a later tax on 8, against (using the full marital deduction) a tax on 6 plus a later tax on 14. Minimization of the present value of the tax might be achieved by a bequest to the wife of, say, 4, producing a tax on 8 now and 12 later.

Disregarding the time factor, the estate tax is minimized in this sort of case by either (1) dividing the property equally between the spouses before death, with bequests only to children, or (2) if property is unequally divided before death, using enough of the marital deduction to yield an equal division immediately after death. The former choice may cost something in the form of gift tax. The latter choice is not open, of course, if the less wealthy spouse dies first. None of such spouse's property should go to the surviving spouse if the tax is to be minimized (ignoring the time discount), and even then the estate tax will exceed what would have been due if the property had been divided equally before death. Since the order of death cannot be predicted, it would be prudent of the couple to divide the property equally before death (aside from the time factor and the gift tax), assuming that the surviving spouse does not need all the property.

Evidently, despite the presence of a 50 percent marital deduction, the estate tax does exert some pressure for equal division before death. Even if the marital deduction were 100 percent (interspousal exemption), some pressure would remain. In the case above, where the husband with 12 dies first, and the wife has 8, a bequest of the entire 12 tax free to the wife would mean more tax than would a bequest of, say, 4 tax free to the wife. If she dies first, she should still leave her 8 to the children rather than tax free to her husband.

If the total amount of property in the family is small, there is economic pressure to leave it all to the surviving spouse, regardless of tax consequences, so that he or she will not become dependent

[3] For simplicity, the decrease of funds caused by tax payment is ignored in these illustrations.

on the children. In such an instance, the marital deduction is of course a boon and will tend to be fully utilized.

The marital deduction does not apply to bequests of terminable interests to the spouse where some third party, typically a child, has an interest that leads to possession or enjoyment of the property after the surviving spouse's interest terminates. Thus a life interest to the spouse, remainder to children, does not qualify the corpus or even the value of the life interest for inclusion in the aggregate of property bequeathed to the spouse that can be deducted up to 50 percent of the adjusted gross estate. The purpose, of course, is to qualify for the marital deduction only that property that will be taxed in the surviving spouse's estate (unless she uses it up or gives it away). To ascertain whether an interest is or is not a "terminable interest" in this sense is sometimes difficult.

It is impracticable politically to return to the 1942-48 practice of no marital deduction and treatment of community property as (roughly) noncommunity property. Moreover, such a move would lack support in practicing law and academic circles. The alternative most discussed currently is complete interspousal exemption.[4]

If the rationale behind the estate and gift taxes is taxation of property once a generation,[5] interspousal exemption does not violate this principle when spouses are of the same generation. Marital departures from the same-generation assumption (for example, husband 70 years old, wife 40) might even increase a little under the stimulus of a 100 percent interspousal exemption. Higher tax rates would be needed on nonspousal transfers in order to maintain the revenue flow, with a consequent increase in avoidance and evasion.

Interspousal exemption would in some cases induce the bequest of a greater fraction of the disposable estate to the spouse than would have occurred under no tax. In some of these instances the results might be deemed socially undesirable, as when the surviving spouse is incapable of acting responsibly. Even a general power of appointment, exercisable by will, may lead to unwise disposition of the property. But the tax pressure thus to endow a

[4] See the proposal in the American Law Institute, Federal Estate and Gift Tax Project, Study Draft No. 1, *Unified Transfer Tax* (1965), pp. xxiii and 58-70.

[5] With respect to other grounds for transfer taxation, see Chap. VIII.

spouse is just as strong, speaking generally, under the present 50 percent marital deduction.

For some taxpayers, an interspousal exemption would have no advantage over the present marital deduction. Suppose that the surviving spouse does not consume capital. If a husband dies possessed of $1,000,000, present law allows him to leave $500,000 to his wife tax free and the other $500,000, taxable, to his children, perhaps in a trust with income to his widow for life. (Or the second $500,000 may be left tax free to a charitable organization.) The widow, on her death, leaves a taxable estate of $500,000. Owing to the progressive rate scale these dispositions will often result in a lower present value of estate tax than would a bequest of $1,000,000 to the widow under interspousal exemption plus a taxable bequest of $1,000,000 by the widow to the children.[6] Only if the widow dies many years later would the time-discount factor overcome the progressive rate factor to make this second disposition the cheaper in tax.

An interspousal exemption would not remove the tax pressure now exerted for an equal division of property before death in order to eliminate the risk of the extra tax that would be payable if the less wealthy spouse died first.[7] The only kind of estate tax that would remove that pressure would be one that yields the same present-value tax whichever spouse dies first. For example, one such tax might be as follows: A complete interspousal exemption is granted. Upon the second spouse's death the taxable part, if any, of the estate of the first spouse (that is, the part of the estate not bequeathed to the surviving spouse) is added to the estate of the second spouse and divided by two. The tax is computed on that one-half and is multiplied by two. Credit is then given for the amount of tax paid by the first estate. There are serious problems

[6] For example, if the tax on $500,000 were 20 percent and that on $1,000,000, 30 percent, and if the time discount were 15 percent (roughly 4 percent for 3½ years), the present value of the tax under the present law would be 20 percent of $500,000 plus 85 percent of 20 percent of $500,000, or $185,000. Under complete interspousal exemption and transfer of all property to the surviving spouse, the present value of the tax would be 85 percent of 30 percent of $1,000,000, or $255,000.

[7] See pp. 51-52.

in this, however.[8] If the surviving spouse inherits a fortune and has received nothing from her decedent spouse, there will be a tax in the upper brackets on her estate at her death that might be considered unfair.[9] If the surviving spouse remarries, perhaps the account will have to be settled by a valuation of her property at the time of her remarriage.

An alternative is to value the surviving spouse's property as of the day before his or her spouse's death, add this to the decedent spouse's estate, divide by two, compute the tax, multiply by two, and collect the tax on a pro-rata basis from the estate and the surviving spouse's wealth. But now a difficult valuation problem is created.[10]

In view of these difficulties, the pressure exerted by the estate tax for an equal division of property between spouses before death may have to be accepted as an unfortunate by-product of the tax. It is unfortunate because in some families, and not in others, nontax considerations will prevent equal division and so may lead to a heavier estate tax. A capricious distribution of the tax burden is the consequence.

For many, perhaps most, married couples complete interspousal exemption is seen to have no great advantage over the present 50 percent marital deduction. This impression is strengthened by the working of the quick-succession relief described below.[11] But complete interspousal exemption does no taxpayer any harm, and if "taxing once a generation" were the only aim of the estate and gift taxes, it would be the logical next step. In fact, however, other aims must be considered. At least one of these, the aim of slowing down or reversing the concentration of wealth, will

[8] For a thorough analysis of the interspousal transfer problem, see G. S. A. Wheatcroft, ed., *Estate and Gift Taxation, A Comparative Study,* Chap. IV (by Professor Wheatcroft), "Proposals for a System of Estate and Gift Taxation," (London: Sweet and Maxwell, 1965), pp. 137-43.

[9] ". . . who is to pay the increased duty on *A*'s estate consequent on its aggregation with *B*'s? There is also an almost insuperable difficulty when *B* remarries after *A*'s death." *Ibid.*, p. 141.

[10] And a potential problem of death-bed marriage. *Ibid.*

[11] The impression is weakened a bit when the decedent leaves minor children. See the section on "Transfers to Sons and Daughters" below.

in certain instances become more difficult to achieve if complete interspousal exemption is granted.[12]

Length of Time Between Transfers[13]

If the recipient of property from a taxed estate dies shortly thereafter, some death tax laws, including that of the United States, allow a certain amount of tax relief. If, on the contrary, the lapse of time between the two estate taxes is extraordinarily long, symmetry might suggest an additional tax. No taxing jurisdiction imposes one, however, so far as the author is aware.[14]

In the United States, the relief, in the form of a credit against tax, extends over a ten-year period, but is "100 percent" relief only for the first two years following the transferor's death. The credit is stepped down by 20 percentage points every two years, becoming zero at the start of the eleventh year.

This "quick succession" relief is permitted where the prior decedent was the spouse of the present decedent, but not with respect to the amount that was allowed as a marital deduction. Insofar as the deaths of spouses tend more to produce quick successions than do deaths of other pairs of transferor-transferees, there exists at present more interspousal exemption than the marital exemption alone would imply.

In one way the credit is somewhat biased against the taxpayer (the transferee), and in another way extraordinarily in his favor.

The transferee is allowed to credit only the smaller of (1) the portion of the transferor's estate tax attributable to the net value of the prior-transfer property and (2) the portion of the transferee's estate tax attributable to that value. And the two tax portions are not computed on the same basis. The portion of the transferor's tax attributable to the property in question is computed by applying to it the average rate paid by the estate. The portion of

[12] See Chap. VIII below.

[13] For a detailed examination of this problem, see American Law Institute, *Unified Transfer Tax* (cited in note 4 above), pp. 89-95, 113-118.

[14] In its draft of a "successions tax" (see Chap. III, the section on "Solutions to the Problem"), the American Law Institute (*op. cit.*, pp. 184-85), calls for taxation of the term interest at the end of each thirty years, and a tax after each thirty years of mandatory accumulation of income.

the transferee's tax is computed on an incremental basis, using the marginal rate or rates that apply on the assumption that the prior-transfer property was the "last" property in the transferee's estate. A transferee does best if the prior transfer has come from an estate so large that its average rate is not less than the transferee's marginal rate.[15] This result may reflect a desirable, if unconscious, social policy. But except for that advantage, there is no particular logic in using average rates for the transferor and the incremental approach for the transferee. The rule for restricting the credit to the smaller of the two attributable taxes is an indirect but very crude device for rate progression.

The extraordinary favor shown the transferee is that the credit is granted even if the prior-transfer property has been given away, lost, or consumed by the transferee and never appears in his estate. This has not always been so. Before 1954 the prior-transfer property had to be identified and traced into the transferee's estate. The change appears to have been made because of the difficulty of tracing specific parcels of property. When the property received has been turned into cash, for example, how can one know whether consumption has come out of that cash? The difficulty goes even deeper. If the transferee keeps intact the prior-transfer property, say a parcel of real estate, it does seem to be in his estate; but if he had not received it, he might have consumed less, and left, perhaps, about as large an estate as he in fact did. And if the prior transfer had come to him tax free, hence in a larger amount, he might have consumed that extra amount.

There is really no way of knowing, in most cases, whether the transferee is subject to a larger estate tax than he would have been if he had not received the prior-transfer property. Because of this problem, perhaps the net value of the prior-transfer property might be reduced by one-half in computing the credit.

With respect to the prior-transfer credit granted as between spouses, aside from the amount taken as marital deduction, there are no data available on the percentage of widows and widowers who die within one year, two years, and so on, of the death of their spouses. Hence there is no way of knowing to what extent the law grants what is in a way a supplementary marital deduc-

[15] An estate's marginal rate is always above its average rate.

tion. This factual question may be of some importance in deciding how much spouses would gain in the case of a complete interspousal exemption.

No credit is given against *B*'s estate tax for the gift tax paid on a prior transfer by *A* to *B*. Nor is any credit given against the gift tax for an estate tax paid on a prior transfer. If the gift tax were heavier, or if wealthy persons gave more than they do, this gap in the credit structure would be important. It seems unlikely that the low level of giving is due to any great extent to the existence of this gap.

Transfers to Sons and Daughters

Gifts or bequests to sons or daughters receive no special treatment under the federal estate tax. On the other hand, inheritance taxes, which are levied on the recipient instead of on the transferor, commonly provide low rates, if not exemption, to children. Technically the estate tax could easily do the same. Bills have been introduced in Congress in recent years to modify the estate tax in this way.[16]

Again, policy should be consistent with the aim of the tax. If the tax is designed to tax transferred wealth once a generation, complete exemption cannot be granted to all bequests to sons and daughters. But if the rationale of the tax is to strike windfalls,[17] bequests to minor children can claim special treatment. Bequests to them finance maintenance and educational expenses that the decedent would have defrayed directly had he lived. Indeed, a bequest to a minor child may be viewed in somewhat the same light as an interspousal transfer, at least that part of the bequest that will be used for his support and education. An inter vivos gift cannot make the same claim to exemption, since the donor parent is still living and can meet these expenses without making a gift.

[16] See especially H.R. 1845 introduced Jan. 14, 1963, by Congressman Utt of California, which would allow deduction, in computing the taxable estate, of bequests to children, to a maximum per child of 5 percent of the gross estate after subtracting expenses, claims, losses, and marital deduction. See also *Children's Estate Tax Deduction,* Hearing before the House Committee on Ways and Means on H.R. 7924, 86 Cong. 1 sess. (July 10, 1959).

[17] See Chap. VIII.

Because (1) a minor child cannot himself normally use his bequest directly for his own support, and (2) bequests larger than are needed for this purpose should be taxed, a simpler way of caring for minor children would be to provide:

1. Complete interspousal exemption. The decedent can then leave as much as he needs to (or as much as he has) tax free to the surviving spouse to be used to the extent necessary to raise their children, and

2. Where there is no surviving spouse, a deduction from the estate for bequests to dependents, the deduction to vary inversely with the age of the dependent. For example, a $3,000 deduction could be allowed for each year the dependent's age, at the decedent's death, fell short of 21.[18] Thus the estate of a widower leaving two children, ages 7 and 16, would obtain an exemption equal to $3,000 (14 + 5) = $57,000.

More generally, an amount could be allowed as a deduction that would buy terminable annuities to care for the children until their majority, or until the completion of their education.

A deduction might also be allowed for permanently incapacitated dependent children of any age, as well as for incapacitated dependent brothers and sisters, parents, and grandparents. In these instances, actuarial data on the expectation of life of the beneficiaries would be used to compute the size of the deduction.

"Dependent" could be defined in somewhat broader terms than under the income tax.

The $60,000 exemption can be regarded as in part a device to insure that some tax-free amount can be left to children, even though the exemption is not restricted to decedents with children.

An allowance for bequests to minor children would probably induce some reduction in the present level of inter vivos gifts to children, and possibly some reduction in the amount of property put in trust with children as life beneficiaries, though, with the amount of the allowance recommended here, this effect would probably be negligible.

[18] A provision of this sort was inserted in the Puerto Rico Estate Tax Law of 1946 at the suggestion of Professor William Vickrey. It was also part of the recommendations on transfer taxes in Carl S. Shoup and associates, *Report on Japanese Taxation by the Shoup Mission* (Tokyo, September 1949), pp. 147-48.

The problem of treatment of transfers to children is an important one. The special study of 1957 and 1959 returns shows that the majority of decedents did make transfers to children, during life or at death, except in the two lowest gross-transfer classes ($0-$100,000 and $100,000-$200,000), where the proportions were 44 percent and 48 percent, respectively. This proportion rises fairly steadily as the size of gross transfers rises, reaching 61 percent for the $900,000-$1,000,000 gross transfer class and 71 percent for the top class ($10 million or more).

In value terms, no such trend appears. The fraction of total noncharitable transfers (after tax) represented by transfers to children was about one-third for all size classes. Considering only those decedents who did transfer something to children, however, a definite trend does emerge. In the lowest gross-transfer group ($0-$100,000), those decedents who transferred something to their children, either during life or at death, gave them, on the average, some 74 percent of the total value of their noncharitable transfers. Those in the highest transfer group ($10 million and over), who transferred something to their children, gave them, on the average, only about 42 percent of the value of their total noncharitable transfers. In between, the percentage declines fairly steadily as gross-transfer size rises. As Dr. Jantscher notes, this trend is understandable:

> Fewer decedents in the lowest wealth ranges transfer anything to their children (husbands usually transfer everything to their wives), but those who do transfer property to their children transfer a lot (presumably most of these are widowers or widows). In higher wealth classes most everybody is transferring property to their children, but not as much.[19]

Transfers to Charitable Organizations

An unlimited deduction from taxable estate or taxable gift is granted to "contributions," a term used here to cover all transfers, during life or at death, to (1) the United States, any State, Territory, or political subdivision thereof, or the District of Columbia; (2) veterans' organizations; (3) corporations organized and oper-

[19] Jantscher, *op. cit.*

ated exclusively for religious, charitable, scientific, literary, or educational purposes, or for the prevention of cruelty to children or animals; or (4) a fraternal society or association operating under the lodge system. Further conditions are that: transfers under (1) must be exclusively for public purposes, and under (3) and (4) must be for the religious, etc. purposes named in (3); and the net earnings of organizations in (2) and (3) must in no part inure to the benefit of any private shareholder or individual. The transfers must in any case involve a public, not a private, benefit; a transfer to an educational trust for the benefit of the decedent's grandnieces and grandnephews has been held not deductible.[20]

The organizations need not be created under domestic laws; this contrasts with the income tax provisions.

In returns filed in 1961 from gross estates totaling $14.6 billion, $1.0 billion[21] was subtracted in the charitable deduction. This is larger than the amounts deducted either as funeral and administration expenses ($600 million) or as claims, mortgages, and other indebtedness ($700 million), though much smaller than the marital deduction ($2.8 billion).

In the 1957 and 1959 special study, data were gathered on the distribution of transfers among the various types of transferee organizations, by size of gross estate (small, medium, millionaire) and by size of gross transfer within the millionaire estate.

Save in the very highest wealth categories, most of the decedents did not respond to the unlimited deduction. Of the small-estate returns (gross estate of $300,000 or less), 86 percent of the 1957 returns reported no contributions at all, either during life or at death. Even when allowance is made for under-reporting or legitimate nonreporting of inter vivos contributions, this percentage is striking. The 1959 percentage is similar—87 percent. Medium-estate contributors ($300,000-$1,000,000) were somewhat more numerous relatively; 74 percent (72 percent in 1959) reported no contributions. Even more surprising is the fact that in the millionaire group, slightly over half the decedents reported no contributions, either during life or at death. To be sure, most of the very

[20] James B. Lewis, *The Estate Tax* (Practising Law Institute, 1964), p. 129, note 32.

[21] Figures here and following are to the nearest $100 million.

wealthiest were contributors; of the 52 decedents (1957 plus 1959) with over $10,000,000 gross transfers, only 5 reported making no contributions.

The percentages of total gross transfers that were contributions were correspondingly small: 3 percent, 5 percent, and 15 percent in 1957 for the three size groups (in 1959, 3, 4, and 15 percent). Those in the subgroup with over $10,000,000 gross transfers, however, contributed 32 percent in both 1957 and 1959.

For the three groups combined, in 1957, 16 percent of the decedents reported contributions, and the contributions were 7 percent of total gross transfers (in 1959, 15 percent and 6 percent).

Those who did make contributions were fairly generous, however. They gave roughly from 20 to 30 percent of their gross transfers. It should be remembered that gross transfer includes gift tax and estate tax paid. This percentage going in contributions seems to be about the same for decedents with small, medium, and large estates, though there is some tendency for the percentage to increase from the lowest to the highest category.

The small-estate decedents ($300,000 or less) gave the bulk of their contributions to charitable organizations: 71 percent in 1957 and 52 percent in 1959. "Charitable organization" means here one concerned primarily with benefits to, and the social welfare of, the community. The millionaire estates indicated a wider range of interests. In 1957 they gave 31 percent to charity; 26 percent to scientific, literary, or educational organizations; 6 percent to religious organizations; and 37 percent to "others," including the "basket" type of organization whose aims are stated in terms too general to categorize them here. The 1959 percentages were, respectively, 47, 28, 7, and 19.

The religious organizations did better, in these terms, with the lower wealth groups: 21 percent and 17 percent of the small- and medium-estate contributions, respectively (34 and 23 percent in 1959).

The degree to which "private" charitable organizations are used as donees is significant. These are organizations that receive all or substantially all their funds from the decedent, his ancestors, or his estate. The decedent or his family usually controls the organization. Of the contributions at death by the millionaires, 43 percent (in 1959, 41 percent) went to private organizations. The bulk of these private-fund contributions was to the "other, including 'basket' " type of organization in 1957; in 1959 about half went to the "charitable" group. There are many possibilities for abusing the contribution deduction through the use of private charitable organizations, and they are currently under investigation by Congress. This problem will not be developed further here.

Allowing the charitable deduction is in a sense the same as using tax revenue to subsidize these organizations, without executive and congressional decision as to precisely how much money shall be so spent and how it shall be allocated among the organizations or used by them (within wide limits). Such by-passing of the budgetary process is advisable when, although the purpose served is a public one, decisions made through the governmental process would create dangerous social and political tensions, or would proceed in virtual ignorance of the merits of thousands of claimants. Both these conditions are fulfilled in the present instance.[22] The law itself and the regulations need to be carefully worded so that this type of subsidy will not be extended by individual decisions to areas and programs that Congress never intended to benefit.

The chief issues in the United States with respect to the charitable deductions are:

1. Are socially undesirable ends being fostered because the definitions in the law are too broadly drawn?

2. Is it desirable for the government to pay a larger share of the contribution, the wealthier the taxpayer concerned?

The role played by "private" foundations (see the special-study data summary above), the size of some of the nonreligious organizations, and the extent to which education is supplied by one of the religious groups have led to differences of opinion as to the desirability of the deduction. The issues are too complex to be developed here. They are not tax-equity issues primarily; rather they are problems of public expenditure that appear in the guise of tax issues because the financing technique is one that bypasses the ordinary budget process.

[22] The investment credit under the income tax, viewed as an alternative to congressional appropriations, is presumably based on the second condition.

Possible alternatives to the present deduction are (1) a tax credit or (2) a deduction effective only for low-bracket rates. Such a comparison uncovers tax-equity issues and problems of incentives and government sharing. If the aim is to induce the largest amount of charitable transfers with a given revenue loss to the government, the reverse of the existing arrangement is preferable. To someone who is contemplating a bequest of $100,000 to a charity, the competing claims of relatives and friends who would lose out because of this bequest will seem weaker in his mind if he has $10,000,000 to dispose of than if he has only $200,000. For the small estate, the government might have to share, say, 50 percent of the cost, to induce a $100,000 bequest to charity; for the large estate, perhaps only 25 percent of the cost. Yet under the present law the government assumes 76 percent of the cost for a $10,000,000 estate[23] instead of the 25 percent share considered necessary, in our illustration, and only 30 percent[24] of the cost for the $200,000 estate instead of the 50 percent share needed. The result in this hypothetical case is: total charitable bequests, $100,000; revenue loss to the government, $76,000. This amount of revenue loss could have produced $200,000 of charitable bequests if the distribution had been $25,000 to the large estate and $50,000 to the small estate, with $1,000 left over for the Treasury.

Essentially the same argument applies if the government's aim is considered to be to obtain a certain total of charitable bequests with a minimum revenue loss.[25]

To be sure, the larger estates have more to give than the smaller. This fact would be recognized by increasing the percentage of deduction the more the larger estate gives—that is, the closer it reduces itself (after the charitable bequest) to the level of the smaller estate.

In effect, to achieve either of the aims stated above (to maximize charitable bequests or to minimize revenue loss), the gov-

[23] The rate for the $8 million to $10 million bracket is 76 percent.

[24] The rate for the $100,000 to $250,000 bracket is 30 percent.

[25] The incentive or substitution effects noted here are to be distinguished from the income effects of the tax. If less total revenue were required from the estate tax, much of the money released for disposition by decedents might be given to charities. C. Lowell Harriss points out that, in this sense, the incidence of some part of the estate tax may well be on the poor. "Sources of Injustice in Death Taxation," *National Tax Journal* (December 1954), p. 296.

ernment would have to completely reverse the progressive rate scale in computing the tax relief to be given for a bequest to charity. A compromise would be to deduct at the effective rate.

What aim may be inferred from the present law? Perhaps none at all; or possibly a desire to induce bequests to charity only when the socially more important task of caring for one's heirs has been accomplished, and to increase the inducement, as the size of the estate increases and more is available beyond the needed bequest to heirs.

Another possible explanation is more in terms of tax equity. If the heirs of a large estate commonly get more than the heirs of a small estate (this of course is not necessarily so), the heavy losses suflered by the large-estate, wealthy heirs through the extra-powerful inducement given under the present system to charitable bequests by the decedent can be just as easily borne by these wealthy heirs as the small losses can be borne by the small-estate, modest-wealth heirs.

The foregoing comments by no means exhaust the issue, but they serve their purpose if they raise questions in the reader's mind about the aims of the charitable-bequest provisions and the criteria for implementing them. It is important to be clear on the purposes and the criteria of the tax even in discussing the much less radical reforms (not examined here) of changing the deduction to a flat-rate credit or limiting it to some percentage of disposable estate.

Life Insurance Proceeds

If at the time of his death a decedent possesses no incidents of ownership in an insurance policy on his life, and if the insurance proceeds are not receivable by his executor, the proceeds are not taxable in his estate. Under the Revenue Act of 1954 this rule applies even if the decedent has been paying the premiums on the policy. From 1942 to 1954, either payment of premiums or possession of incidents of ownership was enough to make the insurance proceeds includable in the estate.

Under the new dispensation an insured can assign to his spouse or other beneficiary all incidents of ownership that he possesses, at the cost only of making a taxable gift of the then value of the policy, roughly the reserve value, not the face value. Each subsequent payment of premium is a taxable gift. (Or, if the $30,000 lifetime exemption has been exhausted, the $3,000 exclusion can be used by giving money to a trustworthy beneficiary who will use it to pay the premiums.)

In support of this new favorable treatment it is said that there is an exact analogy here with any other inter vivos transfer of property. In opposition, it is maintained that an insurance policy is usually not intended for lifetime use, through surrender of the policy, borrowing on it, etc., and is thus "testamentary" in nature. "For the essential function of insurance is to serve as a will."[26] As Bittker points out, there are a number of types of transfer that are held incomplete for estate-tax purposes, despite "the donee's ability to turn the gift into cash during the donor's life."[27] The common feature is that "the transfer is testamentary at its core," and this includes the insurance case.[28]

One might have thought, with Eisenstein, that "Hence insurance proceeds should virtually disappear from the estate tax base."[29] But, whatever the reason, insurance proceeds in estates filed in 1961 totaled $755 million, about 5 percent of gross estate in 1961 returns. For taxable returns only, insurance was $551 million, or 4 percent of taxable gross estate.[30] (See Table IV-1.) In

[26] Louis Eisenstein, "The Rise and Decline of the Estate Tax," in U. S. Congress, Joint Committee on the Economic Report, *Federal Tax Policy for Economic Growth and Stability* (U. S. Government Printing Office, 1955), p. 841.

[27] Boris I. Bittker, "Recommendations for Revision of Federal Estate and Gift Taxes," in U. S. Congress, Joint Committee on the Economic Report, *op. cit.*, pp. 868-69.

[28] *Ibid.*, p. 869. In Britain life insurance proceeds from policies on which the decedent paid the premiums are included in his taxable estate even if he gave the policy to his wife or some other donee before his death. If the deceased, although paying the premiums, *never* had any beneficial interest in the policy, the proceeds are still taxable, but as a separate estate (aggregating the proceeds for any one beneficiary, if there is more than one policy). G. S. A. Wheatcroft, "The Anti-Avoidance Provisions of the Law of Estate Duty in the United Kingdom," *National Tax Journal* (March 1957), p. 54.

[29] Eisenstein, *op. cit.*, pp. 841-42.

[30] U. S. Treasury Department, Internal Revenue Service, *Statistics of Income, 1960*, Fiduciary, Gift, and Estate Tax Returns Filed During Calendar Year 1961, Table 2, p. 46.

comparison, consider the estate tax returns filed in 1950 (for those who died on or after October 22, 1942): gross estate, $4,124 million; taxable insurance, gross, $259 million, or 6 percent.[31] Perhaps the reason why no great change in the amount of taxable insurance has occurred following the 1954 provision is that: (1) insurance is not a form of wealth-holding that appeals to the ultra wealthy; and (2) to those of lesser wealth, loss of ability to borrow on the policy, to change the beneficiaries, etc., may be too high a price to pay for the modest tax savings they can gain by transferring ownership of the policy.

Correlation of Transfer Taxes with the Income Tax[32]

In transfer tax language, "integration," as was pointed out in Chapter II, means combining the estate and gift taxes in some manner, while "correlation" means defining a taxable transfer, under either of these taxes, in a way that will harmonize with the definition implied in income tax law. The term here is "harmonize with," not "coincide with." Depending on the aim in view, it may be desirable to call a transfer effective for transfer tax purposes, but ineffective for changing the taxable recipient of income from the transferred property, or vice versa.

There are at least five major questions involved in "correlation":

1. To prevent shifting of taxable income from a high-bracket donor to a low-bracket donee when little real change in the actual beneficiary of the income occurs, it may be desirable that certain inter vivos intra-family gifts be declared ineffective for shifting taxable income, but at the same time, in order to safeguard transfer tax revenue, that the transfer be declared effective for gift tax. The United States income tax law does not, in fact, use the family relationship test, though the married couple in effect uses it when they file a joint return for splitting income. But the income tax

[31] U. S. Treasury Department, Internal Revenue Service, *Statistics of Income, 1949,* Part 1, p. 354. For certain other years, see Table I-4 in Chap. I above.

[32] See U. S. Treasury Department, Advisory Committee, and Office of Tax Legislative Counsel, *Federal Estate and Gift Taxes: A Proposal for Integration and for Correlation with the Income Tax* (U. S. Government Printing Office, 1947).

TABLE IV–1. Life Insurance Proceeds Reported in Estate Tax Returns Filed in 1961, Taxable and Nontaxable Returns, by Gross Estate Classes

(Dollar amounts in thousands)

Size of gross estate	*Number of returns*	*Amount*
Taxable returns		
Under 60	—	—
60 under 70	816	$4,690
70 under 80	1,541	9,984
80 under 90	1,388	10,598
90 under 100	1,152	10,164
100 under 120	1,850	19,734
120 under 150	3,546	56,378
150 under 200	4,227	91,997
200 under 300	3,957	114,331
300 under 500	2,635	93,264
500 under 1,000	1,550	74,457
1,000 under 2,000	564	37,781
2,000 under 3,000	132	10,326
3,000 under 5,000	99	9,820
5,000 under 10,000	42	5,154
10,000 under 20,000	16	1,674
20,000 or more	6	774
Total	23,521	551,126
Nontaxable returns		
Under 60	5	$54
60 under 70	2,390	22,802
70 under 80	2,029	25,301
80 under 90	1,909	29,215
90 under 100	1,578	27,519
100 under 120	2,642	51,963
120 under 150	1,273	31,372
150 under 200	303	8,499
200 under 300	132	3,785
300 under 500	52	1,776
500 under 1,000	28	1,228
1,000 under 2,000	10	399
2,000 under 3,000	2	6
3,000 under 5,000	1	27
5,000 under 10,000	—	—
10,000 or more	1	85
Total	12,355	204,031
Grand total	35,876	755,157

Source: U. S. Treasury Department, Internal Revenue Service, *Statistics of Income, 1960,* Fiduciary, Gift, and Estate Tax Returns Filed During Calendar Year 1961, p. 47.

law does use an incomplete-gift test which is sometimes more, sometimes less rigorous than those that sweep incomplete gifts and gifts made in contemplation of death into the estate. If the estate and gift tax were integrated so completely that the double-inclusion sections on incomplete and contemplation gifts could be eliminated, the income tax law would still need its own provisions for not recognizing certain transfers that would be recognized for the integrated tax.

At present there seems to be room for more correlation.[33] A transfer under which the transferor retains a power of control over the property that is exercisable only in conjunction with someone who has a substantial adverse interest in such exercise is a completed transfer under the income tax and gift tax, but not under the estate tax. If the power is exercisable by a third party alone, the practice is reversed: the transfer is usually incomplete for income tax, but complete for estate tax purposes. The Clifford case[34] led, through the courts and regulations, to the 1954 Internal Revenue Code provisions that determine for trusts what powers and rights can and what cannot be retained by the transferor without making the income attributable to him for income tax; estate tax law allows few such powers to be retained if the gift is to be complete.

2. Income tax loopholes that for political or other reasons cannot be eliminated directly might be deliberately impaired by special provisions in the estate tax, as, for example, in the 1924 amendment on the floor of the House (which was defeated) that would have levied "a special inheritance surtax on that part of decedents' estates consisting of (income-) tax-exempt securities."[35]

3. The rigor of the income tax may be relaxed in order to reduce an excessive strain on liquidity from the transfer tax. For example, in some cases distributions in redemption of stock included in an estate that would otherwise be deemed dividends can be considered return of capital. This is allowed only to the extent

[33] Bittker, *op. cit.*, pp. 869-70. See also *Federal Estate and Gift Taxes,* cited in note 32.

[34] *Helvering v. Clifford,* 309 U.S. 331 (1940).

[35] William J. Shultz, *The Taxation of Inheritance* (Houghton Mifflin, 1926), p. 161.

that such distributions do not exceed the amount of the death taxes and funeral and administration expenses, if made from a closely held corporation owned largely by the decedent who can find no broad market for the stock (there are a number of definite restrictions).[36]

4. The rigor of the estate tax might be relaxed to lessen an undue strain on liquidity caused by the income tax. If accrued capital gains were subject to income tax at death, some proponents of this measure might be willing to endorse reduction of the estate tax on the capital asset producing the gain, or of estate tax rates generally.

5. The major question remains, though it is always far in the background, whether gifts and inheritances should be treated simply as income to the donee.[37] If they were so taxed, should the donor be allowed a deduction from his income? Presumably not; but would a transfer tax continue to be levied?

Only the first of these five questions seems easy to answer. Points three and four might better be taken into account by improving the payment-by-installment provisions. The fifth would require a highly developed averaging system; and it is not obvious that the amount of tax on a gift or inheritance received should be a function of one's income from other sources rather than of one's net wealth or, as under the accessions tax, one's lifetime history of receiving such bounties. This issue is developed further in Chapter VIII.

Capital Gains and Losses at Death and at Time of Gift

A proposal was advanced in the President's tax message of 1963 to include in taxable income the gain accrued at death or at time of gift and to recognize capital losses similarly accrued, except as between certain related persons.[38] This proposal raises some of the

[36] See the section "Effect on Closely Held Firms" in Chap. VII.

[37] As proposed by Henry C. Simons, in his *Personal Income Taxation* (University of Chicago Press, 1938), pp. 56ff. and 134ff.

[38] For details, see the *President's 1963 Tax Message,* Hearings before the House Committee on Ways and Means, 88 Cong. 1 sess., Part 1 (Feb. 6, 7, and 8, 1963), pp. 128-40.

issues that are encountered under the death and gift taxes. It also requires consideration of the combined amount of income tax, or income tax relief, and death or gift tax, in the light of payment problems. It will be argued below that the President's proposal does not involve any question of double taxation or undue tax relief; rather, it repairs a gap that now exists in the combined transfer tax–income tax structure.

That some of the issues raised are similar to those encountered in the transfer taxes can be seen by noting that the amount of the tax on capital gains, and, to a lesser degree, the amount of tax relief on capital losses depends, under the President's proposal, on (1) to whom the appreciated property is transferred (for example, to spouse or to a charity) and (2) what kind of property is transferred (for example, personal residence left to spouse). For transfers at death, the alternate valuation date would be available, and the special provisions of the estate tax law for easing the payment problems in instances of illiquidity would apply.

The combined effect of the capital gains tax, or capital loss relief, and the estate or gift tax would depend on the marginal rates involved. If the decedent were well into the 77 percent estate tax bracket, and if the capital gain were taxed at 25 percent, the net added tax would be 23 percent of 25 percent of the recognized gain, that is, 5¾ percent of that gain. If he had a capital loss instead, and if it were fully allowable as an offset against ordinary income taxed at 70 percent, the computation would be as follows. The tentative income tax relief from a capital loss of $1,000 would be $700. The tax relief would increase the taxable estate by $700, leading to an increased estate tax of $700 × 77 percent, or $539. The net tax relief would be $700 − $539, or $161, that is, 16.1 percent of the loss. If the loss were allowed only against gains, hence to a maximum of 25 percent of the loss, the existence of the loss would bring a net tax relief of only 23 percent of 25 percent, or, as with the gain above, 5¾ percent of the loss.

Clearly, for taxpayers in the very high estate tax brackets, the net additional tax would be only some 5 or 6 percent of the gain (not 5 or 6 percent of the asset), and the net additional relief would be similarly restricted.

A more typical case might be one where the decedent was in the 40 percent estate tax bracket and the capital gains rate applicable was 20 percent. Then the net additional tax arising from recognition at death would be 60 percent of 20 percent, or 12 percent of the gain.

For gifts the net additional tax and the tax relief would be somewhat higher, owing to the lower gift tax rates.

The proposal has been criticized as double taxation.[39] (No one seems to have criticized it as double tax relief, in the case of capital losses.) But double taxation is meaningful only on a comparative basis. The investor who banks dividends and saves until death pays both income tax and death tax on that income. The holder of a growth stock can increase his economic power while paying only death tax. Moreover, the present failure to tax accrued gains at death obtains even when the property is passed tax free, as through the marital deduction. The President's proposal therefore fills a gap in a discriminatory system, rather than imposing double taxation.

In general, there seems to be little or nothing in this income tax proposal that should change one's views as to what reforms are needed in the estate and gift taxes. If anything, it is the other way around. As long as accrued gains are not taxed at death or at gift and accrued losses are not allowed as income tax deductions at death or at gift, there is some argument for introducing differential death or gift taxation and death or gift tax relief, where the transfer involves an accrued capital gain or loss. Rather than try to make the transfer tax compensate for the inadequacies of the present income tax law, however, it would be better to continue efforts to reform the latter.

Other Technical Issues

There are several more or less technical issues involved in defining the tax base, besides that of life insurance, which are not closely examined here.

Joint annuities and joint interests in a parcel of property lead to taxability of gifts that many honest taxpayers are unaware of,

[39] For example, see the testimony of Henry Bison, Jr., *ibid.*, Part 3, p. 1332.

and in more than one instance an unwitting transferor has accumulated unpaid (but unsuspected) gift tax larger than the value of the property. This can happen, for example, in the case of transfers back and forth within the family effected by putting property in joint tenancies.

Powers of appointment, as now treated by the estate tax law, allow the decedent to have very great control over the property and its income during his lifetime, including wide latitude in determining where it should go after his death, without running any risk of having the property included in his estate at death. To be sure, this power comes to him from another; it is not a residue of a former complete ownership by him. But is this a relevant difference? These special powers of appointment should, in general, make the property includable in the estate of the holder of the power, especially if some way can be found to tax property upon the expiration of a life interest.[40]

Under the present law, which taxes appointive property only if the power of appointment is general, taxable powers apparently supply only some $100 million a year of a $15 billion gross-estate tax base.[41]

Real estate located abroad has finally been brought within the taxable estate under both United States and British law.

[40] See Bittker, *op. cit.*, p. 870.

[41] U. S. Treasury Department, Internal Revenue Service, *Statistics of Income, 1960,* Fiduciary, Gift, and Estate Tax Returns Filed During Calendar Year 1961, Table 2, p. 46.

CHAPTER V

Exemptions and Rates

THIS CHAPTER ANALYZES the effect of the exemptions now allowed under the federal estate tax and of the present rate structure of that tax. Changes that might be made to meet certain criteria are also discussed.

The Exemptions

Under the estate tax exemption of $60,000, about 65,000 returns are being filed annually, of which nearly a third are nontaxable.[1] A return is required of a United States citizen or resident if his gross estate exceeds $60,000 in value at the date of his death. The return may prove to be nontaxable because the deduc-

[1] The total number of estate tax returns of citizens and resident aliens filed during 1961 was 64,538, of which 45,439 were taxable. There were 1,251 returns filed by nonresident aliens during 1961, of which 989 were taxable. U. S. Treasury Department, Internal Revenue Service, *Statistics of Income, 1960,* Fiduciary, Gift, and Estate Tax Returns, p. 67. In the United Kingdom, "Since 1946 there has been no duty on estates under £2,000 (£3,000 since 1954), so that the large majority of the 550,000 people who die each year in the United Kingdom are not affected by the tax. The Revenue statistics show between 70,000 and 80,000 new 'estates' each year, and this figure is expected to drop to approximately 50,000 a year when the estates between £2,000 and £3,000 cease to be recorded." G. S. A. Wheatcroft, "The Anti-Avoidance Provisions of the Law of Estate Duty in the United Kingdom," *National Tax Journal* (March 1957), p. 48.

tions (expenses, claims, losses, charitable contributions, marital deduction) exceed the difference between the gross estate value and $60,000, or because a lower alternate valuation date is chosen by the executor, or because of credits against the tax (for state death taxes, gift taxes paid on property interests included in the estate, foreign taxes, taxes on recent prior transfers).

A married couple with a taxable estate of $120,000 can pass it all to their children or others free of tax, even if the property is in the first decedent spouse's name initially. The husband can leave $60,000 tax free to his wife under the marital deduction and the rest to the children tax free under the $60,000 exemption. The widow can pass on her $60,000 tax free under the exemption.

The 45,000-odd taxable returns under the estate tax represent not more than 3 percent of annual adult deaths in the United States.[2] Some adult deaths result in no estate whatsoever or a negative amount. Many other decedents probably leave no more than a few hundred dollars worth of furniture, clothing, and their equity in a car or household appliances.

In 1953, Lampman estimates, 1.6 percent of the adult living population had over $60,000 in assets, but these adults held about 30 percent of the total assets in the personal sector in the United States.[3]

A gift tax return must be filed by any donor who in any year gives to any one person more than $3,000, or who makes any gift of a future interest. The number of gift tax returns being filed each year happens to be not far from the number of estate tax returns filed—some 78,000 in 1961, of which only about 18,000 were taxable.[4] The large proportion of nontaxable returns reflects the fact that the donors are not excused from filing a return because of nontaxability arising from taking part or all of the $30,000 life-

[2] The number of deaths among the adult population 25 and over was 1,541,357 in 1960. U. S. National Office of Vital Statistics, *Vital Statistics of the United States, 1960,* Vol. II, Part B, pp. 9-87.

[3] Robert J. Lampman, *The Share of Top Wealth-Holders in National Wealth, 1922-56* (National Bureau of Economic Research-Princeton University Press, 1962), pp. 18, 23. Included are equities in unincorporated enterprises and in certain financial institutions.

[4] U. S. Treasury Department, Internal Revenue Service, *Statistics of Income, 1960,* Gift Tax Returns Filed During 1961, Table E, p. 29.

time exemption, gifts to charity, the marital 50 percent deduction on gifts to spouse, or gifts to a donee exceeding the $3,000 exclusion. According to the regulations, incomplete transfers of any size call for a return.[5]

A lowering of the $30,000 lifetime gift tax exemption might not bring in many new taxpayers. The pattern of giving could shift readily to accommodate to the new exemption level. For the same reason, a lowering might not bring in much added revenue from those now filing taxable returns. The fact that it would still be cheaper to give than hold and bequeath cannot be accorded much weight in view of the disinclination shown to take advantage of existing tax bargains.

There seems to be little reason for the annual exclusion per donee to be as high as $3,000, especially with the split-gift provision. A spouse can give up to $6,000 a year to each child (or any other donee) if his partner joins formally, even though not actually, without even impinging on the $30,000 exemption ($60,000, for husband and wife together).

The $60,000 estate tax exemption and the $30,000 lifetime gift tax exemption are now worth less than half, in real terms, what they were in 1942, when they were set at these levels. The estate tax exemption is coupled with a rate scale that starts at 3 percent on the first $5,000 of taxable estate, not reaching a marginal rate of above 20 percent until the taxable estate becomes $40,000 (that is, a net estate of $100,000).

At initial rates so low, a lowering of the $60,000 estate tax exemption to, say, $30,000 would not gain much revenue from those estates not now taxable.

Data from the study by Harriss (Appendix D below) concerning the distribution of the estate and gift tax base by *brackets* (not by estate, or gift, or transfer *classes*),[6] show the degree of concentration of the gross tax base[7] in the lower *brackets,* as reported in estate tax returns for 1957 and 1959. These data of course do not include decedents whose estates were so small that no return was filed. About 40 percent of the total gross transfers,

[5] George Craven, *The Gift Tax* (Practising Law Institute, 1960), p. 29.

[6] See the explanation below in the section on "Rate Structure."

[7] Gross tax base is before exemption and certain deductions.

that is, about $4 billion ($5 billion in 1959), fall in the gross transfer *bracket,* $0-$100,000. The figure for *gross transfers,* it will be recalled, is before subtracting the $60,000 exemption, or the marital or charitable deductions, and includes gifts and gift tax and estate tax. Similar computations made from *Statistics of Income, 1959* for gross estate (not gross transfers) for taxable and nontaxable returns show about $5 billion of gross estate in the gross estate bracket, $0-$100,000; over $3 billion of the $5 billion is in the $0-$60,000 bracket alone. In terms of net estate (that is, after all deductions except the $60,000 exemption), there was $2.3 billion in the $0-$60,000 bracket. Thus a 3 percent rate, for instance, instead of the 0 percent rate, would yield only $69 million from those decedents filing returns under the present law.

The most important point in the level of the exemption, $30,000 one way or another, is its value or its shortcomings as a substitute for a change in the rate scale. The lower the exemption, the lower can be the marginal rate on a given gross estate if the same total tax is to be taken from this estate in either case. The lower the exemption, the closer is the marginal rate to the average rate. The lower the marginal rate, the less are the announcement effects, or incentive effects. The income effect (the average rate) remains unchanged, by hypothesis. Accordingly if one welcomes the incentive effects of the tax, one will advocate a high exemption and high tax rates.

If a deduction were allowed for bequests to minor dependents (see the section on "Transfers to Sons and Daughters" in Chapter IV) and if interspousal transfers were completely exempted (see the section on "Interspousal Transfers" in Chapter IV), the $60,000 estate tax exemption might be reduced to, say, $10,000 or $20,000, though the states might object. (See Chapter VI.)

If lifetime giving is to be encouraged at the expense of later bequests, the estate tax exemption should be low and the rates high, and the gift tax exemption high with low rates. These remarks of course apply only to taxpayers who would pay a tax in either case, and indeed the same tax. But the assumption that they would pay the same tax cannot be maintained absolutely, since there will be new taxpayers under a lower exemption. There is, however, a general tendency here that is relevant.

A tax credit instead of an exemption would increase the progressiveness of the present rate scale. But could it accomplish anything that a direct change in the rate scale, yielding the same increase in total revenue, could not? The answer is yes, if reference is to husbands and wives compared with single decedents. A tax credit up to $1,800, in place of the $60,000 exemption, is equivalent to an exemption taken out of the lowest (3 percent) bracket. Under such a credit, but with a lower rate of progression to avoid a change in total revenue, the marital deduction would not mean as much as it would under the present system with the present rate schedule. The marital deduction comes out of higher rate brackets under the present system than it would under the tax-credit, lower-rate-of-progression form of tax.

A tax credit for contributions, with a lower rate of progression to obtain the same revenue, would of course change the distribution of the transfer tax bill. This device would tend to move part of the estate tax bill to the married. While marriage might not be discouraged thereby, contributions might be, though probably not by much.

A credit in lieu of an exemption is sometimes supported on grounds that it allows a lower marginal rate of tax relative to a given effective rate. But under an assumption of equal revenue, this conclusion is not valid as a general rule, in contrast to the conclusion reached above on lowering the exemption with an equal-revenue constraint. A numerical illustration will indicate the nature of the problem.

Assume that a given taxpayer is faced with the following rate and exemption schedule: first $1,000, exempt; second $1,000, 10 percent; third $1,000, 20 percent; fourth $1,000, 30 percent.

If he has a net estate of $3,000, the tax bill will be $300. He is faced with a marginal tax rate of 30 percent on the upside, 20 percent on the downside. If the exemption of $1,000 is replaced by a credit of $100, his tax bill will be $600 minus the credit, or $500. To reduce this to $300, the rate scale would have to be changed as shown on the following page:

	Rates	Tax
First $1,000	*10* percent	$100
Second $1,000	*10* percent	100
Third $1,000	*20* percent	200
Fourth $1,000	*30* percent	—

The tax bill in the hypothetical example, before the $100 credit, would now be $300; and the taxpayer would still be faced with a marginal rate of 30 percent on the upside and 20 percent on the downside.

A vanishing exemption would allow a still lower rate scale, but every vanishing exemption has this shortcoming: the marginal rate of tax would be higher on a smaller estate, one in the range where the exemption is vanishing, than on the larger estates just beyond the point where the exemption vanishes.

A change in the federal estate tax exemption is included in some plans for revising the present credit allowed for state death taxes.

Rate Structure

The appropriate rate structure for an estate tax to meet certain criteria cannot be determined without some knowledge, or at least an assumption, as to the incidence of the tax. If at one extreme the tax is viewed as always burdening the heirs rather than the decedent during his lifetime, graduation of the tax by size of estate rather than by size of donee's share can have little to do with relative ability to pay.[8] This extreme assumption on incidence may be untenable, but it seems closer to the truth than does the other extreme,[9] which would place the full force of the coming estate tax on the decedent-to-be, inducing him to restrict his consumption and to work more.

When a large estate goes chiefly to one beneficiary, graduation may be applied formally to the estate as a substitute for graduation according to donee's share. Perhaps some such reasoning is an implicit rationale for graduation of the estate tax. If preventing

[8] See the discussion of inheritance taxes in Chap. II.
[9] See Chap. VII.

TABLE V–1. Effective Rate of Estate Tax, by Gross Estate Class, on (a) Gross Estate Less Debts and Mortgages and (b) Taxable Estate—Taxable Returns Filed in 1961[a]

(Dollar amounts in millions)

Gross estate class (In thousands of dollars) (1)	Number of returns (2)	Amount of gross estate (3)	Number of returns (4)	Amount of debts and mortgages (5)	Gross estate less debts and mortgages (col. 3 minus col. 5) (6)	Net estate tax (after credits) (7)	Effective rate (col. 7 divided by col. 6, percent) (8)	Taxable estate (net estate after exemption) (9)	Effective rate (col. 7 divided by col. 9, percent) (10)
Under 60	—	—	—	—	—	—	—	—	—
60 under 70	2,051	$137.4	1,618	$1.2	$136	$0.2	0.2	$6.7	3.3
70 under 80	3,874	290.4	3,277	5.0	285	1.9	0.7	35.5	5.5
80 under 90	3,414	289.8	2,947	6.9	283	4.5	1.6	59.0	7.7
90 under 100	2,792	265.1	2,443	7.5	258	6.6	2.6	69.9	9.5
100 under 120	4,398	481.4	3,925	14.7	467	18.9	4.0	158.8	12.0
120 under 150	6,523	879.9	5,670	25.8	854	38.9	4.6	260.0	15.0
150 under 200	7,183	1,238.7	6,468	48.1	1,191	75.5	6.3	429.9	18.0
200 under 300	6,575	1,596.0	6,132	76.1	1,520	142.5	9.4	693.1	21.0
300 under 500	4,469	1,696.5	4,225	81.7	1,615	212.9	13.0	902.2	24.0
500 under 1,000	2,684	1,822.4	2,613	92.5	1,730	281.1	16.0	1,084.5	26.0
1,000 under 2,000	966	1,311.3	945	66.8	1,244	235.6	19.0	827.4	28.0
2,000 under 3,000	242	589.1	239	27.7	561	118.5	21.0	376.4	31.0
3,000 under 5,000	165	618.2	164	20.7	597	134.6	23.0	389.1	35.0
5,000 under 10,000	65	442.9	65	16.8	426	107.2	25.0	262.1	41.0
10,000 under 20,000	26	351.2	26	11.9	339	84.9	25.0	183.1	46.0
20,000 or more	12	723.1	12	16.6	706	154.5	22.0	276.8	56.0
Total taxable returns[b]	45,439	12,733.5	40,769	520.0	12,213	1,618.5	13.0	6,014.5	27.0

Source: U. S. Treasury Department, Internal Revenue Service, *Statistics of Income, 1960,* Fiduciary, Gift, and Estate Tax Returns Filed During Calendar Year 1961, Table 3, pp. 47-50.

[a] Citizens and residents only.

[b] Details may not add to totals due to rounding.

concentration of wealth is the aim, graduation by size of total estate is again not justifiable unless the estate goes chiefly to one heir.

A small estate can produce only a small inheritance. Low initial rates under the estate tax can be based on this fact. A huge estate will almost inevitably give rise to at least one large inheritance and probably several. Perhaps these considerations justify an estate tax rate scale that (1) starts at a level low enough to be proper for a small inheritance, though the present 3 percent level seems too low in any case; (2) moves to higher but not much higher levels for estates that may easily go either way; and (3) climbs to high levels—77 percent maximum in the present law—for estates so large that they inevitably give rise to large inheritances.[10]

The effective rates of the federal estate tax are, of course, much lower. Table V-1 shows effective rates for 1961 returns, by gross estate class. The effective rate on taxable estates of $20 million or more is 56 percent. The effective rate on the gross estate less debts and mortgages is 22 percent.

For estimating rate schedules that would yield the same revenue, but with differing degrees of progression, the bracket-distribution tables computed by Harriss and referred to above, are indispensable.[11]

If the burden of the tax rests on the donee, his wealth and income are relevant for determining the rate applicable to his inheritance. A cumulative accessions tax moves some distance in this direction. More directly to the point is a tax collected from the donee and graduated by the size of the donee's net wealth including the gift or inheritance.[12]

[10] The British estate tax rates go to still greater extremes: from 1 percent on estates between £3,000 and £4,000 to 80 percent on estates over £1 million. These are effective (average) rates, not bracket (marginal) rates. Wheatcroft, *op. cit.,* p. 48.

[11] The tables will be found in Appendix D.

[12] As proposed by Nicolas Kaldor, with a starting rate of 10 percent and a top rate of 80 percent, in his *Indian Tax Reform,* Department of Economic Affairs, Ministry of Finance, Government of India (June 1956), pp. 16 and 50. For an earlier, similar proposal, with the definite aim of causing "the curve representing the individual distribution of private wealth" to tend "towards symmetry with relation to the *Modus,*" see Vasco N. P. Fortuna, "The Sociometric Theory and the Estate Duty," *Public Finance* (No. 3, 1951), pp. 267-71. Kaldor would give the donee the option to include the gifts (and inheritances?) of any one year in taxable income. *Op. cit.,* p. 51.

Taxing estates that themselves are traceable to inheritance more heavily than first-generation estates is a familiar idea in academic literature (Rignano, Pigou, Dalton), but it has received no serious attention in practice. The tracing problem is, to be sure, formidable, but surely not insurmountable, with the aid of some reasonable presumptions. If an aim of death and gift taxation is to prevent large fortunes from growing ever larger by a series of inheritances, the possibility of graduation on this basis should be explored, whether or not the top rate is set, in effect, at 100 percent, as Rignano would have it.

Guides that have been suggested for the graduation of tax rates on income probably do not fit well the death and gift taxes.[13]

[13] See, for example, the formulas discussed by William Vickrey in his *Agenda for Progressive Taxation* (Ronald Press, 1947), Appendix VII.

CHAPTER VI

Federal-State Relations[1]

THE CREDIT CURRENTLY allowed against the federal estate tax for state death taxes paid is limited to an amount equal to 80 percent of what the federal estate tax would be if it were applied to the currently defined base before exemption (for example, after the marital deduction), but after the 1926 exemption of $100,000, not $60,000, and at the 1926 scale of rates.

Most of the 49 states that impose death taxes do so at rates, and with exemptions, that cause the state tax for many decedents to exceed the amount that can be credited. Of the $411 million death tax revenues of the states in 1961, less than 40 percent was creditable against the federal estate tax. About 20 percent was not creditable because the estate was under $100,000 (the 1926 federal exemption), yet was taxable by the state. The remainder, over 40 percent of the total state death tax bill, was noncreditable because the states' tax rates were so high and/or their exemptions so low that the estates in question (those over $100,000) owed more tax than 80 percent of the 1926 federal estate tax.[2]

The states differ widely in the kinds of death tax they impose.[3]

[1] See also Chap. I above.

[2] U. S. Advisory Commission on Intergovernmental Relations, *Coordination of State and Federal Inheritance, Estate and Gift Taxes* (U. S. Government Printing Office, January 1961), p. 48.

[3] *Ibid.*, Table 3, p. 35.

Hence an executor may have to work through not just two death tax laws, but several. The states sometimes conflict in asserting their respective rights to tax certain types of property, notably intangibles (securities, notes, etc.). Aged persons of wealth and some not so aged find it pays to shop around for state of death, since the degree to which the state tax exceeds the federal credit differs among states. The crediting device has indeed prevented the states from competing with each other to the point of lowering state death taxes below the credit level (except for unregenerate Nevada), but that is all it has done.

Disillusionment with the credit has not prevented it from remaining unchanged in substance for nearly forty years. Any move to any other form of federal-state coordination is bound to affect someone adversely, and he will always protest more loudly than others will acclaim, unless the Treasury is the loser under a deliberate federal policy. If it were possible to start afresh, the arguments for exclusive federal use of the tax would be overwhelming. But that path now seems impossible politically in view of all the vested interests right down to the local probate official, in sparsely populated areas, who has much to do with setting the value on taxable properties and who gains some local political power and fees that way.

The Advisory Commission on Intergovernmental Relations has recommended that the present credit "be replaced with a two-bracket credit to earmark for the States a large share of [current] Federal tax liabilities in the lower tax brackets [that is, notably below the $100,000 level] and a small share in the higher brackets,"[4] provided that each state raises its death tax "in an amount corresponding to the estimated aggregate increase in the tax credits on Federal estate tax returns filed" in that state.[5] The new credit would be limited to estate-type death taxes to encourage uniformity. Over the longer run the Commission hopes for exclusive federal collection plus sharing of the revenue with the states.[6] It recommends against a federal gift tax credit for state gift taxes.[7]

[4] *Ibid.*, p. 16.
[5] *Ibid.*, p. 18.
[6] *Ibid.*, p. 22.
[7] *Ibid.*, p. 23.

Given the political and other limitations within which the Commission had to operate and the fact that they wanted prompt action, one can appreciate the recommendations. But prompt action has not been forthcoming, and none is in prospect. The best course is probably to aim at once for the long-term goal of an exclusive federal tax, with or without sharing with the states.

CHAPTER VII

Economic Effects

A TAX USUALLY comes partly out of saving and partly out of consumption. That is, it reduces both the taxpayer's consumption spending and his saving (or increases his dissaving) from the levels they would have reached in the absence of the tax.

Effect on Saving[1]

A tax may be devised, however, that will come entirely out of saving or that will go further and cause the taxpayer to reduce his saving by more than the tax. He will then increase his consumption by the difference, assuming his income to be unchanged. For example, if the taxpayer's income before tax is 100 and would be 100 if there were no tax, and if he would in that event spend 90 and save 10, he might, under a certain tax of 5, consume 98, pay a tax of 5, and dissave by 3. Such a reaction might occur if the tax were an expenditure tax, the rate of which was scheduled to increase with time: say 5 percent this year, 10 percent next year, and 15 percent the third year and thereafter.

Suppose instead that the expenditure tax is put on the statute books now, but will not take effect until three years from now, at

[1] See Appendix F.

a rate of 15 percent then and thereafter. The tax collected this year is zero, yet the pattern of 90 spent and 10 saved if no tax at all had been announced might be replaced by a pattern of 105 spent and 5 dissaved. And in the year the tax first takes effect, spending might drop to, say, 74, and the former dissaving of 5 change to a saving of 15, the tax (15 percent) being 11.

Finally, suppose that the tax announced today is to be levied on the expenditure of just the third year from now, not the second, and not the fourth, fifth, and so on, and will be at a high rate, say 30 percent. Spending this year and next might rise to 120, dissaving being 20 each year, drop to, say, 50 in the third year, and rebound to a normal (nontax) level of 90 in the fourth year.

This last, and peculiar, type of expenditure tax is hypothesized because it throws some light on the death tax, which is closely analogous for certain types of decedents and heirs. The time of death is the "year" of the tax; the amount transmitted to heirs is the amount "spent." For the type of decedent in mind at the moment, this kind of spending, coupled with the benefits of power, etc. (see the section "Why So Little Lifetime Giving?" in Chapter II), from holding property until death, has a close substitute in ordinary consumption; if there is a tax on the "spending" at death but none on ordinary consumption during life, the decedent substitutes the latter for the former. Note that there is no possibility of the decedent's saving anything in the year of death, if transfers are counted as expenditures, and that the date of that year cannot be foreseen.

Conceivably then a death tax could induce an increase in ordinary consumption by the decedent-to-be, compared with what it would have been if no such tax had existed. The increase would take place over the years prior to his death, at the expense of the saving in those years that would have been devoted to enjoying power etc. meanwhile, and to "spending" (passing to heirs) in the year of death. The increase in ordinary consumption might be so great as to result in dissaving. Whether it did or not, it would exceed the tax for those years prior to death, which is zero.

"Spending" in the years before death may for present purposes be defined as the sum of ordinary consumption and gifts inter vivos (plus gift tax), since, like ordinary consumption, such gifts lessen the tax at death.

In national income accounting terms, the point here is that an estate tax may at one extreme not only "come out of saving" in the sense that saving over the years is reduced by the amount of the tax below what it would have been in the absence of the tax (consumption is not decreased), but may go further: saving may be reduced by more than the tax (consumption is increased by the tax). The extreme case would occur if the tax was avoided entirely by consumption of all the potential estate before death. This result, saving decreased by more than the tax, is even more likely to occur if consumption is defined to include lifetime gifts; but this definition, though useful from some points of view, has no direct significance for economic growth.

In all this analysis, income before tax is assumed to remain unchanged. The possibility that the death and gift taxes might induce a change in income is discussed in the section on "Effect on Amount of Income," below.

For other types of decedent, however, the reaction to the estate tax may be quite different. Suppose that for one kind of decedent, ordinary consumption is not a close substitute for holding property for power, etc., and passing it to heirs at death. A death tax may even induce such a decedent to consume less than he would have in the absence of the tax, though perhaps not enough less to make up for the tax in full. And even inter vivos gifts may not be for him a close substitute for holding property for power, etc., then passing it at death.

Surprisingly little property is passed inter vivos, despite bargain tax rates. Does this imply that the property owner's heirs are not prominent in his thoughts as he works and saves? Not necessarily so. The accumulator who likes power may give little during life, but he may still be concerned over what will happen to his heirs after his death. He would not necessarily be inconsistent in giving so little during life, yet reacting to a rise in estate tax rates by consuming somewhat less and saving somewhat more, especially since more saving means more "consumption" of power meanwhile.

But the behavior of the heirs-to-be should not be neglected in our preoccupation with the decedents-to-be. In the absence of a tax, they have certain more or less well defined expectations of inheritance. The tax is announced, and these expectations decline. The present value of a future "income effect" weighs on them; what will they do in consequence? Nothing they can do themselves will change the amount of the tax, there is no substitution effect. Following the usual reasoning, we should expect the heirs-to-be to work harder (see the section on "Effect on Amount of Income" below) unless they are quite well-to-do. They would probably save a large part of their additional income and might even save more of the rest of their income than if no tax had been announced. For example, suppose that a tax of 100 percent were imposed on bequests and gifts. Many fairly well-off adults in their thirties and forties would surely begin to retrench, and those with little capital and modest incomes might even strive to get more income, as the prospect of inheritance disappeared.

So little is known about how people do react to the threat of a distant but inevitable tax that it is impossible to assert confidently that the estate tax will on balance reduce saving by the prospective decedent and his prospective heirs, viewed together. Of course, if the tax is heavy, both saving and consumption will presumably be reduced. (This is not based on reasoning on a macro level here, only on a view of one small part of the economy.) But instances are conceivable where the prospective decedent will reduce his consumption in an effort to lessen the future impairment by the tax of his heirs' net wealth. The prospective heirs also will reduce their consumption in a duplicative effort to reduce that threatened impairment. Together, decedent and heirs might increase their net wealth, after tax, over what it would have been if no such tax had existed.

Finally, there remains the possibility that the heirs, in the years following the death and the tax, would keep their consumption at a lowered level in an effort to recoup part of the impairment.

This analysis does not imply that what the decedent has saved by the time he dies has been saved merely with the heirs in mind.

Indeed, another group of decedents may be postulated who save mightily, but not for heirs. As was noted in Chapter II, the direct exercise of power and other desirable intangibles that come with possession of wealth are strong inducements not to consume. And they are goods whose value to the decedent-to-be is not lessened by the inevitability of a death tax.[2] Only the satisfaction from forming a dynasty of power is impaired by that tax. Very wealthy persons may be near satiation with respect to consumption as defined in national income accounting and may be impressed by the likelihood of spoiling their heirs by further gifts. They then purposefully devote most of their income over the years until death to saving in order to obtain ever more power and may plan to leave the bulk of their estates to charity. On the consumption and inter vivos giving of such persons an increase or decrease of death tax rates or gift tax rates can have little or no effect. The prospective heirs of such decedents-to-be, meanwhile, may not take the same view at all; they may retrench a bit if death tax rates go up. And their consumption in the years following the death may well be lower than if there were no death tax. A donee's propensity to consume out of gifts and bequests may be high, in contrast to David Ricardo's world, where the heirs strove to keep intact whatever capital net of tax they did receive, but did not attempt to make up for the tax by more work or lower consumption.[3]

The bulk of the estate tax revenue, as the tax is presently constituted, may well be coming from combinations of decedents and heirs of the type just described. According to *Statistics of Income,* the taxable estate tax returns filed in 1961[4] showed a total gross estate of $12.7 billion ($6.3 billion in corporation stock, $2.2 billion in real estate) with debts and mortgages of $0.5 billion, incurring a net estate tax liability, after credits against tax, of $1,619 million. Nearly half of the latter ($741 million) attached to net es-

[2] For emphasis on the importance of this group of accumulators, see Dr. Fiekowsky's analysis in Appendix F. See also his paper, "On the Significance of Successors' Welfare as a Motivation for the Accumulation of Wealth," *Proceedings, Western Economic Association* (1956), pp. 42-48.

[3] See Carl S. Shoup, *Ricardo on Taxation* (Columbia University Press, 1956), pp. 46-48, 205-06.

[4] Citizens and resident aliens.

tates (before specific exemption) of $1,000,000 and over.[5] When it is recalled that the net estate is after the marital deduction ($2.2 billion for 1961 taxable estates; $487 million for net estates of $1,000,000 and over) and minus the community property of a surviving spouse, and is also after the charitable deduction ($748 million for 1961 taxable estates; $385 million for net estates of $1,000,000 and over), and when it is recalled also that much property is in trusts and does not appear even in the gross estate, is it too much to say that this $741 million of estate tax came from decedents and heirs of the type last described above? (If one goes down to the $500,000 *net* estate level, $1,003 million of the $1,619 million tax can be accounted for.) If this is so, the estate tax does come out of saving (the decedents' reaction), but this effect is counterbalanced to some degree, though not entirely, by retrenchment by heirs. And it may be inferred that, for the type of decedent just discussed, the net effect of the tax is certainly not to decrease the economy's saving by more than the tax.

Effect on Amount of Investment[6]

The effect of a tax on saving is no clear indication of its effect on investment. Investment spending decisions are to some extent made by persons who cannot make corresponding decisions on saving. They spend, on investment, other people's money, including newly manufactured bank money. Consequently an increase in the estate tax, or any other tax, if it did decrease saving, might at the same time have little or no influence on investment spending. Indeed it is conceivable that a certain tax measure might decrease saving and simultaneously increase investment. To be sure, saving must always equal investment spending for the economy as a

[5] U. S. Treasury Department, Internal Revenue Service, *Statistics of Income, 1960, Fiduciary, Gift, and Estate Tax Returns Filed During Calendar Year 1961*, Table 4, pp. 51-52. For a historical series, see Tables I-2 and I-3 in Chap. I above.

[6] "Investment" is here used in the national-income sense, not in the securities-market sense. An investor is one who buys producers' goods (machinery, plant, and, on a net-increase basis, inventoried goods). A disinvestor is one who sells such goods. Gross investment is the amount of producers' goods created during the period (but inventoriable goods are computed on a net-increase basis). Net investment is gross investment less depreciation, depletion, and obsolescence.

whole. If a tax measure does change saving by one amount and investment by another, the other fiscal or monetary measure that goes with it (change in another tax, change in government expenditure, change in government debt or cash balance), along with consequent changes in private-sector spending, must iron out the potential discrepancy. But we are not studying these other measures. Our attention is riveted on the death and gift taxes, as we conduct a partial-equilibrium analysis.[7]

Insofar as investment spending decisions are indeed conditioned on the level of saving of the investment spender, the above remarks do not hold, and a tax that decreases saving will thereby decrease investment. A closely held business without ready access to the capital market may easily be checked in its growth by an estate tax. If the estate tax were repealed, such a firm would invest more. (In a policy analysis on the macro level, one would then have to ask: would this increase in investment spending be at the

[7] Ultimately evaluation of a tax always means comparing it with some other source of revenue, or, if not that, with some change in government expenditure, borrowing, or new-money finance. Action can be taken sensibly only in the light of alternative measures available. Yet the analyst would be intellectually paralyzed if he had to observe this rule, essential though it is for the policy maker. The analytical process instead is commonly this: some feature of the tax is assumed to be changed, and the economic, social, and administrative consequences are conjectured on the *ceteris paribus* assumption; the environment is assumed, for the time being, to be unchanged. For example, since the present estate tax law does not tax the corpus of a trust upon the expiry of a life interest, we ask what would be the consequences of adopting the British practice, but without considering the lowering of estate tax rates that might follow if the total revenue from the tax were stipulated to remain unchanged. On the broader economic issues discussed in this chapter, for example, the effect of the estate tax on the volume of saving, we conjecture what would happen to the volume of saving if the entire estate tax were removed and no other change were made in the fiscal system as to revenue, expenditure, or borrowing. Of course, some such change would have to occur. But each of these changes in turn can be analyzed in appropriate studies, on the same supposition—that all other things are unchanged. These other analyses are not a part of the present study, except for some very general pronouncements offered here and there in passing.

The policy maker then constructs a package of two or more compatible changes (taxation of expiry of life interests, corresponding reduction of estate tax rates) and, with the aid of the analyst, sets the effects of the one against those of the other, notes the cancellations of opposing effects or the reinforcing of common ones, takes account of the more important of the interaction effects produced by the two changes in combination, and reaches a conclusion on the net result.

expense of investment spending somewhere else in the economy, or would it be met by reduced consumption, or would such reactions be avoided by the use of unemployed resources, or capital imports? But these questions lie beyond the scope of the present analysis.) How large this kind of investment is, relative to total investment spending, we do not know, but it cannot be very large; it does not include investment spending by widely held corporations.

There remains for consideration the incentive effect of the transfer taxes. Does the prospect that any earnings that may result from an investment will be lost in part to gift and estate taxation if they are not consumed deter investment spending, even though the money, one's own or someone else's, is at hand?

There may be instances of such an effect, but introspection and common observation suggest that they are rare. The decision makers of widely held corporations are not likely to be influenced by prospective death taxes on stockholders. The owner of a closely held corporation may be induced to lower his rate of saving, as has been seen, but that is not the question here. The question is, assuming that he saves a certain amount, does the death-gift tax induce him to hold his saving uninvested, when in the absence of the tax he would have invested it? Here investing, as was noted earlier, is in the national income sense: direct spending for newly created plant, equipment, inventories, and foreign financial assets. If the death-gift tax is to reduce investment because of its effect on incentive, we must postulate the case of a potential demand for tangible capital goods (or foreign financial assets) that does not develop because the would-be purchaser is discouraged by the death and gift taxes. Such a result seems unlikely.

Effect on Type of Investment

The estate tax has been charged with diverting investment from risky ventures into safe, rentier-like securities, and with causing a business firm to be managed with unusual caution.

This latter phenomenon is said to occur when the decedent's majority interest in a firm remains in an executor's hands for a considerable period, perhaps owing to estate tax difficulties.[8] Getting the business interest out of the estate quickly is easier than it used to be, thanks to the use of buy-sell agreements and the stock redemption provisions of 1950; both of these are discussed below, under "Liquidity."

The former is the more serious problem; it arises from the tendency of the estate tax law to cause property to be put in trust. The extent to which this occurs has been discussed above, and measures to reduce the tax pressure in this direction have been suggested. It is important to recall here that we have no idea of the extent to which trusts would still be employed even if the estate tax system were quite neutral in this respect. The income tax and a number of powerful nontax forces stimulate the use of trusts. We should also recall, what seems to be ignored too frequently, that no one knows whether national income would in fact be increased or decreased if the current investment pattern were altered to increase the number of risky ventures at the expense of safe ventures. How can we be certain that we are not currently wasting (in some sense or other) large amounts of investment on risky ventures?

Effects on Closely Held Firms

The closely held firm poses several problems under death taxation. Each appears in a somewhat different light depending on whether the firm is a sole proprietorship, a partnership, or a corporation.

Valuation

Since there is no active market, indeed no market at all, for the ownership interests in these firms, a wide area is open for dispute between the tax administration and the estate's representative. A majority owner in a family corporation will often see to it that his interest in the corporation is reduced to less than 50 percent before his death, so that his executors can claim the disadvantages of

[8] Harold M. Somers, "Estate Taxes and Business Mergers," *Journal of Finance* (May 1958), p. 202.

a minority stockholder in urging a low valuation. A difference of only a few percentage points in the rate of capitalizing current earnings can of course mean a large percentage difference in the capital value.

Buy-sell contracts can often avert valuation disputes. Thus the owners of a closely held corporation will bind themselves to sell only to each other, the stock on death to be sold only to the surviving owners; and this agreement establishes either the value of the shares or a reasonable method of arriving at the value. (Each owner takes out insurance on the lives of each of the others; this is a problem of liquidity, which will be discussed below.) Such a contract is perhaps found most often for two- or three-owner corporations. Similarly partners may establish values or methods of valuation. "Such established valuation . . . is controlling on the tax collector, if it is arrived at by arm's-length bargaining and creates a binding contract to buy and sell."[9]

Liquidity for Payment of Tax[10]

By now, the estate tax law has been so amended in the direction of meeting liquidity problems of an estate consisting largely of an ownership share in a closely held business, especially if that business is incorporated, that there would seem to be not very much estate tax pressure to merge with large corporations before the death of a large stockholder or to break up the business at a disadvantageous price after his death. But these remarks are largely conjecture; not enough experience has yet been accumulated, and little intensive research has been done.

After the "preliminary notice" on Form 704, the return, Form 706, must be filed within fifteen months of death. The local District Director of Internal Revenue may extend this *filing* time (not tax payment time) up to six months more. Payment of the tax is due fifteen months after death. Certain United States Treasury bonds may be redeemed at par for payment of the tax.

[9] Joseph Trachtman, *Estate Planning* (Practising Law Institute, 1961), p. 165. But Trachtman warns against "indiscriminate use of the business insurance trust," p. 166.

[10] See James B. Lewis, *The Estate Tax* (Practising Law Institute, 1962), pp. 178-81.

No doubt, fifteen months is not always enough to find a "willing buyer" who will pay a "fair" price for the decedent's ownership interest or some part thereof. But the pressure is lessened by a provision that the District Director may extend the date for payment by one year for the part of the tax that the executor shows would impose "undue hardship" on the estate, which usually means substantial financial loss. The interest charge is only 4 percent. And the extension may be renewed, year by year, for up to ten years. But the executor cannot know in advance how many renewals, if any, he can get; if there are only a few potential buyers of the ownership interest, they can put pressure on him to accept an unfavorable price. As Professor Harriss says, "In principle, the line of solution is simple—allow as a matter of right to every estate generous time (up to perhaps 5 years) for payment of tax on assets of low liquidity (with modest interest rates, none at all perhaps if the asset yields no income); additional time would be given on proof of need."[11]

Payment of a deficiency tax may similarly be postponed up to four years.

Payment of the portion of the tax attributable to a reversionary or remainder interest in property may be postponed until six months after termination of the precedent interest(s), but this provision is of little concern for the question at hand.

The biggest steps so far toward reducing the liquidity problem to a minor status are:

(1) Permission given to the executor by the law of September 2, 1958, with respect to estate tax attributable to a closely held trade or business, whether proprietorship, partnership, or corporation, to pay that part of the tax in from two to ten equal installments, as he may elect, at 4 percent interest.

(2) Permission granted to the executor, by legislation enacted in 1950, to treat redemption of the decedent's stock in a closely held corporation, up to an amount sufficient to cover estate and inheritance taxes and funeral and administrative expenses, as a sale subject to capital gain and loss provisions rather than as a receipt

[11] C. Lowell Harriss, "Economic Effects of Estate and Gift Taxation," in U. S. Congress, Joint Committee on the Economic Report, *Federal Tax Policy for Economic Growth and Stability,* Panelists' Papers (Nov. 9, 1955), p. 862.

of dividends.[12] Moreover, the basis for computing gain or loss is the market value at date of death, or at the alternate date (at disposition, or one year after death). Hence, in practice, there is normally not even a capital gain to attract tax. This provision is of direct importance only for the income tax due by the estate, but it eliminates a tax deterrent to the flow of liquid funds from the corporation into the estate. It is therefore helpful if the corporation itself has enough liquidity. It is not applicable to partnerships and proprietorships; there the owner's share of the year's earnings is attributed to him in full, and no exception is made for an estate.

For either (1) or (2), the decedent must own a minimum proportion of the corporation's stock. Certain other requirements also must be met.

Evidently, before these provisions were enacted, the liquidity problem was a significant, if not always the most important, factor in inducing owners of closely held businesses to transfer, some time before death, ownership of the firm or its assets to a corporation whose stock had an active market.[13]

Effect on Amount of Income

If, as is commonly asserted, inheritance induces a slackening of effort, it follows that a death tax induces an extension of effort by the disadvantaged heirs. They face no discouraging substitution effect in their capacity as heirs. *In that capacity,* they can keep all they get in their effort to make up partially for what the transfer tax deprives them of. The decedent is not in the same unambiguous position. His income effect is accompanied by a substitution effect. Also, without denying that it is more blessed to give than to receive, one might expect that the income effect on him will be less powerful than on his heirs.

But most heirs who suffer at all under the existing transfer taxes are still left with enough property to yield an income that takes care of essentials when coupled with the incomes they are already receiving. We may assume, therefore, that in practice the

[12] See Chap. IV, the section on "Correlation of Transfer Taxes with the Income Tax," Question 3.

[13] Somers, *op. cit.,* pp. 201-10, and sources cited therein.

tax results in little if any increase in income through extra work. If the exemption were as low as $5,000 or $10,000, the story might be different.

As for getting more income from investment, the questions involved have largely been covered above. The income effect of the tax might induce some desperate heirs to invest their funds in more risky ventures, but this would seem to be an uncommon reaction.

Effect on Liquidity Preference

A death tax may well influence the shape and location of the curve of demand for cash balances. At any given level of aggregate real income, households are assumed, in modern macro analysis, to want to hold a certain amount of money, given the interest rate. (The higher the interest rate, the less the amount of money they are willing to hold.) An estate tax, with its threat of a requirement for liquid funds at some inevitable but absolutely unknowable date in the future, may alter this demand for cash balances. At a given interest rate (and national income) households may want more cash. The liquidity preference curve may shift to the right, on the usual diagram where the interest rate is plotted on the vertical axis, and the amount of money demanded is plotted on the horizontal axis. Then the curve for the demand and supply of money (vertical axis, interest; horizontal, national income), derived from the intersection of a supply-of-money curve with successive liquidity preference curves reflecting different levels of national income, will be shifted up and to the left by the estate tax. Its intersection with the expenditures curve (derived from the investment curve as a function of the interest rate, and the consumption function) is moved up and to the left. A new equilibrium is reached at a higher interest rate, hence at a lower level of national income.[14]

More briefly, by causing more hoarding of cash, the death tax may send interest rates up and national income down. But the

[14] See, for example, Martin J. Bailey, *National Income and the Price Level* (McGraw-Hill, 1962), Chap. 2.

monetary authorities should be able to counter this effect without getting the economy into a dangerously liquid position.

Certain United States Treasury bonds may be tendered at 100 in payment of federal estate taxes, if they are owned by the decedent at the time of his death, for instance (with market prices as of March 1, 1965, given in parentheses, to nearest dollar), the 2½'s of 1962-67 ($97), 1963-68 ($95), 1964-69 ($94), 1965-70 ($93), and June ($90) and December ($90) 1967-72, and the 3's of 1995 ($85).[15] "Purchases in contemplation of death" can reduce the cost of a part of the estate tax by as much as 15 percent, with only a modest risk of capital value fluctuation in the interim. No good reason is apparent for catering to this particular form of liquidity, to the substantial benefit of this particular group of taxpayers.

[15] Information, except that on prices, from Aubrey G. Lanston and Company, Inc., market letter (April 13, 1956).

CHAPTER VIII

Evaluation and Recommendations

AN ENGINEER WOULD not think of designing a machine or of appraising an existing one if he were not aware of what the machine was supposed to accomplish or by whom it was to be operated. Appraising a tax is even more difficult, for a tax is closer to a living organism than it is to a machine; it absorbs, as it were, from those who legislate it, those who administer it, and those who pay it the uncertainties and conflicts of ends and the technical imprecision of means that mark all men in their dealings with one another, somewhat in contrast to their dealings with inanimate nature. Yet the attempt must be made. The appraisal of the estate and gift taxes attempted here is based on what appear to be the chief aims of those who support taxation of gifts and transfers at death. The appraisal also takes into account certain criteria that are commonly set for taxes of any kind: for example, the absence of a deterrent effect on the amount of labor offered and, more generally, the absence of undesired effects on the allocation of resources ("excess burden"); the observance of certain canons of equity; and administrative convenience.

Three Aims of Transfer Taxation

Three themes are found in most discussions of the death duties and gift taxes: (1) taxation of windfalls, (2) taxation of property once a generation, and (3) taxation to reduce concentration.[1] A fourth is sometimes mentioned, that a gratuitous transfer demonstrates the existence of a special capacity to pay tax. By giving, the donor indicates that he has a surplus that the state can tap; by getting something for nothing, the donee becomes exceptionally able to pay. This segment of ability-to-pay doctrine, however, has too many reservations to be useful here. Insofar as ability to pay justifies transfer taxation, it is better expressed through the aims of taxing windfalls and taxing property once a generation.

The ordinary meaning of windfall, something unexpected by the one who receives it, disregards the feelings of the transferor. If the transferor intends to make the gift or bequest and will enjoy doing so, he will suffer psychic injury from announcement of a prospective tax on that transfer, and his conduct may be altered by the tax.

Taxation of property once a generation through gift and death taxes has special appeal in a country where a low-rate annual tax on personal net wealth is difficult to enact or administer. In the United States this tax is not possible at present; the Constitution prohibits direct taxation by the federal government unless the tax is apportioned by states on a per capita basis.[2] A tax on gifts and transfers at death is at best an imperfect substitute; it can never reach that large proportion of the country's wealth that is consumed later by the saver. Moreover, it fails with respect to property that passes over one or more generations, either through skipping by the use of trusts (the subject of Chapter III above) or by direct transfer, as to a grandchild. It also fails when the annuity device is used. The decedent leaves to the next generation an annuity for life, giving to the next generation beyond a cash amount adequate to purchase an insurance policy on the in-between generation's life in an amount equal to the capital value that would otherwise have passed directly to that in-between generation.

[1] This study does not analyze data on the degree of concentration and changes in that degree over time. Dr. Seymour Fiekowsky has been exploring this area, but his findings had not become available at the time this book was written.

[2] Such apportionment would mean high tax rates in poor states and low tax rates in rich states. The income tax is exempt from this provision under the Sixteenth Amendment to the Constitution.

To eliminate these sources of failure to tax once a generation would require an ambitious attempt to make any kind of timing device ineffective by basing the transfer tax on relative ages, as in the bequeathing power succession tax proposed by William Vickrey.[3] This powerful instrument has never received the attention it deserves; a sympathetic but intensive critique of it by lawyers and economists is needed to ascertain whether its cost would be reasonable in terms of administration and compliance and in terms of certain equity and economic aims that it foregoes, for example, graduating the tax by relationships. A worthwhile study of the Vickrey plan, or of some related plan should be undertaken as a research project extending over several years. For the moment, it can only be said that the bequeathing power succession tax appears to be the only fairly loophole-proof formula that has yet been devised to assure transfer taxation once a generation and no more. As it stands, however, the plan needs further refinement even before it is subjected to the study suggested above and accordingly cannot be included among policy measures to be accepted or rejected in the near future.

Taxing to reduce concentration is usually difficult to accomplish without at the same time restricting private-sector spending in the aggregate. The death tax in some of its forms probably accomplishes this aim better than almost any other tax. It therefore has a special attraction for those who fear that economic growth through automation will tend to intensify concentration of income in the hands of a few wealth holders. A case is made by Professor James E. Meade for "measures . . . to increase the total of tax revenue without any adverse restriction of total private expenditure on goods and services," in order "to maintain a sufficiently high surplus of tax revenue over current budgetary expenditure to ensure that there is the desired rate of gradual socialization of property ownership," if "a socialist state" is deemed the best means of "combining an efficient level of the real wage rate with an equitable distribution of income."[4]

[3] *Agenda for Progressive Taxation* (Ronald Press, 1947), Chap. 8 and Appendix IV. See also Vickrey's earlier formulations of this proposal in "An Integrated Successions Tax," *Taxes* (August 1944), and "The Rationalization of Succession Taxation," *Econometrica* (July-October 1944).

[4] *Efficiency, Equality, and the Ownership of Property* (London: George Allen and Unwin, 1964), pp. 73, 72, and 66.

The death and gift taxes are also especially appropriate if the aim is to restrict concentration of inherited wealth, particularly after several generations.

Is the transfer tax needed to achieve these aims? Other taxes no doubt satisfy these criteria in part, but taxation of gifts and bequests is a powerful aid. The point to be made here is, rather, that the kind of transfer tax selected must depend on the relative weights given to these aims, for they tend to be mutually contradictory with respect to some of the issues discussed in the preceding chapters. For example, consider intra-family outright transfers, intra-family transfers in trust, the basis of rate progression, and the order of preference among an accessions tax, an inheritance tax, and an estate tax. Table VIII-1 indicates broadly how the answers to these issues may differ, depending on the aim assigned to the tax. For example, should an outright transfer to spouse be taxable or exempt? The answer is that it should be exempt if the aim is windfall taxation or taxing property once a generation; it should be taxable perhaps if restricting concentration is the goal. A trust with a child and grandchild as life tenants, the remainder going to a great grandchild, should be taxed upon the expiration of each life interest under the once-a-generation approach. It should be taxed upon expiration of the second life interest if a crude kind of windfall taxation is the aim, and probably exempted or lightly taxed under the anticoncentration goal on the grounds that the more distant the recipient generation, the more widely is the property ordinarily dispersed.

The reader may disagree with some of the answers in Table VIII-1 and may consider other technical decisions equally relevant, yet concede that until the fundamental aim of transfer taxation, or some mixture of aims, is agreed upon, the present federal estate and gift taxes cannot be appraised. Those taxes, when judged by Table VIII-1, make a poor score under the once-a-generation approach: 2½ out of 8, counting one point for each time these taxes satisfy the 8 answers in the first column. The present system also does poorly under the anti-concentration aim (3½), and still more poorly as a windfall tax (2½). The table is crude and incomplete, but the figures do indicate either that the present system is not very good no matter what the aim or that it reflects a complex mixture of aims.

TABLE VIII–1. Influence of Basic Aims on Answers to Selected Technical Questions in Death and Gift Taxation

Item	*Basic aim*		
	Taxing property once a generation	*Anti-concentration*	*Windfall taxation*
1. Transfer outright:			
a. To spouse	exempt	tax	exempt
b. To children	tax	tax	exempt
c. To grandchildren	tax doubly	exempt	tax
2. Upon expiration of each life interest in trust:[a]			
a. Wife life tenant, children remaindermen	exempt	tax	exempt
b. Children life tenants, grandchildren remaindermen	tax	exempt	tax
c. Children, grandchildren life tenants; great grandchildren remaindermen	tax	exempt	tax once or twice
3. Basis of rate progression	none	heir's wealth	relationship and "age" of wealth (Rignano)
4. Order of preference: accessions, estate, inheritance tax	E, A, I	A, I, E	I, A, E

[a] Assuming that the transfer to the trust has been taxed.

General Criteria To Be Satisfied

Leaving aside for the moment the three chief aims attributed to transfer taxation and returning to certain criteria that are commonly applied to taxes of any kind, the transfer taxes score relatively high. Compared with most taxes, they have few effects on the allocation of resources and hence impose little excess burden. They tend less than other taxes to check entrepreneurial drive. They have little tendency to push investors either toward or away from risk taking. They are collected at times and under circumstances that are relatively convenient for the taxpayer and tax administrator. They do, however, give rise to the most complex maneuvers by those who are bent on minimizing tax.

Nothing has yet been said explicitly about equity. Equity is implicit in the three major aims listed earlier. Beyond that, equity demands that a tax should not strike capriciously. Tax equity has been defined as equal treatment for similarly circumstanced taxpayers, and this aim is no doubt desirable, but only if "similarly circumstanced" is implicitly defined. More useful is the criterion given by Harriss: the avoidance of large inequalities in one's tax bill created by "slight inequalities in personal position."[5] Harriss points out that "To most of us, justice (equity, fairness) in taxation is probably associated with continuity and gradualness. Big changes, big breaks, large discontinuities are more likely to be a source of . . . injustice . . . A relatively small and insubstantial difference should not give rise to a large substantial difference in tax."[6]

We may rephrase this criterion by stipulating that the tax-bill function must be continuous with respect to its monetary variables, and not too discontinuous with respect to its nonmonetary variables. For example, the taxpayer's bill should increase or decrease continuously, without jump or gap, as the dollar value of his net estate changes, or as his foreign tax paid changes.[7] Discontinuities are especially damaging for a death tax since no opportunity is afforded to repair the damage, at least for that particular decedent.

At present the estate and gift taxes contain a number of discontinuities that impair their equity. An example is the 5 percent rule on reversionary interest;[8] the small difference between a 5 percent and a 6 percent interest gives rise to a large difference in

[5] C. Lowell Harriss, "Sources of Injustice in Death Taxation," *National Tax Journal* (December 1954), p. 291.

[6] *Ibid.*

[7] Continuity of the tax-bill function implies roughly—to borrow from Allen—that we can graph the curve of the tax bill (against the amount of the variable in question) without taking pencil point from paper. R. G. D. Allen, *Mathematical Analysis for Economists* (Macmillan, London, 1963), p. 100. For a more exact statement of continuity for functions of two or more variables than that above, see *ibid.*, p. 269. Ordinarily tax functions should also be "smooth" (with respect to money variables). That is, the tax bill should have no sharp points marking a reversal of direction. The function should have a first derivative everywhere (*Ibid.*, p. 147); but smoothness seems to be a much less fundamental principle of equity than continuity.

[8] See Chap. II, the section on "Policing Gifts in Contemplation of Death and Incomplete Gifts."

tax. Not all the discontinuities can be removed, but some of them might be transformed into graduated discontinuities of several small steps each.

The following is another test of tax equity. The tax bill of any one taxpayer under a given tax is a function of several variables; does every taxpayer face the same function? If not, something other than the variables specified has been allowed to influence the tax bill of one or another taxpayer, giving rise, *prima facie,* to inequity. An estate tax bill, for example, may be made explicitly a function of (1) size of net estate, (2) number of dependents, and (3) foreign death tax paid. If, of two decedents for whom the values of these three variables are precisely the same, one pays less tax than the other, because (for example) he dies as a resident of a community property state, a *prima facie* case of tax inequity exists.

If the function explicitly excludes some characteristic that appears very much like one of the characteristics in the function, the Harriss test may indicate that something analogous to a discontinuity exists. An example is real estate located outside the United States (until recently, nontaxable) and real estate located in the United States. (See Chapter IV.)

Ultimately equity is a system concept; what looks like inequity in a certain tax may be only an attempt to compensate for an opposite type of inequity in another tax, or in the distribution of some government service or transfer payment. Or a tax may have the minor virtue of not repeating the kind of inequity shown by a sister tax. Thus state and local securities, exempt from federal income tax, are fully includable in the taxable estate. If the estate tax is added to the income tax, there is a smaller disparity in the treatment accorded these securities or in that accorded capital gains and losses. Again, a gift tax may in this equity sense "protect" the income tax revenue.

Another criterion that should be considered in any exhaustive evaluation of the transfer taxes is coordination with foreign transfer taxes, a topic which has not been explored in this study.[9]

[9] See Harvard University, International Program in Taxation, *World Tax Series: Taxation in the United States* (Commerce Clearing House, 1963), pp. 186-92, 234-38 (nonresident aliens), pp. 232-34 (credit for foreign death taxes), and pp. 264-67 (gift tax).

A Proposed Transfer Tax System

An attempt will now be made to construct a transfer tax system that will take account of the three aims of (1) taxing windfalls, (2) taxing property once a generation, and (3) reducing concentration, especially concentration due to a series of inheritances.

The task falls into two parts. First, the three aims must be fitted into one framework, though they seem to produce conflicts on specific policy issues. (See Table VIII-1 above.) The aims must be weighted in some manner. The solution adopted here is to weight them, roughly, according to size of transfer, size of accumulated transfers, and amount of wealth.

Second, it must be stipulated how the several specific policy issues will be resolved to achieve consistency within this framework. Shall the gift and death taxes be integrated? And if so, shall gifts inter vivos be given favored treatment? Shall the corpus of a trust be taxed upon expiry of a life interest? Answers to the questions are given on pages 111-17 below.

The present section is frankly normative, reflecting the author's personal weighting of what he takes to be the chief aims of transfer taxation. The following section, "The Technical Issues Evaluated," is technical in its attempt to implement the normative framework.

It is assumed that in the lower wealth ranges restriction of the tax to windfall transfers is the primary aim. Accordingly a $10,000 bequest to a low-wealth, but surprised, distant relative or stranger would be taxable. Surprise itself cannot be made the criterion, but other attributes—lack of relationship for example—may be. The anti-concentration aim need not be involved as long as the recipient's wealth is low. Taxation of property once a generation has limited appeal at these low levels of transfer to spouse because property taxation itself has limited appeal when the taxpayer is an elderly rentier with a modest income. If the $10,000 goes to a low-wealth son or daughter instead of a spouse, there is a case for taxation under the once-a-generation criterion, but it is over-ridden by the nonwindfall element, that is, the expectation.

As the size of the bequest rises somewhat, and as the total net wealth of the recipient increases, the contrast between anticipated transfers and windfalls seems less relevant to a decision whether to tax lightly or heavily. The mass of property invites taxation once a generation in either case. Yet the amounts involved may be well below the level at which concern arises over undue concentration of wealth. A bequest of $500,000 to a wife is so large that even if she has no other property, the distinction between anticipated transfer and windfall transfer has faded relative to the aim of taxing wealth once a generation. But that aim is not to be achieved by taxing transfers to spouses; the three-layer structure of aims thus calls for no tax on such a bequest. If the $500,000 transfer is to a son or daughter, the once-a-generation test calls for taxation, unless it is held to be outweighed by the anticipations (nonwindfall) test. It may be assumed that anticipation of the tax on the last $100,000 or so of this $500,000 transfer will exert little influence on the actions of transferor or transferee. As the level of wealth and size of transfer rise, increments of transfer tend not to affect action through anticipation. This is so even for transfers to spouse. Meanwhile the importance of taxing all wealth once a generation grows.

Finally at high levels of transfer, with high levels of wealth of recipient, the anti-concentration aim becomes dominant. A bequest of $20 million to a wife could well be treated (at least as to the last $10 million) just the same as a bequest of $20 million to a distant and unexpecting relative, and at rates more severe than those justified by taxing property once a generation. Our existing social values insist upon some limit, or some restraining force, on the accumulation by any one person of wealth through gift or inheritance. (If anyone thinks this is not so, let him keep doubling an amount that he considers acceptable for any one person to control.) These values probably also call for some restraint on the first-generation type of accumulation, that is, wealth acquired by work and investment. The transfer tax, however, cannot check accumulation at this stage.

What kind of a transfer tax system does this three-layer structure of aims imply?

If we are limited to an estate tax integrated with a gift tax, the structure would at best be imperfect. A deduction would be allowed for transfers to spouse, up to some ceiling. When this was reached, either through cumulation of gifts or in a bequest on top of the gifts, further transfers to spouse would be taxed, or at least the exemption would begin to vanish. A similar deduction would be allowed the donor for gifts and bequests (cumulated) to children, but it would diminish with the age of the donee, vanishing partly or entirely when the donee was, say, 21 or perhaps somewhat older. These provisions, and no doubt a few other like ones, would take care of the first aim, to tax only windfalls. The initial rate of tax applicable would be, say, 20 percent instead of the present 3 percent.

As the cumulated amount of taxable transfers by any one donor increased, the rates would increase consistent with whatever is desired in taxation of wealth once a generation. Finally, beyond a certain level, say $1,000,000, anti-concentration provisions would come into play. A tentative tax would be computed by a continuation, at higher rates, of the progressive rate scale started in stage two (taxing wealth once a generation), but the donor would be allowed to reduce this tax substantially, though not to the level at the top of stage two, through fragmentation of his transfers. The larger the number of donees, over his lifetime, the less would be the total transfer tax. The final reckoning could not be made until his death, but some allowance for fragmentation could be given while he was making lifetime gifts.

Evidently implementation of the three aims is crude as long as we are limited to a tax on the transferor. Such a tax is not a function of the wealth of the transferee.

Changing the estate tax to an inheritance tax while retaining the gift tax as a lifetime cumulated tax on the donor is probably not advisable, as it attempts to merge two disparate bases.

An inheritance tax alone, without a gift tax, would leave perhaps too much of an escape route. But assume for the moment that not too much advantage would be taken of it, and consider how an inheritance tax, coupled with information on the inheritor's wealth, would implement the three aims of taxing windfalls, taxing property once a generation, and reducing concentration. In the case of heirs of low wealth, the inheritance tax could implement fairly well the first aim, taxation of windfall transfers, and in the case of heirs of medium wealth, the second aim, taxation of wealth once a generation. Instead of asking for a net worth statement each time the taxpayer in these low- and medium-wealth ranges receives an inheritance, the crude substitute might be used of cumulating the inheritances of any one person through his lifetime. This makes for some complication for the low-wealth inheritor, who would have to cumulate his windfall inheritances separately from his nonwindfall inheritances; the cumulative rate schedule would not be the same for both.

In the high-wealth ranges, to pursue the anti-concentration aim, progression of the cumulated tax on inheritances would be by amount of wealth at the time of inheritance, including the inheritance, and not by size of current or prior inheritances alone. The accompanying need to ascertain the taxpayer's total wealth each time he received an inheritance might not be too difficult, though there would be troublesome cases, such as those involving rights in complex trusts, closely held business firms, certain kinds of real estate, and perhaps annuities. A net worth statement would be needed only from heirs whose net worth surpassed a certain amount, say, $500,000. Such a tax might, however, be held a direct tax, in violation of the constitutional requirement for apportionment among the states by population.

To assume that the exemption of lifetime gifts would not be too damaging to this tax structure seems, on balance, unrealistic. Moving from an integrated donor tax (estate tax plus gift tax), the next step would probably be to an integrated donee tax, that is, an accessions tax. How can an accessions tax be made to satisfy the three-layer structure of aims?

In the low-wealth ranges each donee would have to build up two tax bases: one for windfall transfers and one for expected transfers. After his total accessions from both sources had reached a certain level, say $100,000, all his accessions, windfall or not, would be merged, and he would be transferred to a new rate scale to satisfy the aim of taxing property once a generation. This rate scale might be progressive according to cumulated accessions, but it would be better if it were progressive according to total net wealth. However, appraisals of net wealth might have to be made inconveniently often. Again, a constitutional question might be involved. For transferees with net wealth above $500,000, for example, progression by amount of net wealth would be indispensable for the anti-concentration aim. Transition from a dual rate schedule for accumulated accessions below $100,000 to a single progressive schedule after that point might give rise to so much additional tax as to call for some form of marginal relief and perhaps even tax refunds. Alternatively, the separate windfall tax rate schedule might be retained up to the level where the anti-concentration aim becomes dominant.

The Rignano approach (which would tax wealth the heavier, the more times it had already passed by inheritance) could be incorporated in the lowest wealth range part of the tax by defining windfall transfers to include those that came from the transferor's inherited wealth. The tracing problem should be disposed of in a rough way, though not as roughly as does the existing provision with respect to property previously taxed.[10] An acceptable compromise would be to assume that the transferor made one-half of any transfer, inter vivos or at death, out of taxable gifts and bequests he had received up to that point, until those cumulated gifts and bequests had been thus used up. Under the alternative suggested just above, the Rignano approach could be maintained in the second range of wealth, where the aim is to tax property once a generation, thus retaining the dual rate schedule until the anti-concentration range is reached. In that latter range, the rates would be so high that the Rignano approach would not be needed.

The Technical Issues Evaluated

It is important now to consider the technical problems posed in Chapter II and the following chapters and to consider solutions that would be consistent with the three-aim structure. At the same time, some attention will be devoted to the more modest goal of making the present estate and gift taxes more acceptable.

Integration

The present lack of integration has scarcely anything to be said for it, except that to make a change would be costly. The benefits

[10] See Chap. IV, the section on "Length of Time Between Transfers."

to come from integration of the present system are not impressive, since progression would be based only on the cumulated total of the donor's transfers, without reference to the donee's status. And if a lower rate were allowed on lifetime gifts, much of the simplicity that might be gained from integration through wiping out the distinction between those gifts and gifts at death would be lost. Under the three-aim structure, integration in some form or other would be essential.

The Trust, and Outright Bequests That Skip Generations

The accumulating trust and the discretionary trust impair progress toward any of the goals set forth above or any that are implied in the existing transfer tax structure. A quinquennial penalty tax on such trusts, as suggested by Professor Wheatcroft (see Chapter III, the section on "Solutions to the Problems"), is advisable, even under an accessions tax, with perhaps a few carefully specified exceptions. But what of other trusts, particularly the simplest form, income to A, remainder to B? How shall such trusts be treated under a cumulated accessions tax designed for the three-layer structure of aims?

At lower-wealth levels, where substantial taxation would be restricted to windfall transfers under the three-layer plan, the accessions tax might be levied, and at low rates, only on the value of the life interest received by the life beneficiary, unless that interest were a windfall. If the beneficial interest were a windfall, the value of the corpus would be taxable to the life tenant as he received his life interest, but the corpus would be liable for payment of the tax. The windfall definition would be framed in terms of the relationship between settlor and life beneficiary. In either case, windfall or not initially, the full value of the corpus would be taxed to the remainderman when his interest matured, but the rate scale (in this lowest wealth range, if that is where he was) would depend on whether this was a windfall transfer to the remainderman.

If nonwindfall treatment were to be accorded the life

beneficiary, the life interest would need to be a limited, genuine one, not one approaching full power over the property under provisions allowing invasion of the corpus.

Where taxation of property once a generation would be the predominant aim, that is, in the medium-wealth category of transferee, no exception would be made to taxation of corpus upon receipt of a life interest, excepting only those life interests of roughly the same generation or an earlier generation than that of the settlor. If the sole life tenant were two generations removed (down) from the settlor, the tax on the corpus at the time of initiation of the life interest would apply twice. (It will be recalled that the lower-wealth category of transferees is not affected.)

On outright transfers that skip a generation, the integrated accessions tax in this intermediate wealth range would take account of this fact by including in the transferee's tax base some multiple, between 1 and 2, of the amount transferred.

If the three-layer structure of aims is not followed, the corpus of any trust, except one subject to the penalty tax, should be included in the estate of the expiring life tenant, the incremental tax thereby incurred to be paid from the trust corpus.

Interspousal Transfers

Under the three-aims plan, accessions by a spouse would be exempt in the lower range of wealth of spouse, on the assumption that no such transfers at these wealth levels can be windfalls. They would continue exempt in the second range of wealth under the once-a-generation policy. Only in the anti-concentration range of wealth would such accessions be taxable, but they would then be taxed heavily. "Wealth" here refers to the amount of wealth held by the donee after the accession.

If the existing structure is retained, no change from the present marital deduction formula seems imperative, even if this structure is deemed to reflect chiefly the once-a-generation view. The reasons for this conclusion are given in Chapter IV above, the chief one being that many decedents would not find it to their advantage to use the full exemption. Admittedly the once-a-generation aim does imply full interspousal exemption, and, if the changeover would develop no serious transitional or other problems, such exemption could be accepted.

Length of Time Between Transfers

Under the three-layer structure of aims, the length of time between transfers could be disregarded. It is irrelevant to the windfall criterion. It is relevant to taxing only once a generation, but in the interests of consistency an extra tax should be applied when particularly long periods supervene. The marital deduction probably gives enough relief in what is most frequently the case—that of quick succession.

If the existing structure is kept, the quick succession relief should be matched by an extra tax in the case of slow succession; and the tracing problem should be solved by assuming that only half the property previously transferred is in the second estate.

Transfers to Sons and Daughters

In the lowest wealth range, accessions from a parent would be exempt up to an amount equal to the purchase price of an annuity sufficient to yield, say, $5,000 a year from the date of accession to perhaps age 30 or 40. An age level beyond 21 is suggested here as being more in accord with our nonwindfall, no-tax concept. In the middle and upper wealth ranges, gifts or bequests from parents would be given no exemption, whatever the child's age.

The existing federal tax probably would be improved by a deduction from the estate, over and above the basic exemption, similar to the exemption described immediately above, but with age 21 substituted for age 30 or 40.

Transfers to Charitable Organizations

Under an accessions tax, charitable organizations could be exempted, but public policy might dictate some limit to the size of the organization, beyond which the exemption would disappear or taper off.

If the existing tax is retained, the deduction for transfers to charitable organizations should be allowed only at the average rate on the entire estate, for estates above a certain level (say, $500,000), for the reasons given in Chapter IV in the section on "Transfers to Charitable Organizations." It might be even better to allow the deduction at rather more than marginal rates for the low-value estates and even less than average rates for the high-value estates, with a regressive deduction in between.

Current abuse of this deduction with respect to private foundations should be corrected; in general, donors and their heirs should not benefit from deductions and at the same time retain control, directly or indirectly.

Life Insurance Proceeds

Under an integrated accessions tax the proceeds of a life insurance policy would be included in the beneficiary's annual return of accessions, even if he had paid the premiums and possessed all the incidents of ownership. The argument would follow that in opposition to the present law given in Chapter IV in the section on "Life Insurance Proceeds." The proceeds would be exempt, or taxed at a nonwindfall rate, only if the decedent were of a class (for example, father) such that an outright transfer from him to the recipient of the proceeds would have received the same treatment.

The existing law, as just indicated, provides too lenient a regime for life insurance; the premiums-payment test, in some form, should be reinstated.

Correlation With Income Tax

Some further correlation of the transfer taxes with the income tax seems advisable, whatever the structure of the former; see the comments in Chapter IV in the section on "Correlation of Transfer Taxes with the Income Tax."

Exemptions

Under the three-layer structure of aims, no general exemption would be called for, except a small annual exemption of up to, say, $500 a year per taxpayer, to eliminate accounting for small gifts. The accessions tax contemplated under this structure of aims would be as general a one as administrative techniques would allow. There seems to be no reason, other than administrative, for granting an exemption to windfall accessions in the lower wealth group, and no reason for an exemption of any kind for the two upper wealth groups.

Exemptions of gifts or bequests from spouse or parents have been covered above.

With respect to the present law, one's view on exemptions depends somewhat on what he believes to be the aims of these estate and gift taxes. If an exemption is granted to bequests to minors, and the marital deduction is continued, there does not seem to be much reason to continue an exemption as high as $60,000 under the estate tax. It might well be decreased to $20,000, while the gift tax lifetime exemption could be reduced to, say, $10,000, and the annual exclusion per donee to $500.

Rate Structure

Under the three-aims tax suggested here, the donee would be subject to a progressive rate scale cumulated through his life and death. In the lowest wealth range, where there would be a distinction between windfall and nonwindfall accessions, the donee would be subject to one or the other of two rate scales, as described above.

If the present structure is retained or an integrated donor tax is substituted for it, the starting rate should not be as low as 3 percent. The starting rate should be 10 or 15 percent. There seems to be no need to reduce the 77 percent rate, at least as long as anticoncentration motives play some part in support of the tax.

Credit for State Taxes

Until the federal government can take exclusive jurisdiction over the transfer taxes, any new system must arrange to credit substantially as much of the state taxes as the present system does. Equivalence in this sense would be difficult to reach under the kind of accessions tax that is proposed here, but a rough approximation could be made. The chief problem is that the amount of federal accessions tax could easily be less, perhaps much less, than the unchanged state inheritance and estate taxes, on all kinds of transfers.

Under the existing type of federal transfer tax, there is not much to be done about the credit for state taxes except to leave it unchanged until the federal government takes over this tax as part of some general agreement with the states on federal-state-local fiscal relations.

Transitional Problems

A formidable problem of transition will arise if a cumulated accessions tax is substituted for the existing tax on donors. The higher progressive rates of the newly introduced accessions tax would not become effective until enough time had elapsed for donees to have received appreciable cumulated amounts. The revenue from transfer taxation might decline sharply over a number of years. The decline would be mitigated, under the tax proposed here, by the use of wealth as a criterion for graduation, and by the classification of certain accessions as windfalls. Yet some problem would remain, and retention for a number of years of the existing donor tax on a much reduced level might prove advisable.

CHAPTER IX

Summary of Conference Discussion

THE CONFERENCE OF experts dealt chiefly with the following: (1) the aims of death and gift taxation, (2) integration of death and gift taxes into a unified tax, (3) the problems posed by so-called generation-skipping through the use of trusts, and (4) the treatment to be accorded to interspousal transfers. Some discussion also developed with respect to transfers to children, the regime for capital gains and losses accrued at death, and the liquidity problems encountered by closely held business firms consequent upon the estate tax levied at the death of a principal owner.

There was an implicit assumption by the conference participants that taxation of transfers at death and by inter vivos gift, at progressive rates, will remain a part of the United States federal revenue system indefinitely. Some of the conferees evidently thought the present rate schedule too high, but some remarked on the modest levels reached by the present effective rates, expressed as percentages of the estate before the marital deduction.

The possibility of replacing the transfer taxes by including gifts and inheritances in the donee's taxable income, as suggested by Henry Simons, was mentioned with some approbation by a few conferees. No substantial support for this proposal developed, however.

Some of the conferees expressed the view that any attempt to reform the transfer taxes now would lead to substantial reductions in the rates of, and revenue from, these taxes.

Objectives of Transfer Taxation

There was general agreement on the need to discover or formulate the aims of death and gift taxes, aims that could not as readily be achieved by other taxes (for example, by replacing the transfer taxes with an increase in income tax rates). The chief aims discussed were those of reducing concentration of wealth, of taxing property once a generation, and of taxing a special type of ability to pay—that resulting from the receipt of a gift or inheritance. The British death tax was said to reflect the idea, already taken account of in the British income tax, that one who is living on a portfolio income is able to pay more tax than one whose income comes from his own exertions. The death tax, of course, adds the idea that an inherited portfolio indicates further ability to pay. It was pointed out, however, that in a growing economy especially, not more than a fraction of the total wealth in existence at any one time is destined to pass by gift or bequest, since much of it will have been accumulated for spending later in old age, illness, or emergencies. In general, the discussion reflected an unwillingness to view the death and gift taxes as close substitutes for a low-rate annual tax on net wealth. The fact that the wealth in question was being inherited recurred in the justifications given for the transfer taxes.

More general acceptance of the anti-concentration aim was evident if this goal is interpreted to mean hindering or even preventing accumulation beyond some unspecified amount by wealthy individuals or, in the view of some, wealthy families. Again emphasis was on wealth accumulated by inheritance, not by the first generation. The discussion seemed to imply that the anti-concentration principle is not a goal with respect to estates in the small and moderate ranges, say, up to $500,000 or $1,000,000, and that even in higher ranges the aim is a fairly modest one. None of the discussants suggested a top limit to concentration, and none supported a type of tax that would wipe out inheritances on the second or third round.

It was pointed out that very little is known about the influence of inheritance on concentration and that, in general, inheritance has been a neglected field of study.

Other aims suggested by one or more conferees were:

1. Encouragement of transfers to charitable and similar institutions. The question was raised, but not pursued, whether such transfers are indeed greater than they would be if there were no transfer taxes.

2. Encouragement of inter vivos giving to transfer economic power to a younger, possibly more dynamic generation and to reduce concentration of wealth.

3. Taxing indirectly accumulations from certain kinds of income that have obtained unduly favorable treatment under the federal income tax; depletion allowances and interest on state and local government debt were cited as illustrations.

4. Avoiding the kind of distortions of economic decisions that are said to characterize the income tax.

The question was raised to what degree gifts and inheritances come from donors whose incomes are in the higher ranges of the progressive part of the income tax rate schedule. No direct information is available on this point, and it was suggested that some future study might try to match estate and gift tax returns with income tax returns of the decedents or inter vivos donors.

Opinions differed somewhat as to whether the transfer taxes are in general accepted as good taxes to the degree that the income tax is.

Intra-Family Transfers

The treatment of intra-family transfers, especially transfers to spouse and to children, continues to be a difficult and perplexing one for transfer tax policy. The federal estate tax allows a spouse to pass up to one-half of the estate tax free to the surviving spouse, and the question arises whether this "marital deduction" should be enlarged to a complete interspousal exemption. Also one-half of an inter vivos gift to a spouse is free of gift tax; should the entire gift be tax free?

Insofar as the aim of the estate tax is to tax inherited wealth once a generation, no more and no less frequently, a complete interspousal exemption is appropriate, save in the few cases where older men marry much younger women. Such marriages might in theory be fostered by a complete interspousal exemption, but the conferees were inclined to discount this possibility.

For some families of more than moderate wealth a complete exemption would be no more useful than the present 50 percent exemption. They are the ones who, because of the progressive feature of the estate tax, prefer to pass the family wealth to the younger generation in two equal parts. Thus if the husband owns all the family property and dies first, he can pass half the property to his widow, tax free, and the other half, taxable, to their children, perhaps in a trust with income to the widow for her life. On the widow's death she passes to the children, taxable, the one-half she received from her husband. A complete interspousal exemption might not induce the husband to pass the entire estate to the widow, since it would all be taxable at progressive rates at her death. But for families of moderate or small wealth it may be necessary to pass all the property to the surviving spouse anyway, regardless of tax considerations. In these cases the complete interspousal exemption would be an unequivocal benefit.

If the poorer of the spouses dies first, there can be no even split of the property in order to pass it to the younger generation in a way that minimizes tax. To avoid this possibility, the couple should see to it that the family property is divided more or less equally before either spouse dies. But this action may be undesirable for certain nontax reasons. Is the tax influence strong enough, in fact, to induce many couples so to rearrange their property holdings, or at least to make them worry about it? On this the opinions of the conferees seemed to differ, and no clearcut picture emerged of what is in fact occurring.

Assuming that there is some tax-induced property shifting, or concern over the need for it—or a feeling of injustice at the tax results where equal division had not been achieved—is there any way of getting the tax results of equal division without actually forcing such division? The majority of the conferees thought that there was not, after considerable discussion of proposals for achieving that end. The two chief plans discussed were:

1. An option plan, which would allow the estate of the first spouse to die to pay tax on some or all of the property that would be exempt under a 100 percent marital deduction; the segment of property thus voluntarily subjected to tax would be subtracted from the estate of the second spouse. This plan has the weakness that it cannot give the tax results of an even split if the poorer spouse dies first. But it does allow the full property of a spouse who owns all the property to be passed to the surviving spouse with as much tax saving as if part had been diverted at once to the children.

2. Aggregation and splitting of some sort. This would probably involve taxing the first estate on what is left after a complete interspousal exemption, adding that taxed part of the estate to the second estate, dividing by two, computing the tax on one-half, multiplying this tax by two, and crediting the tax paid on the first estate. This procedure might give rise to a tax refund on the second death. If the first to die leaves nothing to the spouse, who later inherits a substantial amount, say, from her father, the question arises whether it is fair to make the second tax on that inheritance (that is, when the widow dies) depend in part on the size of her husband's estate.

If the spouse remarries, then dies, the amount available to the survivor will depend on the size of the earlier decedent's estate. Is this reasonable? And what of the tax due on the death of the survivor?

If the marriage is a second marriage for both and both have children by their first marriages, to whom they regard their respective properties destined, there is no true community of property that can justify aggregation and splitting, it was argued.

A majority of the conferees seemed to favor complete interspousal exemption, while recognizing that by itself it would not eliminate the tax penalty incurred when the less wealthy spouse dies first.

Transfers to Children

Transfers to children pose a problem because, on the one hand, taxation seems called for since the property passes from one generation to the next, yet, on the other hand, exemption seems called for if the children lose, by death of the parent, the income needed to support them and educate them. The problem is thus predominantly one of transfers to minors, or to children who have not finished their education.

One view expressed was unfavorable to an exemption for transfers to children, even minor children, provided a complete interspousal exemption were allowed and the rates were moderate in the lower brackets. Another conferee noted that the specific basic exemption might be regarded as a partial substitute for an exemption of transfers to children. It was remarked, however, that if the second spouse to die left minor children, there could, of course, be no interspousal exemption to reduce tax, and that, even when there is a surviving spouse, children of a prior marriage may not in fact be adequately safeguarded by an interspousal exemption.

Some conferees believed that if the rate scale were not higher than it is at present for the lower brackets, an exemption for minor children would result in an unacceptably low level of revenue from the estate tax. Others looked at this from another point of view. They felt that just because the rates were no higher, the revenue loss from the exemption alone would not be important. Some conferees expressed preference for the Canadian law, which grants the exemption whether or not any transfer is in fact made to the child. There also seemed to be some difference of opinion as to whether the minor child's expectation of support could form a valid basis for an exemption. Doubt was expressed as to the need for this exemption by a tax lawyer, who said he had never encountered a case of hardship to a minor caused by the estate tax. And why should not grandchildren be included in the exemption? Where would the line be drawn?

The present tax is on the transferor. Suppose that the tax were instead on the donee, with graduated rates. Then the larger the number of children among whom a given estate was split, the smaller would be the aggregate tax owing to the progressive rate feature. Also each child would have his own basic exemption. Of course, the transferor might change the pattern of his transfers because of the new tax pattern, but the conferees who spoke on this question thought such a change unlikely.

The tax on the donee, which in its most general form is called an accessions tax (embracing both gifts and bequests), would strike heaviest where there is the greatest likelihood of concentration—for example, in the one-child family compared with the many-child family. At least one conferee, however, was not very favorably impressed by this means of preventing concentration of wealth.

A majority of the conferees was against making the tax smaller, the larger the number of children of any age to whom transfers were made, but was in favor of doing it in the case of minor children—on the assumption that the tax rates were high enough to make this a significant issue.

Trusts and Generation-Skipping

A decedent can put property in a trust, income from the property to go to his child during the child's lifetime and title to the property to pass from the trust to the grandchild at the child's death. The property is subject to estate tax upon going into the trust, but is not taxed upon coming out of trust. It is not taxed again until the grandchild dies. Thus the estate tax skips a generation (that of the child), although that generation benefits from the property through use of the income from it. This result has been attacked as unjust; moreover, a strong tax incentive is provided to put property in trust instead of passing it outright to the child.

According to the Treasury's special study of 1957 and 1959 estate tax returns (see Appendix B), there is a considerable amount of one-generation skipping, especially of the kind illustrated above, but not much skipping of two or more generations.

There was some discussion of possible reasons why there has not been even wider use of the trust instrument than the data revealed. One explanation offered was that many of the wills might have been drawn some time ago and not revised in the light of later legislation or increased awareness of benefits from estate planning; the 1957 and 1959 data did not include the dates of the wills. The advanced age of many of the wealthy decedents and the difficulty experienced by tax lawyers in persuading clients to revise wills drafted long ago (expressed forcefully by one conferee) would tend to support this theory.

That a smaller proportion used trusts in 1957 and 1959 than did in 1945 is one of the phenomena revealed by the data. Some of the conferees felt that this was not surprising since the 1948 marital-deduction provisions gave more incentive to leave some property outright to the spouse. It was pointed out, however, that the tax pressure to leave the nonmarital part of the estate in trust (income to spouse for life, remainder to children) was as strong as ever. Hence the number of estates making at least some use of the trust might be expected to remain high. More understandable than the data on proportions of decedents using trusts in some degree is the finding that the percentage of disposable estate passing in trust form is lower in the 1957 and 1959 data than in the 1945 or 1951 data.

Some of the tax lawyers from metropolitan centers reported that in their experience the use of trusts is clearly increasing as knowledge of the possible tax savings becomes more widespread. Others said their experience was that trusts had always been used fairly extensively, as far back as the 1930's. In general, it proved difficult to obtain a clear impression from the experiences related by the conferees as to whether the use of trusts had changed much over the past few decades.

There was general agreement that tax saving is currently a common motivation in the setting up of trusts. At the same time it was emphasized that trusts serve useful purposes apart from tax saving and might be unduly restricted by a tax reform measure. One conferee pointed out that there are very good nontax reasons for putting property in trust for daughters.

Some surprise was expressed over the relatively modest use made of powers of appointment, as indicated by the special study data. A power of appointment is that given by an owner of property to another person to decide to whom title to the property shall pass, and when. Often the life beneficiary, for example the child in the illustration above, is the holder of the power of appointment. So long as he does not have the power to appoint the property to himself or his estate or to creditors of either ("nongeneral power"), he can hold and exercise the power without thereby giving rise to a transfer tax. Even if the power is of a taxable type ("general power"), its flexibility makes it of potential use.

A direct bequest to a generation twice removed is an alternative to a trust that skips generations. Not all the conferees considered such outright bequests to be "skipping." But there seemed to be agreement that the two methods were in some degree substitutes for each other (actually, perhaps, substitutes available to wealthy families only), so that discouraging use of one method would promote use of the other. This illustrates the difficulty of constructing an estate tax that will not influence patterns of disposition. The truly neutral tax was described as one based on the Vickrey bequeathing-power formula,[1] so that no matter how the property has been transferred in the interim, the accumulated tax would be the same.

Several conferees warned against what they considered the danger of pushing testators into the direct-bequest method of getting title to the property into the hands of grandchildren. On the other hand, some of the conferees urged that neutrality in this regard (direct-bequest versus trust) was not a prime objective of transfer taxation. In this view, even if all present trusts would still be in existence had there never been a transfer tax, it would still be appropriate to exert some tax pressure against trusts insofar as trusts might be considered a threat to the fundamental aims of death and gift taxation.

One conferee noted that occasional early deaths give rise to an estate tax that could have been avoided if the decedent had been made a beneficiary of a trust for a stated period of years, instead of having the property pass to him outright, the remainder to pass to him upon expiration of the trust. An example is a trust that provides income to the child until he reaches, say, 40, the remainder going to that same child. (This kind of trust was not counted as a trust in the Treasury special study tabulations.) Another example is a case which provides for income to children until the last child dies, the remainders going to the grandchildren; the estate of a grandchild who predeceases one of the children, since it does not include any interest in the trust property, does not owe any estate tax with respect to that property.

Following the above discussion, the unanimous sense of the

[1] William Vickrey, *Agenda for Progressive Taxation* (Ronald Press, 1947).

meeting was that, whatever specific measures one might support or oppose, the present degree of use of generation-skipping trusts does pose a problem for the estate and gift tax that is worth exploring. But there was no consensus on whether the broader phenomenon—generation-skipping in the widest sense—should give rise to a heavier tax, as in the case of an outright bequest from decedent to grandchild; the conferees appeared about evenly divided on this issue. Some of the conferees expressed the view that enjoyment of income by a generation was a minimum requisite to taxation; in the absence of such enjoyment, no charge of "skipping" could be substantiated. And one suggested that a heavier tax on an outright bequest to a grandchild could be justified only if children were living at the death of the testator, for only then would the testator have a real choice.

Integration of Estate and Gift Taxes

The estate and gift taxes now have their own separate progressive rate schedules (lower for the gift tax) and their own exemptions. They differ in still other ways. This state of affairs opens a broad avenue for avoiding high brackets of estate tax by making substantial gifts during life. In fact, however, wealth transferors do not use this escape route as much as might be expected. Still, should it be closed by integrating the two taxes into one tax with one rate schedule? All gifts and transfers at death by one donor would be cumulated to determine the rates applicable.

The conferees discussed first the question whether, if integration were adopted, lifetime gifts should be given some tax advantage compared with transfers at death. Omitting the gift tax from the tax base was viewed by some as a tax advantage and, in one view, a very unequal advantage, meaning little to the families of little wealth and a great deal to high-bracket taxpayers. But at least one conferee considered this omission to be simply a partial offset to the disadvantage of paying a tax at an earlier date than if the transfer had been postponed to death. A compromise suggested was that the gift tax be included later in the estate.

It was pointed out that the data available on gifts suggest that a very large tax differential would be needed if a significant amount of such giving were to be induced; but one of the tax lawyers expressed the opinion that the amount of lifetime giving is in fact far larger than the official data indicate and that the immediate need is to enforce the present gift tax. (A question on the federal income tax return form regarding gifts made during the year was suggested.) Moreover, another lawyer interpreted the data on giving to mean that even the nonintegrated gift tax is very effective in discouraging gifts. But still another thought that the gift tax was a poor "policeman" because of the many ways of legally passing property through the gift tax screen (for example, taking a son into partnership). There was some opinion that integration *per se* would discourage gifts, as the donor would consider the fact that each gift would increase the tax rate to be imposed eventually on what was left to give to the spouse. Completely free interspousal transfer was suggested as a way of removing this psychological barrier to gifts to children.

There was some support for lower gift tax rates simply to induce more lifetime gifts, part of this support being on anti-concentration grounds. An objection was raised that a separate rate scale would continue the need for making a careful distinction between complete and incomplete gifts for gift tax purposes. In any case, the decision has to be made whether to encourage outright giving only or to include gifts in trust.

An overwhelming majority of the conferees agreed that some sort of integration of the taxes is needed in order to avoid undue tax pressure for inter vivos giving with its consequent tax avoidance, distortion of patterns of transfer, and increased complexity of law and regulations.

Accrued Capital Gains and Losses at Death

The problem here is an income tax problem, but it is relevant to transfer taxes because of the alleged financial strain that might result from simultaneous imposition of the two taxes. This possibility arises when a decedent holding property that has gained in value since he bought it passes it on to his heirs. If they sell it, they calculate a gain (or loss) by subtracting from the sales price, not the cost to the transferor, but the value used for estate tax purposes. The capital gain accrued during the lifetime of the transferor is thus exempted (by death) from the income tax; and a loss similarly accrued gives no income tax benefit. For lifetime gifts, however, the present rule is different. For a capital gain the rule requires the donee to use the cost to the donor if he sells property that appreciated in value both while the donor held it and while the donee held it. But if the property depreciated during both periods, only the depreciation suffered by the donee is allowable as a capital loss.

The question now arises, if the estate tax and gift tax are to be integrated into one tax, which set of rules shall be used? Or shall a third set be chosen? For example, should the accrued gain or loss be brought to account, upon any transfer, and the gain taxed or the loss allowed (under the income tax) accordingly?

One conferee noted that the additional tax levied through realization upon transfer, though it might not be a large percentage of the gross estate in the high-bracket cases, was a large percentage of what was left after tax and would add to what he felt was already a difficult problem of liquidity. The ten-year deferral possibility now permitted under law is of little practical use. His tax office has never been able to use it. Just as no fiduciary would buy on margin, so an executor, faced with a fixed amount of tax to pay and holding assets that can fluctuate in value, will sell as promptly as possible in order to pay the tax as soon as possible. In contrast, two conferees expressed the view that realization upon transfer would be feasible, with respect to liquidity, under an integrated transfer tax with moderate rates in the lower and middle brackets.

Taxing capital gains at death, unless a family corporation were exempted, would increase concentration among business firms by forcing sale of the concern to a larger firm. In rebuttal, it was suggested that just as with the homeowner under the property tax, the liquidity problem becomes less serious once taxpayers know what to expect and know that they have to plan in order to be liquid enough to pay the tax.

Another conferee remarked that his experience indicated that closely held businesses are sold chiefly because of lack of a succeeding generation of managers or executives in the family. The tax-rate examples cited were said to need restatement in terms of effective rates, not marginal rates.

The point was also made that, by failing to tax gains at death, the law creates a lock-in effect before death that discourages the owner of a closely held business from trying to find a buyer during his lifetime. But some of the tax lawyers said that their experience had never indicated such a result from the lock-in effect.

A majority of the conferees favored realization for income tax purposes of gain or loss on transfer inter vivos or at death, with an integrated transfer tax.

Transfer Taxation and Accumulation

Is the amount of wealth in the United States affected appreciably by the estate and gift taxes? There is about $2 trillion worth of personally held wealth in the United States. The total death and gift taxes collected by federal and state governments is less than 0.2 percent of this amount. The participants in the testamentary and gift transfer process constitute only from 4 to 6 percent of the total population of the United States. Their wealth behavior through life is atypical in that they do not, as do most persons, first save and then consume all their wealth before they die (or all above the exemption level). According to the analysis of one conferee, the evidence indicates that the behavior of the first group has not been affected by the transfer taxes; their accumulation of assets is associated more with their lifetime aspirations than with concern over how to hand on their possessions to their children and grandchildren or spouse. British data indicate that although wealthy decedents generally come from wealthy families, the size of their wealth at death is not closely correlated with the size of their inheritances. The amount of wealth at death thus reflects largely their own ability and drive. A tax on their wealth that is postponed until their death allows them to make use of their wealth-creating capacities in a way that an annual net wealth tax would not. The effect of the tax on passive inheritors may be a more or a less rapid decumulation of wealth; on active inheritors the effect is small, as they build up most of their estates-to-be by their own efforts.

According to this analysis, lifetime gifts are not good substitutes for bequests—for holding property throughout life and parting with it only at death. Hence the analysis is said to remain valid even though the records give evidence of a desire to reduce the gift tax, in the form of large bursts of lifetime giving at times when the transfer tax rates are about to rise.

The view recapitulated above was challenged by some of the conferees, especially with respect to a hypothetical tax of extremely high rates—up to 100 percent. Such a tax, it was asserted, would surely affect capital accumulation.

As to the distribution of wealth and the concentration pattern, even the present transfer tax system exerts a significant influence, one conferee emphasized.

Taxation of Donee

The conference concluded with a brief discussion of the proposal to tax the donee, rather than the transferor, through an ordinary inheritance tax or by a cumulated accessions tax. Questions were raised about the possible lapse of time between tax collections while in transition to the donee tax; the time of collection of tax on a future interest, and the need for generally higher rates if the revenue is to be maintained. A majority of those willing to express a view on this matter favored having the Treasury seriously consider an accessions type of transfer tax.

Summary

In general the conference felt that:

1. Transfer tax problems are complex, and no easy solution to them is in sight.

2. The majority of the conferees favored an integrated tax, with an interspousal exemption, and some method of dealing with generation-skipping through trusts.

3. In principle, the conference seemed disposed to favor imposing such a tax on the donee (an accessions tax), but recognized that such a change might prove too formidable in practice and might also lower the already relatively small yield of the transfer taxes.

4. Some allowance should be given for transfers to minor children, but not to children generally.

5. There was disagreement on the best treatment at death of accrued capital gains and losses under the income tax.

6. Some felt that the liquidity problem, for payment of the tax, was still serious for an estate consisting principally of a closely held concern.

List of Conference Participants

Donald C. Alexander
Taft, Stettinius and Hallister

John H. Alexander
Mudge, Stern, Baldwin & Todd

Robert Anthoine
Winthrop, Stimson, Putnam & Roberts

Boris I. Bittker
Yale Law School

Walter J. Blum
University of Chicago Law School

Gerard M. Brannon
U. S. Treasury Department

Robert D. Calkins
The Brookings Institution

A. James Casner
Law School of Harvard University

Norris Darrell
Sullivan & Cromwell

Louis Eisenstein*
Arnold Fortas & Porter

Wirth F. Ferger
U. S. Internal Revenue Service

Seymour Fiekowsky
Center for Naval Analyses

Richard Goode
International Monetary Fund

* Died January 5, 1966.

C. Lowell Harriss
Columbia University

Gerald R. Jantscher
University of Manchester (England)

Robert J. Lampman
University of Wisconsin

James B. Lewis
Paul, Weiss, Rifkind, Wharton & Garrison

Alan T. Peacock
York University (England)

Joseph A. Pechman
The Brookings Institution

Joseph S. Platt
Porter, Stanley, Treffinger & Platt

Alan R. Prest
University of Manchester (England)

Richard C. Pugh
School of Law
Columbia University

Carl S. Shoup
Columbia University

Dan Throop Smith
Graduate School of Business Administration
Harvard University

Conference Participants (*Continued*)

Joseph T. Sneed
School of Law
Stanford University

Lawrence M. Stone
U. S. Treasury Department

Stanley S. Surrey
U. S. Treasury Department

William S. Vickrey
Columbia University

Robert W. Wales
Cleary, Gottlieb, Steen & Hamilton

David E. Watts
Dewey, Ballantine, Bushby, Palmer & Wood

David Westfall
Law School of Harvard University

G. S. A. Wheatcroft
London School of Economics and Political Science

Laurens Williams
Sutherland, Asbill & Brennan

Laurence N. Woodworth
U. S. Congress, Joint Committee on Internal Revenue Taxation

APPENDIXES

APPENDIX A

The Treasury Special Study of 1957 and 1959 Estate Taxation

RICHARD M. BIRD, GERALD R. JANTSCHER, and CARL S. SHOUP

OVER THE PAST fifteen years, three extensive studies of the amount and form of private wealth transfers have been made by the Internal Revenue Service of the United States Treasury, based upon data obtained from federal gift and estate tax returns. These surveys attempted to match with each estate tax return all gift tax returns that had been filed by the decedent during his lifetime. Relevant wills, trust instruments, and other supporting documents were also examined. The information thus obtained constitutes a broad data base for describing the amounts of wealth transferred, transfer taxes paid, the form in which transfers were made (whether in trust or outright), and the classes of beneficiaries (for example, relatives of the transferor or charitable institutions). The first of these special studies dealt with estate tax returns filed in 1945;[1] the second, with returns filed in 1951; the latest, with returns filed in 1957 and 1959.[2] Only the first and third surveys encompassed all sizes of estate tax returns filed; the second included only those with net estate[3] before exemption of $300,000 or more.

[1] See Joseph A. Pechman, "Analysis of Matched Estate and Gift Tax Returns," *National Tax Journal,* III (June 1950), pp. 155-64, and *Revenue Revision of 1950,* Hearings before the House Committee on Ways and Means, 81 Cong. 2 sess. (1950), Vol. I. Nothing has yet been published from the other two special studies. For a brief comparison of certain of the 1945 and 1951 findings with those of 1957 and 1959, see Appendix E.

[2] In every case, the decedents to whom the returns investigated relate presumably died within the fifteen months preceding the date on which the return was filed.

[3] "Net estate" is "taxable estate" plus the specific exemption of $60,000.

Individually and collectively, these surveys are primary information sources of potentially great value to economists and tax officials interested in private economic behavior affected by taxes on the transfer of wealth by gift or bequest. Initially the surveys were undertaken by the Treasury in an effort to estimate the estate tax "loss" resulting from the use of gifts and trusts. This objective remains an important one. But the surveys have also been important in judging the effectiveness of the present federal estate and gift tax system and possible methods of improving it.

The 1957 and 1959 Studies

The central office of the Internal Revenue Service instructed all district offices to submit a list of all estate tax returns filed in 1957 and 1959 (except for nonresident aliens). A punch card was then prepared for each return (46,249 filed in 1957 and 54,293 in 1959) showing gross estate per revenue agent's report if it had been audited, or per return if not audited. After sorting cards by district, and by size within districts, random samples were selected on a systematic interval basis at the agreed rates: 1 in 100 for returns with gross estate under $300,000, 1 in 6 for returns with gross estate over $300,000 and under $1 million, and 100 percent for $1 million and over. Sample lists were sent to all district offices with instructions to ship to a Service Center all sample returns. The offices were also instructed to associate with the estate tax returns all gift tax returns for the decedents on file in the office. On the returns with gross estate of $1 million and over, they were instructed also to associate gift tax returns filed in other districts, to the extent that there was evidence that such returns had been filed. (In most cases of the larger returns this had already been done as far as possible when the return was audited.)

When the returns were received in the Northeast Service Center, transcript sheets were prepared giving all information needed for compiling the tables. The transcribing involved minute examination of wills, trust instruments, etc., as well as returns and audit reports. Some thirty-five clerks worked about ten weeks, under the technical direction of two statisticians thoroughly conversant with the broad objectives of the study and with the continuing assistance of three or four experienced estate tax examiners from the field offices. Printed transcribing instructions had been prepared, which were amended and supplemented as unforeseen problems arose and new interpretations and decisions had to be made. After each transcript sheet was completed, it was checked for internal consistency and then verified by an independent verifier. In the meantime steps were taken to obtain returns that were not immediately available because they were under investigation or in litigation. Out of 5,000-odd estate tax returns in the sample for the two years, only twenty were finally unavailable or too incomplete to be used.

The final sample of returns transcribed and tabulated was as follows:

Gross Estate	1957	1959
Under $300,000 (Small)	398	471
$300,000 and under $1,000,000 (Medium)	876	968
$1,000,000 and over (Large)	1,119	1,137

As transcript sheets were completed, punch cards were prepared averaging 3.5 cards per return, and the usual consistency checks were applied. On 17,550 cards, thirty-three errors were thus discovered and corrected. In the meantime the programs had been prepared for the electronic data processing machine to compile and print the basic tables.

The machine runs of the tables showed all data separately for the three sampling strata, and for all three combined, the universe. This allowed the identification of those data cells in the universe tables where the sampling variability was so large as to make the data unreliable.

Limitations of the Data

While the 1957 and 1959 studies were planned and carried out with great care, it should be emphasized that there is a serious deficiency in the data. Information on gifts made by the decedents during their lifetimes is incomplete. Difficulty in this field was anticipated from the beginning of the study. In contrast with the situation in the 1951 study, when the gift tax returns for the whole country were kept in a central file in Washington, the files are now decentralized to the sixty-two district offices, and it is difficult, when an estate tax return is filed, to find out where earlier gift tax returns may have been filed by the decedent—in other districts and perhaps under a different name. For returns that are audited (most of those with gross estate in excess of $500,000), the examiner as a routine part of the audit tries to obtain all associated gift tax returns. But this is not always possible. The estate tax return does not require a complete listing of lifetime gifts of the decedent, and executors do not always comply with such requirements as there are. Even when the listing is given, the information is sketchy and never complete enough for the purposes of this study. If the latest gift tax return is available, it is supposed to show in Schedule B a list of all such returns filed previously and the district where filed. This schedule was often found to be incomplete, however, or it had been interpreted to apply only to prior *taxable* gifts, in excess of the lifetime exemption. Even with unlimited time available for a more intensive followup of all possible leads, it would have been impossible to assure anything like full coverage of lifetime gifts made by the decedents in the study. There is evidence that the available data is very incomplete.

To understand the limitations of the available data, one must establish clearly the limits of their reliability. These limits depend on the definitions of terms and measures used and on the data collection procedures. For the 1957 and 1959 data, the Internal Revenue Service has prepared a set of technical notes (reproduced below) which define the terms used. Operational definitions of terms and measures in such a study are necessarily narrowly circumscribed by the nature of the information reported in estate and gift tax returns and by the need to maintain comparability with previous studies. Each user of the data must confront the problems posed by these definitions on terms appropriate to his purpose.

The most recent special study differed from the earlier ones both in the information collected and in the statistical procedures followed. More detailed information was collected on charitable foundations benefiting from gifts and bequests and also on the form of trust instruments, the use of powers of invasion, etc., than in the 1945 and 1951 studies. Although all sizes of estate tax returns with a gross estate of $60,000 or more filed in 1957 and 1959 were included, as in 1945, the examination of returns with a gross estate of less than $1,000,000 was on a sample basis, as was explained above. In contrast to the two earlier studies, audited data were used wherever they were available, and no account was taken of gifts made before 1932.

Sampling Variabilities

The thirty special study tables, on which the summary tables in the following appendixes are based, contain information for the millionaire group separately and for all three groups combined into what are called the "universe" tables. (Thus there are sixty basic tables in all.) For the universe tables, the data were combined by using weights inversely proportional to the sampling rates to make the frequencies and dollar quantities shown comparable in size to the results that might have been obtained from a complete canvass of returns.

Certain questions of reliability inevitably arise in any sample study, among them the question of sampling variability. According to the criterion of "excessive" sampling variability used by the Treasury,[4] a good deal of the information in the data cells of the universe tables proved too unreliable to be published. For this reason, much of the detailed discussion in the appendixes below is confined to the returns with a gross estate of $1,000,000 or more, and only the "summary by strata" figures (suitably deflated to yield the actual sample figures) are freely used from the universe tables. The millionaire returns, of course, are not subject to sampling variability in the sense used in the special study since the sampling rate was 100 percent.

But in another, larger sense what is taken to be the population in the special study is merely a sample from a larger universe, so that even the millionaire estimates are subject to sampling variability. In this larger sense, estate tax returns filed during some particular time interval are drawn as a sample from the universe of wealth-holders subject to estate tax, at rates equal to the probability of dying of those individuals (given each one's age, sex, etc.) in that year. Viewed from this broader perspective, the estate tax returns of any particular period, whether all returns or some randomly selected proportion of the total are taken, may be used for such purposes as:

1. *Estimating the number of (potential) estate taxpayers and the total amount of wealth they hold and transfer.* Since mortality rates are functions of age and sex—to mention only two generally significant determinants—if these functions are known, and the age and sex of estate tax returnees can be determined, it is a simple matter to infer the number (and other characteristics) of (potential) estate taxpayers in the living population. Of course, if the estate tax returns filed have been subjected to an additional stage of random sampling, the rate of this sampling is needed also if the number, etc., of potential estate taxpayers is to be estimated. Sampling variability for this purpose has a quite different meaning and dimension from the concept of sampling variability used by the Treasury in the special study.

2. *Estimating the effects of age, sex, marital status, and wealth on the patterns of lifetime and testamentary dispositions of property.* It is with hypotheses of this sort that we are most concerned here. For these

[4] The criterion defines "excessive sampling variability" as that in excess of 50 percent at a confidence level of 95 percent. Possible alternative criteria that might have been preferable for some purposes are explored below.

purposes all, or any randomly selected portion of, estate tax returnees of a given year or years showing a given age, sex, etc., are a sample of an (abstract) universe of all such individuals. Since such an abstract universe is infinite in size, mortality rates or subsampling rates are irrelevant to a statistical analysis of the data; all that affects the estimation of relationships is the number of observations available—the absolute size of the sample. In this usage[5] sampling variability has a meaning and dimension different from either of the two concepts of variability mentioned above. This point is elaborated below in the section on the "Distinction Between Tabulations A and B."

Comparison with *Statistics of Income*

It is interesting to compare the information on which the 1957 and 1959 study is based with that published in the U. S. Treasury Department's *Statistics of Income* (SOI). The number of possible checks and reconciliations is more limited in this special study than in its 1945 and 1951 predecessors owing to the omission of certain items of information for each return, notably gross estate. Table A-1 lists the items in the two tabulations for 1959 returns that can be compared; and a quick glance will show that not all the differences can be ascribed to sampling. Note first the deficiency in total returns. The SOI reported 1,181 more returns filed in 1959 by citizens and resident aliens than are enumerated in the special study universe tabulations, most of these apparently in the small estate group. The explanation for a good part of this discrepancy and for those noted below is that the "frame" from which the special study samples were drawn differed slightly from that used in the SOI. In some districts, for example, only the audited figures were made available for the special study. Since some estates tend to fall below $60,000 on audit, one would expect there to be fewer small estates in the special study than in the SOI.

There are further discrepancies in the amounts of charitable bequests reported. Possibly the $65 million deficiency in millionaire bequests to charity is due in part to the omission of four such estate tax returns from the special study sample, owing to the failure of district offices to send in all the requested returns. Alternatively, the $65 million deficiency may reflect undiscovered errors in one or more stages of transcription, or the SOI rather than the Treasury study may be wrong. More generally, these figures, like those for gross estate and for

[5] It is this meaning of sampling variability that is used in the *B* tabulations in the Jantscher study mentioned on p. 144.

TABLE A-1. ***Comparison of Estate Tax Returns Filed in 1959 as Reported in Statistics of Income (1958) and in the Treasury Special Study of Matched Gift and Estate Tax Returns***

(Dollar amounts in thousands)

Item	Statistics of Income	*Special study*
Number of returns, total	55,685	54,504
By size of gross estate		
Under $300	48,656	47,472
$300–$1,000	5,888	5,895
$1,000 and over	1,141	1,137
Charitable bequests, total	$ 668,900	$ 594,758
By size of gross estate		
Under $300	127,766	138,184
$300–$1,000	137,609	118,030
$1,000 and over	403,525	338,544
Marital deductions, total	$2,176,137	$2,259,872
By size of gross estate		
Under $300	1,184,295	1,261,689
$300–$1,000	564,898	574,359
$1,000 and over	426,944	423,824
Number of husbands	26,463	26,496
Number of wives	4,528	3,731

Sources: U. S. Internal Revenue Service, *Statistics of Income, 1958,* Fiduciary, Gift, and Estate Tax Returns, pp. 58–60 and 62–68; and U. S. Treasury Department.

marital deduction, reflect differences arising from the use of audited returns, wherever possible, in the special study.

Distinction Between Tabulations A and B

The data compiled from the 1957 and 1959 study by the Treasury may be divided into two groups, labeled here *A* tabulations and *B* tabulations.

The *A* tabulations are those made by the Internal Revenue Service from the 17,711 punch cards representing the estates in the 1957 and 1959 studies. The *B* tabulations were made by Gerald Jantscher at Columbia University from a duplicate set of the punch cards, with the facilities of the Columbia University Computer Center.

The *A* tabulations are reproduced in condensed form in Appendixes B and C. The *B* tabulations will be found in *Trusts and Estate Taxation* by Gerald R. Jantscher (to be published in 1966 by the Brookings Institution).

The following distinctions between the two sets of tabulations are presented here for the reader who is interested and who will be comparing the data in Appendix B, which uses the Internal Revenue Service tables, with the data in Jantscher's book. Even those who may not see the Jantscher study will understand better the purposes and limitations of the Internal Revenue Service tables by considering the alternative concepts and uses employed by Jantscher.

The two sets of tabulations are derived, of course, from the same underlying data taken from the tax returns, but they differ in the following two chief respects:

1. The *A* tabulations compare results for decedents in different gross transfer groups within the millionaire gross estate group, and compare the latter as a whole with two other gross estate groups: $0 to $300,000 and $300,000 to $1,000,000. The reader is cautioned to distinguish always between gross transfers and gross estate. "Gross transfers" includes all inter vivos gifts reported and gift tax paid, but is after deduction of claims against the estate and expenses of administering the estate. "Gross estate" does not include inter vivos gifts, except those that are swept into the estate because they were incomplete or were made in contemplation of death, but it is before subtraction of claims against the estate and expenses of administering the estate.[6]

Accordingly, in the *A* tabulations, wherever the data are subdivided by size groups shown in the column farthest to the left, that column will be in terms either of gross transfers (for the millionaires) or of gross estate (to compare millionaires as a group with the $0-$300,000 and $300,000-$1,000,000 gross estate decedents).

The *B* tabulations, on the other hand, disregard gross transfers, and make much less use of gross estate classifications. The data from all three of the gross estate size groups usually are lumped together and then subdivided. When they are subdivided by size, it is either by (1) size of adjusted gross estate or (2) size of disposable estate. Adjusted gross estate is gross estate (including inter vivos gifts swept in) less claims against the estate, funeral and administrative expenses, and losses from casualty or theft.[7] None of the punch cards shows the gross

[6] See James B. Lewis, *The Estate Tax* (Practising Law Institute, 1962), pp. 9-10.

[7] But "adjusted gross estate" in these tabulations includes whatever community property may be in the estate; to this degree, it differs from "adjusted gross estate" as defined in the estate tax law. See Lewis, *op. cit.*, p. 142. The data on the special study punch cards did not distinguish community property from other property, for any estate.

estate; although this was the quantity used for grouping the returns into the three groups just noted above, it was not entered on the cards. Each card contains the data on disposition at death and taxes paid, and so, by addition, the amount of adjusted gross estate for each return can be obtained; but the cards do not contain data on funeral expenses, administrative expenses, and claims against the estate. Hence a gross estate figure for each estate cannot be constructed.

Disposable estate is adjusted gross estate less taxes paid by the estate.

The *B* tabulations present certain data separately for estates of decedents resident at their death in community property states and decedents not so resident. The *A* tabulations do not make this distinction; the two kinds of returns are lumped together.

2. The *A* tabulations are concerned with stating, or inferring, what did occur among the returns filed in 1957 or 1959, with no inferences drawn regarding estate tax returns of other years.

The *B* tabulations, on the other hand, view the 1957 and 1959 estate tax returnees as simply samples of a much larger universe of estate tax returnees, continuing indefinitely over many years even though its composition is continually changing. In this view even the "100 percent sample" of millionaires is only a sample, and far less than 100 percent, of a much larger population of millionaire returnees. Certain variations in pattern from one row of a table (usually a size-class row) to the next row are observed. These variations from row to row might be due simply to random factors operating in the drawing of the sample (the 1957 plus the 1959 returns) from the much larger parent population of potential returns. We set up a hypothesis that the variations are in fact due merely to randomness and apply statistical tools to ascertain whether there is a high probability that this hypothesis is correct. If the answer is yes, the row-to-row variations in pattern are considered not significant in the statistical sense, for they do not signify that some theory other than randomness in choosing the sample is needed to explain the variations. But if the statistical techniques indicate that there is not a high probability that the variations are due to chance, an association between the variables, a dependence of one upon the other, is assumed.

Let us explore a little further the implications of this latter approach in the *B* tabulations.

As economists, we are interested less in cataloging the behavior of a particular group of past decedents than in inferring from their behavior the behavior of a larger group of decedents. Even if all of the property transfers of 1957 and 1959 estate tax returnees were known, such knowledge would from this point of view be of little intrinsic worth in itself. It would be valuable instead in permitting insights into the patterns of disposition of decedents of other years and in furnishing a basis for predicting the testamentary transfers of decedents to come.[8] The goal in the *B* tabulations is not merely to reconstruct the characteristics of the particular populations of decedents whose estate tax returns were filed in 1957 and 1959, but to penetrate still farther to a more fundamental population. Death itself is a sampling process, selecting from the living its samples of decedents whom we conveniently aggregate on an annual basis. The parent population behind these samples, the population of the living viewed as potential estate tax returnees, is the one we are looking for in this concept of the sampling process.

We can postulate a parent population of all persons who might be estate tax returnees in any year, from whom those who actually become estate tax returnees are selected. The group of actual estate tax returnees can be considered a random sample of the larger population. For purposes of the present study, we have further abridged the available sample for returns under $1,000,000 by selecting only a fraction of the actual returnees for analysis; but there is no fundamental difference between the small subsample and the full sample of all estate returnees of one year if both are regarded simply as samples of a larger parent population of potential estate tax returnees.

From this point of view, our sample is actually more informative of the dispositions that might have been made by members of the parent population with gross estates of less than $300,000 than it is of the potential dispositions of "millionaires," despite the fact that our sample of the least wealth decedents was selected by a sampling rate of just one in one hundred whereas all of the "millionaire" decedents from 1957 and 1959 are included; for it is the absolute size of the sample, rather than the fraction of the parent population that it includes, that fixes confidence limits on the inferences one may make about the parent population.[9] There are only a few "millionaires" in our sample because only a few "millionaires" died in 1957 and 1959, as in any year; but many decedents are included whose gross estates were less than $300,000. In general, more secure conclusions can be reached con-

[8] A skeptical reader might convince himself of this by asking of how much interest these 1957 and 1959 data would be to him if he were convinced that the dispositive patterns of decedents fluctuated wildly and irregularly over time.

[9] This is strictly true only when the samples include small fractions of the parent population, as we may assume is the case here.

cerning the characteristics of the parent population of less wealthy decedents than of very wealthy decedents.

Of course, the characteristics of the parent population may change over time, as decedents leave it and new members join. Many of the decedents in our sample must have died nearly a decade ago, and the changing fashions of estate planning, modification of law, or, more generally, subtle changes in the climate of living will combine to encourage new patterns of disposition. It is doubtful, however, that many of the descriptions in our study would need to be modified to describe as well the dispositive patterns planned by the present parent population. Certainly there have been no dramatic changes in the law since these decedents died that would affect most persons' testamentary planning, no changes comparable even with those enacted in the 1951 Powers of Appointment Act.[10]

The distinction between the 1957 and the 1959 decedents in our sample has not been maintained in the *B* tabulations. It would have been possible to perform all of these analyses separately on samples of each year's decedents and to test whether they implied significantly different patterns in their respective parent populations; but a casual examination of these data suggests that the patterns revealed in each are similar and that the additional effort to analyze both separately would probably uncover few differences. Moreover, either sample is only one-half the size of the combined sample, so that fewer statistically significant patterns could be detected than if both were combined and analyzed together. If both were analyzed separately, there would remain the task of interpreting any significant differences observed between them. It would seem incautious to infer a secular trend on the basis of two observations so near in time. These considerations suggested that the limited resources available to the project for the *B* tabulations could be more efficiently expended by analyzing only the combined sample of 1957 and 1959 decedents; and that course was followed.

[10] It can be argued that time is required before the changes of law embodied in the 1948 Revenue Act (including, among other changes, the marital deduction provisions) and the 1951 Powers of Appointment Act will have become so well known that they will be reflected in the conventional estate planning of most lawyers. This is probably true, but it is surprising how frequently the records of decedents in our sample already indicate a familiarity with the amendatory provisions of these acts.

Technical Notes

The following are definitions of the most important terms used in the 1957 and 1959 study:

Audited data. Unlike the *Statistics of Income* reports for estate and gift tax returns filed in 1957 and 1959, and unlike the 1951 study of estate and gift tax returns, audited data were used in the 1957 and 1959 study whenever they were available. Examiner and Appellate Division reports and computations were the major sources for the audited data. Audit reports were available for most estate tax returns with gross estate in excess of $500,000.

Bequests. The term "bequest" is broader than the legal concept. All real and personal properties included in the estate which were transferred at death, other than as payment of debts and expenses, were treated as bequests. Bequests may include non-probate items, such as jointly owned property, life insurance, and certain gifts made prior to death. They include any lifetime gifts required to be brought into the estate. (See *Gifts* below.)

Bequests in trust. The two terms "bequests in trust" and "trusts created at death" have the same meaning in this study, as was also the case in the 1951 study. The "creation" really applies to the bequest, rather than the trust (that may have been in existence prior to the death of the decedent). The dual wording was retained in order to show that the concept is identical with that in the 1951 study.

For the definition of "trust" used in this study, see the paragraph below on *Trusts.*

Charitable bequests and gifts. The term "charitable," when used as a classification of bequests or gifts (in contrast to "noncharitable"), is used in the broad sense of any bequest or gift that qualified for the "charitable deduction"—including transfers for religious, scientific, educational, etc., purposes.

All charitable bequests and gifts are shown in the tables as "other than in trust"; all bequests and gifts "in trust" are tabulated as noncharitable. In the exceptional cases where a trust set up a charity as either the remainderman (frequently) or the life tenant (occasionally), the amount of the charitable deduction was determined on the basis of the actuarial value of the charitable bequest or gift, and this amount was tabulated as a charitable bequest or gift "other than in trust." Only the remaining value of the noncharitable bequest or gift was considered as "in trust."

Gifts. Subsequent to June 6, 1932, property transferred during life, required to be reported on a gift tax return (Form 709), is considered to be a gift, with one exception. A lifetime (inter vivos) gift in this study is a present interest gift, usually in excess of $3,000, made to a single donee in any one year. A future interest gift of any amount which involved a trust was included. However, it was decided to exclude the infrequent future interest gifts "other than in trust" if they were $3,000 or less.

The one exception is where the amount of a gift was required to be included in the estate of the decedent because of any of six causes, such as having been made in contemplation of death, made to take effect at the decedent's death, etc. Gifts that are includible in the estate of the decedent are listed in Schedule G ("Transfers during Decedent's Life") of the estate tax return. These gifts were excluded from the sum of lifetime gifts to avoid double counting, as well as to retain the logic of the estate tax credit for federal gift taxes. This adjustment to avoid duplication is the reverse of the adjustment made in the 1951 estate and gift tax study, where the amounts were counted as gifts and deleted from bequests.

Gifts attributable to spouse. Since the study relates to gross transfers of the decedent alone, any part of gifts of his spouse included for tax splitting purposes on *his* gift tax return was excluded. Likewise the whole of his gifts was included, even though parts of them were "attributable" to his spouse (lines b and d of Schedule A of Form 709).

Gross estate. Gross estate is the value of the estate before subtracting debts or any other use or disposition of the estate. This figure was the key control item in the collection of the data, as noted below.

It is obvious that the gross estate bears no necessary relation to the gross transfers that serve as the basis of the size distribution in many of the tables. A decedent who made no lifetime gifts, with a gross estate of $2 million, may have had debts, funeral and administrative expenses, etc., of $1.5 million, so that bequests and federal, state, and foreign death taxes (gross transfers) total only $500,000. On the other hand, if a decedent with a gross estate of $100,000 had made lifetime gifts of $2 million, his gross transfers would appear in the study as well in excess of $2 million (including gift taxes paid).

Gross transfers. "Gross transfers" is the total of the estate less debts, and funeral and administrative expenses (but including all bequests and death taxes) plus gifts during life and gift taxes paid. This figure, which bears no necessary relation to the "gross estate" for any given decedent, was the major classification variable used. Its usefulness is somewhat impaired by the incompleteness of the data on matched gifts. Gross estate itself would have been a still less satisfactory category for size classifications, in view of (1) the varying amounts of indebtedness included in that gross figure and (2) the omission of all lifetime transfers not included in the gross estate.

Gross transfers at death. These consist of bequests (as defined above) plus all death and inheritance taxes paid by the estate.

Gross transfers during life (gifts plus gift tax). Subsequent to June 6, 1932, lifetime gifts made by the decedent *plus* any gift taxes paid by the decedent, *less* any gifts (and taxes related thereto) forming part of the estate in Schedule G ("Transfers during Decedent's Life") fall in this category.

Intestate decedents. For citizens or residents who died with no will, the descent and distribution of real and personal property were determined by the provision of the laws of his domicile. The reference used for obtaining digests of the laws was *Martindale-Hubbell Law Directory,* Vol. IV (1962).

Marital deduction. The amount tabulated is the marital deduction allowed in the estate tax return and has no reference to the marital deduction allowed in gift tax returns. The marital deduction frequently equals bequests to spouse. However, the marital deduction may be smaller than bequests to spouse on (1) community property returns and (2) other returns where the marital deduction is limited by the Code to 50 percent of "adjusted gross estate." For estates consisting solely of community property, there is no marital deduction.

Nonrelatives. In the classification of recipients of bequests and gifts the following were considered as nonrelatives: stepchildren, godchildren, and all categories of in-laws. Adopted children were classified as children.

Number of years in which gifts were made. This refers to the number of years, beginning with 1932, in which the decedent previously made lifetime gifts. These need not necessarily have been made in consecutive years.

Even though the amount of the gifts and/or the amount of the total gift taxes were not always available (see section on "Limitations of the Data" above), it was sometimes possible to ascertain the number of years in which gifts had been made from the answers to the questions at the top of Schedule G ("Transfers during Decedent's Life") on the estate tax return, Form 706.

Trusts. The type of trust pertinent to this study is property for which the initial transfer (gift or bequest) is taxable, but no tax is imposed upon the termination of the tenancy. Following this concept, the amounts classified as trusts are transfers of real or personal property involving a tenant which is a different person or organization than the remainderman. Of course, there can be more than one life tenant and more than one remainderman.

This definition of a trust is both broader and narrower than the legal concept of a trust. It is broader in the sense that the transfer of certain property, notably real estate or life insurance, may involve a tenant and a remainderman—each a different person or organization—even though no true trust instrument exists. It is narrower in the sense that, even though a trust instrument exists, transfers where the *same* person or organization is *both* the tenant and the remainderman are excluded from this definition. Also excluded from the category of bequests in trust are those cases where the spouse was named as the life tenant *if the bequest in trust qualified for the marital deduction* (because, for instance, she was given a general power of appointment over the remainder). In this case there is no generation-skipping, since the bequest becomes part of the estate of the surviving spouse and is included in her gross estate.

Information for each bequest or gift in trust was tabulated separately, regardless of the number of trusts established by the decedent (or grantor).

Trusts—duration. The duration of a trust refers to the number of generations (or a term of years, or both) represented by the trust income beneficiaries, before the trust is terminated and the corpus is transferred to the remainderman (remaindermen). It represents the number of generations of beneficiaries involved where no new gift or estate tax is payable on the cessation of the temporary interest and the succession of a new interest. Thus neither the grantor (donor or decedent) nor the remainderman is counted in determining the number of generations (duration) of a trust, but only the intervening trust beneficiaries.

Ten categories of "duration" are used in this study, ranging from "Trust for a term of years only" to "Trust for three generations and a term of years."

One-generation trusts are those with one tenant, such as the wife for life, or those with two or more tenants of the *same* generation, such as sons and daughters for life.

Two-generation trusts are those with tenants belonging to two *different* generations, such as (1) children for life and at their death to grandchildren for life, or (2) wife and son concurrently (the trust to terminate on death of son).

Three-generation trusts are those with tenants belonging to three *different* generations, concurrently or successively.

Trusts—life tenant (or tenant for a term of years). This is the person or organization that is entitled to enjoy the use of trust property or to receive the net income from a trust. If a power to invade the trust exists, the life tenant may also receive a portion of the corpus of the trust. For trusts in this study, the life tenant is a *different person or organization* than the remainderman. Of course, there can be more than one life tenant. Many types of tenants were classified separately.

Trusts—remaindermen. When the trust terminates, the remainderman is the person or organization entitled to receive the corpus of the trust. For trusts in this study, the remainderman is a *different person or organization* than the life tenant. (For instance, if a gift or bequest was made to "my son John, to receive the income until he reaches the age of 25, and then to receive the principal or corpus," the gift or bequest was regarded as "other than in trust," since there was no generation-skipping involved, and no avoidance of tax.) Of course, there can be more than one remainderman. Many types of remaindermen were classified separately.

Trusts created at death. The terms "Trusts created at death" and "Bequests in trust" have the same meaning in this study. See note on the latter above.

Trusts—invasion of corpus. A trust by its terms may or may not give the trustee a power to invade the corpus for the benefit of the tenant. The invasion provisions of the trust agreements for gifts and bequests, usually applicable to the trustee, were classified as follows:

1. Unlimited power.
2. Power limited by standard. This refers to an ascertainable standard, such as to allow the tenant funds for (a) educational purposes or for (b) support or maintenance in case of a catastrophe, injury, or illness. These funds are in addition to the specified income the life tenant is to receive.
3. No power.

APPENDIX B

Testamentary Trusts

ROBERT ANTHOINE

USING THE SPECIAL tabulations prepared by the Internal Revenue Service, this appendix summarizes the information on testamentary trusts created by the wills of decedents whose estate tax returns were filed in 1957 and 1959.[1]

The uses of trusts in planning estates so as to accomplish a variety of family and business objectives and to enjoy the tax savings involved are well known to all who are concerned with the problems of "estate planning." Since neither the United States nor any of the states imposes an estate tax upon the termination of a life estate or a tenancy for a term of years, the estate tax advantages to be derived from the use of long-term trusts are obvious.

The principal legal limitation on the use of long-term trusts is the rule against perpetuities, which prevents undue fettering of the alienability of property.[2] Notwithstanding this limitation, through properly constructed trusts it is often possible for property to escape the estate tax for more than a hundred years.

[1] For the definitions of "trusts," "bequests," and other technical terms as formulated for this study (which differ in important respects from both legal and commonly accepted definitions), see "Technical Notes" in Appendix A above.

[2] The rule has been described as being directed against the suspension of the power of alienation and against remoteness of vesting (5 Powell on Real Property, par. 767). Powell states that "Under the common law rule against perpetuities, which is the law in most of the states of the United States, the maximum permissible period is (a) lives of persons who are (i) in being at the commencement of such period, and (ii) neither so numerous nor so situated that evidence of their deaths is likely to be unreasonably difficult to obtain; and (b) twenty-one years; and (c) any period or periods of gestation involved in the situation to which the limitation applies." 5 Powell on Real Property, par. 766[1] (footnotes omitted).

Noncharitable Transfers in Trust

Millionaires

In 1957 there were 1,119 millionaires' returns reporting gross transfers at death of $2.6 billion (Table B-1); and of this number 607 millionaire decedents created 1,119 trusts[3] containing property with a value of $455 million (Table B-4). In 1959 there were 1,137 decedents and $2.5 billion of gross transfers at death (Table B-1). In the returns for that year 646 decedents created 1,334 trusts containing property with a value of $448 million (Table B-4).

In the returns for 1957, the ratio of noncharitable bequests in trust to total noncharitable bequests rises, with some deviations, to a high of 41.1 percent in the $5 million to $10 million category. The highest gross transfer classification of $10,000,000 or more shows a ratio of 33.8 percent. The second highest ratio is in the $1.75-$2 million category, in which the ratio is 37.4 percent. There is a greater use of trusts in the gross transfer classifications above $1,750,000 (noncharitable bequests in trust averaging about 36 percent of all noncharitable bequests) than in the gross transfer classifications from $900,000 to $1,750,000, in which the ratio averages about 28 percent (Table B-1).

In the returns for 1959, the highest ratio of noncharitable bequests in trusts as a percentage of all noncharitable bequests is found in the $3-$5 million class. For decedents with gross transfers of less than $900,000, the ratio is 18.4 percent. This ratio again rises gradually, with deviations, as the gross transfer size increases to the high of 37.4 percent in the $3 million to $5 million category. The two highest gross transfer categories show 28.3 percent and 28.0 percent, respectively.

With respect to 1957, 54.2 percent of the millionaire decedents transferred property to noncharitable trusts (Table B-2). The value of such trust property amounted to 17.8 percent of the value of gross transfers at death and 32.2 percent of the value of all noncharitable bequests. In the 1959 returns 56.8 percent of the millionaire decedents transferred property to noncharitable trusts. The value of such trust property was 18.3 percent of the value of gross transfers at death, and 31.2 percent of the value of all noncharitable bequests.

[3] By an extraordinary coincidence, the number of millionaires' returns in 1957 was exactly the same as the number of trusts created in those returns (1,119). In some returns, no trusts were created; in others, only one; in still others, two or more trusts. In 1959 the totals were 1,137 decedents and 1,334 trusts.

TABLE B-1. *Disposition of Gross Transfers at Death by Selected Ratios, Millionaires, 1957 and 1959*

(Dollar amounts in thousands)

Size of gross transfers	Gross transfers at death: Number of decedents	Gross transfers at death: Amount	Charitable bequests as a percentage of gross transfers[a]	Noncharitable bequests as a percentage of gross transfers[a]	Total taxes as a percentage of gross transfers[a]	Noncharitable in-trust bequests[a]: As a percentage of decedents	Noncharitable in-trust bequests[a]: As a percentage of gross transfers	Noncharitable in-trust bequests as a percentage of gross transfers[a] minus death taxes[b]	Noncharitable in-trust bequests as a percentage of total noncharitable bequests
				1957					
Under $900	47	$ 29,731	3.9	75.6	20.6	40.4	19.0	24.0	25.2
900– 1,000	75	71,284	7.3	70.7	22.0	53.3	19.7	25.2	27.8
1,000– 1,250	260	283,026	5.9	70.4	23.6	51.9	20.0	26.2	28.4
1,250– 1,500	191	247,312	8.0	68.1	23.9	51.8	18.3	24.1	26.9
1,500– 1,750	118	178,234	9.6	66.3	24.1	48.3	15.9	20.9	23.9
1,750– 2,000	78	138,172	9.0	64.2	26.8	57.7	24.0	32.8	37.4
2,000– 3,000	155	356,433	10.6	61.2	28.2	57.4	21.2	29.6	34.7
3,000– 5,000	105	370,080	9.0	59.8	31.2	59.0	19.7	28.6	32.9
5,000–10,000	64	372,531	19.6	47.4	33.0	68.8	19.5	29.1	41.1
10,000 or more	26	508,646	29.2	29.8	41.0	65.4	10.0	17.0	33.8
Total	1,119	2,555,449	14.3	55.4	30.3	54.2	17.8	25.6	32.2
				1959					
Under $900	52	$ 31,944	4.1	76.0	19.9	34.6	14.0	17.5	18.4
900– 1,000	62	59,349	6.7	71.8	21.5	51.6	17.4	22.1	24.2
1,000– 1,250	263	285,836	5.9	70.6	23.5	51.7	19.1	24.9	27.0
1,250– 1,500	190	247,428	6.0	70.6	23.3	54.7	21.2	27.6	30.0
1,500– 1,750	118	179,745	9.2	66.6	24.3	61.0	22.1	29.2	33.2
1,750– 2,000	103	177,878	7.2	67.6	25.2	64.1	22.4	30.0	33.2
2,000– 3,000	162	364,777	14.9	59.3	25.9	59.9	20.8	28.0	35.0
3,000– 5,000	110	373,001	13.4	57.1	29.5	64.5	21.3	30.3	37.4
5,000–10,000	51	308,654	13.6	52.3	34.1	58.8	14.8	22.5	28.3
10,000 or more	26	422,789	29.8	38.6	31.5	76.9	10.8	15.8	28.0
Total	1,137	2,451,401	13.8	58.6	27.6	56.8	18.3	25.2	31.2

Source: U. S. Treasury Department.
[a] Gross transfers at death.
[b] Death taxes consist of: net federal estate tax (that is, after tax credits), gift taxes credited against federal estate tax, state death taxes, and foreign death taxes.

All Decedents

Table B-2 shows the disposition of gross transfers for all decedents by sample strata—small, medium, and large estates, as defined in Appendix A. Table B-6 sets forth the amounts placed in trust by sample strata and the percentage of trust corpora skipping generations.

TABLE B-2. ***Disposition of Gross Transfers at Death by Selected Ratios, Summary by Sample Strata, 1957 and 1959***

Size of gross transfers	Gross transfers at death		Charitable bequests as a percentage of gross transfers[a]	Noncharitable bequests as a percentage of gross transfers[a]	Total taxes as a percentage of gross transfers[a]	Noncharitable in-trust bequests[a]		Noncharitable in-trust bequests as a percentage of gross transfers[a] minus death taxes[b]	Noncharitable in-trust bequests as a percentage of noncharitable bequests
	Number of decedents	Amount (in thousands of dollars)				As a percentage of decedents	As a percentage of gross transfers		
1957									
Small	398	45,182	3.4	91.6	5.0	13.6	8.4	8.8	9.1
Medium	876	387,160	5.0	76.8	18.2	37.0	16.5	20.2	21.5
Large	1,119	2,555,449	14.3	55.4	30.3	54.2	17.8	25.6	32.2
1959									
Small	471	54,786	2.5	91.9	5.6	16.1	9.7	10.2	10.5
Medium	968	439,102	4.4	77.7	17.8	40.3	17.0	20.7	21.9
Large	1,137	2,451,401	13.8	58.6	27.6	56.8	18.3	25.2	31.2

Source: U. S. Treasury Department.
[a] Gross transfers at death.
[b] Death taxes are composed of: net federal estate tax (that is, after tax credits), gift taxes credited against federal estate tax, state death taxes, and foreign death taxes.

In Table B-2 and the following tables, the numbers of returns and the dollar amounts for "small" and "medium" estates are numbers and amounts in the sample, not the "blown-up" figures used in the special study tables in order to facilitate comparisons with the millionaire returns.[4]

The recapitulation for sample strata shows, as would be expected, that the percentage of property transferred in trust is lowest in the smallest estates. Thus, for the small estates (below $300,000) in the 1957 returns, the value of property transferred in trust amounted to only 8.4 percent of gross transfers at death and to only 9.1 percent of all noncharitable bequests. For the medium-sized estates ($300,000-$1,000,000) the figures are 16.5 percent and 21.5 percent.

In the 1959 returns the value of property transferred in trust by the small estates amounted to 9.7 percent of gross transfers at death and to 10.5 percent of all noncharitable bequests. The equivalent figures for the medium-sized estates are 17.0 percent and 21.9 percent.

[4] See the discussion of the sampling problem in Appendix A.

Generation-Skipping by Estate Classification

A major purpose of this appendix is to ascertain the amount of generation-skipping involved in the use of trusts. The tables discussed below are intended to indicate the amount of property that is designed to pass through a given number of generations.

The classifications used in the preparation of the tables are not entirely satisfactory. For example, in the Treasury study (see "Technical Notes," Appendix A above), one-generation trusts are those with one or more tenants of the same generation. Two-generation trusts are those with tenants belonging to two different generations, and three-generation trusts are those with tenants belonging to three different generations, concurrently or successively. It will be noted that under this classification, a trust in which the sole life tenant is a person of the testator's generation, such as the surviving spouse or a sister, is regarded as a trust in which the corpus skips one generation. On the other hand, a trust in which the testator's grandchildren are the sole life tenants is treated as only a one-generation trust. Furthermore, in the tables showing trust duration, no attempt was made to determine whether a generation was skipped between the life tenant and the remainderman—for example, income to surviving spouse for life, remainder to grandchildren.

In the trust duration tables, the only identification of trust beneficiaries is that of the surviving spouse either as the sole income beneficiary or as the first of two or more income beneficiaries in two-generation trusts.

The basic tables in this appendix follow the classifications used in compiling the data on trust duration. In addition, the author has made the following changes for purposes of analysis: A trust which terminates on the death of a surviving spouse who was the sole life tenant is not regarded as involving any generation-skipping. A similar principle is followed where the spouse is the first of two successive tenants.

With respect to the category "a term of years," which the study does not attempt to classify in terms of generation-skipping, it is assumed in every instance that a term of years constitutes one generation.

The author's adherence to the classification of trust duration used in compiling the data may result in understating or overstating the amount of generation-skipping. For example, a trust in which the life tenants are the testator's ancestors or are members of the testator's generation, the remainders passing to members of the generation immediately following that of the testator, should be treated as involving no generation-skipping, rather than as a one-generation trust. A trust in which the testator's grandchildren are the sole life tenants, with remainders to their children, should be treated as a two-generation trust, rather than as a one-generation trust. An effort was made to compensate partially for this analytical failure by ascertaining, insofar as practicable, the value of property transferred to trusts that should be classified in a category different from that used in the study. Data have been assembled from other tables that show the relationships between the testator and the life tenants and the remaindermen. The results of this inquiry are noted below in the section on "Relationship of Tenants and Remaindermen to Grantor."

Millionaires

Table B-3 shows the relative number of testamentary trusts and the relative amounts of trust corpora in each type of tenancy. In both

TABLE B-3. *Percentages of Trusts and of Trust Corpora Skipping Generations by Types of Tenancies, Millionaires, 1957 and 1959*

Description of category	Percentage of total number of trusts		Percentage of total value of corpora of trusts	
	1957	1959	1957	1959
1 generation, spouse sole life tenant (no skip)	23.1	15.7	25.9	19.7
Term of years (1 generation skipped)	2.5	4.0	1.0	3.4
1 generation, life tenant other than spouse (1 generation)	56.7	59.3	49.4	49.8
1 generation plus term of years, spouse life tenant (1 generation)	0.7	2.2	1.4	3.3
2 generations, spouse first life tenant (1 generation)	3.7	3.7	7.1	6.0
1 generation plus term of years, life tenant other than spouse (2 generations)	5.3	5.1	6.3	6.6
2 generations, life tenant other than spouse (2 generations)	4.6	6.3	5.5	5.7
2 generations plus term of years (3 generations)	2.5	2.8	2.4	4.1
3 generations, all life tenants (3generations)	0.7	0.5	0.9	0.8
3 generations plus term of years (4 generations)	0.2	0.3	0.2	0.6

Source: U. S. Treasury Department.

TABLE B-4. *Percentages of Value of Trust Corpora Skipping Generations by Size of Gross Transfers at Death, Millionaires, 1957 and 1959*

(Dollar amounts in thousands)

Size of gross transfers	Number of decedents creating trusts	Number of trusts	Value of trust corpora	Percentages of value of trust corpora				
				No skip (spouse sole life tenant)	1 generation	2 generations	3 generations	4 generations (3 generations plus term of years)
				1957				
Under $900	19	34	$ 5,659	27.1	57.8	8.8	6.3	—
900– 1,000	40	62	14,022	47.2	45.5	4.2	3.1	—
1,000– 1,250	135	203	56,556	31.2	53.5	8.7	6.6	—
1,250– 1,500	99	168	45,274	31.5	57.8	9.8	0.9	—
1,500– 1,750	57	92	28,304	32.9	60.7	6.3	—	—
1,750– 2,000	45	86	33,134	22.8	44.6	20.0	12.6	—
2,000– 3,000	89	172	75,635	22.5	64.2	7.2	6.1	—
3,000– 5,000	62	145	72,910	32.2	48.8	19.0	—	—
5,000–10,000	44	86	72,636	13.1	65.9	18.2	1.3	1.6
10,000 or more	17	71	51,117	21.7	74.1	4.1	—	—
Total	607	1,119	455,247	25.9	58.9	11.7	3.2	0.2
				1959				
Under $900	18	25	$ 4,472	53.7	31.5	13.6	—	—
900– 1,000	32	50	10,304	31.2	60.5	3.1	5.2	—
1,000– 1,250	136	248	54,549	22.5	69.1	8.1	0.2	—
1,250– 1,500	104	187	52,375	26.4	58.1	10.7	3.9	0.9
1,500– 1,750	72	131	39,689	29.4	59.6	4.8	4.7	1.2
1,750– 2,000	66	119	39,880	20.1	63.2	10.1	4.6	1.9
2,000– 3,000	97	223	75,694	16.8	59.1	12.2	10.4	1.4
3,000– 5,000	71	189	79,580	15.8	61.8	18.7	3.7	—
5,000–10,000	30	78	45,732	13.1	59.5	24.4	2.9	—
10,000 or more	20	84	45,738	11.7	75.1	5.8	7.5	—
Total	646	1,334	448,013	19.7	62.5	12.2	4.9	0.6

Source: U. S. Treasury Department.

years more than 80 percent of the value of trust corpora involved either no generation-skipping or skipping of only one generation.

In general the statistics reveal a good deal of one-generation-skipping in most wealth classes but little beyond that. In both 1957 and 1959, the highest gross transfer classification, $10 million or more, had the highest percentage of total trust corpora in trusts designed to skip one generation—74 percent and 75 percent, respectively (Table B-4). For the returns filed in 1957, in other gross transfer categories, the percentage of total trust corpora in one-generation trusts reached a low of 44.6 percent in the $1.75-$2 million class, and a high of 65.9 percent in the $5-$10 million category. For the returns filed in 1959 the lowest percentage of trust corpora to skip one generation was in

TABLE B-5. *Percentages of Trusts and of Trust Corpora Skipping Generations by Types of Tenancies, All Decedents, 1957 and 1959, and Sample Strata 1957 and 1959 (Corpora Only)*

Description of category	Percentage of total value of trust corpora by sample strata					
	Small		Medium		Large	
	1957	1959	1957	1959	1957	1959
1 generation, spouse sole life tenant (no skip)	58.9	51.0	37.4	38.4	25.9	19.7
Term of years (1 generation skipped)	—	2.7	1.9	1.2	1.0	3.4
1 generation, life tenant other than spouse (1 generation)	25.9	33.5	42.5	39.6	49.4	49.8
1 generation plus term of years, spouse life tenant (1 generation)	—	4.0	2.9	3.8	1.4	3.3
2 generations, spouse first life tenant (1 generation)	5.6	3.8	6.1	6.6	7.1	6.0
1 generation plus term of years, life tenant other than spouse (2 generations)	4.5	0.7	2.3	5.2	6.3	6.6
2 generations, life tenant other than spouse (2 generations)	5.1	2.9	4.5	1.5	5.5	5.7
2 generations plus term of years (3 generations)	—	1.3	2.0	3.3	2.4	4.1
3 generations, all life tenants (3 generations)	—	—	0.5	0.5	0.9	0.8
3 generations plus term of years (4 generations)	—	—	—	—	0.2	0.6

Source: U. S. Treasury Department.

the under-$900,000 category—31.5 percent—and the second highest percentage was in the $1-$1.25 million category—69.1 percent.

There does not appear to be a marked propensity to "tie up" property for long periods in trust as the size of the gross transfer increases. In the 1957 returns, in the highest size classification of $10 million or more, there was no trust to last beyond two generations, and only 4.1 percent of the approximately $51 million placed in trust was to be held beyond one generation. In the 1959 returns, in the $10 million or more category, 7.5 percent of the approximately $46 million placed in trust was to last for three generations and 5.8 percent for two generations.

All Decedents

Small- and medium-sized estates show a good deal of one-generation-skipping but, as might be expected, little beyond that (Tables B-5 and B-6). In the returns filed in 1957, the small estates transferred 31.5 percent of trust corpora in trust to skip one generation, 9.6 percent in trusts to skip two generations, and nothing beyond that. The equivalent figures for 1959 are 44.1 percent and 3.6 percent, and in that year 1.3 percent of trust corpora was to skip three generations.

In the 1957 returns, the medium-sized estates transferred 53.3 percent of trust corpora in trust to skip one generation, 6.8 percent to

TABLE B-6. ***Percentages of Trust Corpora Skipping Generations by Size of Gross Transfers at Death, All Decedents, Summary by Sample Strata, 1957 and 1959***

(Dollar amounts in thousands)

Size of gross transfers	Number of decedents	Number of trusts	Value of corpora	No skip (spouse sole life tenant)	Percentage skipping			
					1 generation	2 generations	3 generations	4 generations
1957								
Small	54	65	3,778	58.9	31.5	9.6	—	—
Medium	324	446	64,007	37.4	53.3	6.8	2.5	—
Large	607	1,119	455,247	25.9	58.9	11.7	3.2	0.2
1959								
Small	76	89	5,289	51.1	44.1	3.6	1.3	—
Medium	390	514	74,747	38.4	51.2	6.7	3.7	—
Large	646	1,334	448,013	19.7	62.5	12.2	4.9	0.6

Source: U. S. Treasury Department.

skip two generations, and 2.5 percent to skip three generations. The equivalent figures for 1959 are 51.2 percent, 6.7 percent, and 3.7 percent.

Thus, in the small estates, for 1957 and 1959, respectively, the percentages of trust corpora designed to skip more than one generation are 9.6 percent and 4.9 percent. The equivalent figures for the medium-sized estates are 9.3 percent and 10.4 percent. These may be compared with the figures for the large estates, which for the two years are 15.1 percent and 17.7 percent.

Summary of Trust Corpora Passing Through Generations

Some of the data in the foregoing tables have been recast in Table B-7 in order to summarize for the millionaires' estates the actual dollar amounts of property passing through the given number of generations, and the ratio of such amounts of property to total trust corpora and to total gross transfers at death.

In the 1957 returns, out of total gross transfers at death by millionaires of $2.6 billion, $268 million (10.5 percent) was transferred to trusts that would skip one generation, and $69 million (2.7 percent) to trusts to skip more than one generation.

In the 1959 returns, out of total gross transfers at death by millionaires of $2.5 billion, $280 million (11.4 percent) was transferred to

TABLE B-7. *Summary of Percentages and Dollar Amounts of Trust Corpora Passing Through Generations, Millionaires Only, 1957 and 1959*

(Dollar amounts in thousands)

Item	*No skip (spouse sole life tenant)*		*1 generation*		*2 generations*		*3 generations*		*4 generations*	
	1957	*1959*	*1957*	*1959*	*1957*	*1959*	*1957*	*1959*	*1957*	*1959*
Percentages of value of trust corpora	25.9	19.7	58.9	62.5	11.7	12.2	3.2	4.9	0.2	0.6
Dollar amounts	118,048	88,136	267,930	280,158	53,475	54,821	14,716	22,023	1,078	2,875
Percentages of total gross transfers at death	4.6	3.6	10.5	11.4	2.1	2.2	0.6	0.9	[a]	0.1

Source: U. S. Treasury Department.
[a] Less than 0.05 percent.

trusts that would skip one generation, and $80 million (3.1 percent) to trusts to skip more than one generation.

Revenue Potential of a Tax on Termination of Trusts

A very rough calculation of the amount of revenue that might be collected if a tax were imposed upon the termination of the tenancies was made by Dr. Richard Bird. It is based on the admittedly crude assumptions that (1) the value of the property in trust would remain constant, with no appreciation or depreciation in the value of the trust property itself and with no diminution in the trust property for the taxes borne by the trust upon the termination of prior tenancies, and that (2) the effective rate of estate tax for the millionaires would be 30 percent (this being approximately the effective rate of tax for 1957 and 1959 as calculated from Table B-1).

The value of trust corpora left by millionaire decedents that would be subject to tax is then as follows (in millions of dollars):

	1957	1959
1 generation	268	280
2 generations	53	55
3 generations	15	22
4 generations	1	3

The tax base represented by the trust corpora was then assumed to be the product of their value as shown above and the number of generations skipped (for example, the tax base represented by the two-generation trusts of millionaire decedents in 1957 is $53 \times 2 = 106$). The tax which might be collected was then calculated as follows (in millions of dollars):

	Tax Base	Tax
1957	423	127
1959	468	140

While these are estimates of the revenue to be collected over the next four generations, the bulk of it would come in during the early part of the period. Crude as this calculation is, it gives at least some idea of the relatively small magnitudes involved, even with the rather strong assumptions concerning effective rates made above. One might also expect the use of trusts to decline somewhat if life interests were to be taxed, though this effect should not be particularly strong in view of the evidence on testator motivations presented in this and the other chapters.

Supplementary Data on Family Relationships

Corrected Estimates of Generation-Skipping

Tables B-8 and B-9 show the family relationships in the most significant categories for millionaire decedents. They indicate that the foregoing data overstate the amount of one-generation skipping and understate the amount of two- and three-generation skipping.

For the year 1957 property valued at $22.7 million was transferred by millionaires to trusts in which the only life tenants were brothers or sisters. And $1.5 million was transferred to trusts in which only the parents of the testator were the life tenants. If it is assumed that the remaindermen of those trusts were the children or nephews or nieces of the testator, these trusts should be regarded as involving no generation-skipping rather than one-generation skipping, as they have been reported above. Trusts in which the grandchildren were the sole life tenants held a corpus of $14.3 million. Accordingly the amount of property skipping two generations has been understated by this amount, and the amount skipping one generation has been correspondingly overstated. The amount of $4.7 million was placed in trusts in which the grandchildren and the great grandchildren of the testator were the sole life tenants. The amount of three-generation skipping has therefore been understated by this sum, and the amount of two-generation skipping has been correspondingly overstated. The other categories are difficult to classify accurately in terms of generation-skipping.

For 1959 the figures for the millionaires are similar to those above, except that the amount of property passing into trusts in which the grandchildren were the sole life tenants was higher by about 50 percent, and the amount passing into trusts in which the grandchildren and great grandchildren were the life tenants decreased sharply from the 1957 figure.

From an examination of the foregoing tables, it appears that the amount of one-generation skipping has been overstated and the amount of two- and three-generation skipping understated. The amount of two-generation skipping reported for 1957 is $53.5 million. To this figure should be added at least $14.3 million of trust property to which the grandchildren were the sole life tenants. Similarly, with respect to 1959, to the figure of $54.8 million of two-generation skipping there should be added $21.1 million of trust property to which the grand-

TABLE B-8. *Noncharitable Trusts Created at Death by Relationship of Life Tenants[a] to Grantor, by Size of Gross Transfers, by Principal Categories, Millionaires, 1957 and 1959*

Item	*Total for all tenants*	*Spouse only*	*Children only*	*Brothers or sisters only*	*Grand-children only*	*Other relatives only*	*Non-relatives only*	*Spouse and children*	*Children and grand-children*
				1957					
Number of trusts	1,119	226	357	78	45	91	92	44	33
Percentage in gross transfer class[b]									
Under 500	0.4	1.8					1.1		
500–1,000	8.1	10.2	7.8	7.7		8.8	4.3	20.5	9.1
1,000–2,000	49.1	56.6	52.1	56.4	40.0	39.6	43.5	56.8	33.3
2,000–3,000	15.4	7.1	19.9	12.8	17.8	13.2	23.9	11.4	15.2
3,000–5,000	13.0	8.8	11.2	7.7	8.9	14.3	10.9	6.8	12.1
5,000 and over	14.0	15.5	9.0	15.4	33.3	24.2	16.3	4.5	30.3
Total	100.0	100.0	100.0	100.0	100.0	100.0	100.0	100.0	100.0
Value of trusts[c]	455.2	102.3	153.0	22.7	14.3	30.0	14.1	24.9	15.0
Percentage in gross transfer class[b]									
Under 500	0.2	0.6					2.8		
500–1,000	4.1	6.6	3.1	3.7		3.1	4.1	6.8	3.1
1,000–2,000	35.9	43.9	28.8	48.7	29.6	26.8	38.6	54.5	33.8
2,000–3,000	16.6	11.8	10.4	10.7	11.5	9.9	19.8	16.4	17.1
3,000–5,000	16.0	17.5	18.0	16.9	1.6	18.5	6.2	17.8	8.9
5,000 and over	27.2	19.6	29.7	20.1	57.2	41.7	28.6	4.4	37.0
Total	100.0	100.0	100.0	100.0	100.0	100.0	100.0	100.0	100.0
				1959					
Number of trusts	1,334	208	411	101	79	135	167	56	36
Percentage in gross transfer class[b]									
Under 500	0.2	1.0						1.8	
500–1,000	5.4	10.1	5.6	5.0	6.3	3.0	3.0	5.4	
1,000–2,000	51.3	52.4	59.9	55.4	30.4	40.7	42.5	64.3	33.3
2,000–3,000	16.7	12.5	10.9	22.8	5.1	30.4	23.4	14.3	22.2
3,000–5,000	14.2	18.3	13.1	14.9	26.6	11.9	11.4	10.7	11.1
5,000 and over	12.1	5.8	10.5	2.0	31.6	14.1	19.8	3.6	33.3
Total	100.0	100.0	100.0	100.0	100.0	100.0	100.0	100.0	100.0
Value of trusts[c]	448.0	89.1	157.4	22.5	21.1	27.5	15.1	30.5	25.8
Percentage in gross transfer class[b]									
Under 500	0.1	10.3						0.6	
500–1,000	3.2	6.0	2.7	1.5	2.2	2.8	2.0	3.1	
1,000–2,000	41.6	50.6	42.7	55.2	21.1	23.7	40.2	50.2	22.7
2,000–3,000	16.9	15.9	12.8	16.6	11.0	36.5	20.3	17.1	13.3
3,000–5,000	17.8	12.7	18.3	20.8	17.3	25.9	16.9	18.5	25.0
5,000 and over	20.4	14.6	23.4	5.9	48.4	11.1	20.8	10.5	39.0
Total	100.0	100.0	100.0	100.0	100.0	100.0	100.0	100.0	100.0

Source: U. S. Treasury Department.

[a] Includes tenants for a term of years. [b] Transfer classes in thousands of dollars. [c] Value of trusts in millions of dollars.

TABLE B-9. *Noncharitable Trusts Created at Death, by Relationship of the Remaindermen to Grantor and by Size of Gross Transfers, by Principal Categories, Millionaires, 1957 and 1959*

Item	*Total for all remaindermen*	*Children only*	*Grand-children only*	*Other relatives only*	*Charity only*	*Subject to power of appointment in life tenants*
			1957			
Number of trusts	1,119	160	394	155	120	55
Percentage in gross transfer class[a]						
Under 500	0.4	1.9		0.6		
500–1,000	8.1	9.4	7.4	10.3	4.2	18.2
1,000–2,000	49.1	58.1	49.0	49.7	37.5	52.7
2,000–3,000	15.4	15.6	18.5	13.5	18.3	7.3
3,000–5,000	13.0	7.5	15.2	12.3	6.7	12.7
5,000 and over	14.0	7.5	9.9	13.5	33.3	9.1
Total	100.0	100.0	100.0	100.0	100.0	100.0
Value of trusts[b]	455.2	66.3	181.8	72.1	22.9	19.5
Percentage in gross transfer class[a]						
Under 500	0.2	0.7		0.3		
500–1,000	4.1	5.5	2.8	5.1	4.9	8.4
1,000–2,000	35.9	48.9	29.5	32.3	38.8	37.9
2,000–3,000	16.6	18.5	20.2	18.0	18.3	5.3
3,000–5,000	16.0	11.3	17.7	10.5	11.5	15.5
5,000 and over	27.2	15.1	29.7	33.9	26.4	32.9
Total	100.0	100.0	100.0	100.0	100.0	100.0
			1959			
Number of trusts	1,334	184	399	190	174	101
Percentage in gross transfer class[a]						
Under 500	0.2	1.1				
500–1,000	5.4	12.0	5.5	3.7	3.4	3.0
1,000–2,000	51.3	62.5	55.9	47.4	40.2	52.5
2,000–3,000	16.7	12.0	13.8	28.4	21.8	8.9
3,000–5,000	14.2	7.6	11.5	11.6	19.5	20.8
5,000 and over	12.1	4.9	13.3	8.9	14.9	14.9
Total	100.0	100.0	100.0	100.0	100.0	100.0
Value of trusts[b]	448.0	63.3	167.7	53.8	24.1	30.0
Percentage in gross transfer class[a]						
Under 500	0.0	0.4				
500–1,000	3.2	6.3	2.3	2.3	2.7	1.8
1,000–2,000	41.6	60.5	41.2	41.6	26.3	35.3
2,000–3,000	16.9	11.7	12.4	27.4	22.9	14.2
3,000–5,000	17.8	10.5	17.4	21.4	11.7	24.3
5,000 and over	20.4	10.6	26.8	7.3	36.4	24.3
Total	100.0	100.0	100.0	100.0	100.0	100.0

Source: U. S. Treasury Department.
[a] Transfer classes in thousands of dollars. [b] Value of trusts in millions of dollars.

children were the sole life tenants. As for three-generation skipping, the 1957 figure of $14.7 million does not include the $4.7 million of trust property to which the grandchildren and great grandchildren were the sole life tenants. (There were no trusts in 1957 in which great grandchildren alone were life tenants.) The 1959 figure of $22.0 million does not include approximately $0.7 million in trust corpus of property to which grandchildren and great grandchildren were the sole life tenants and also does not include $0.2 million in trusts where great grandchildren alone were the sole life tenants.

Table B-9 describes the principal categories of remaindermen in terms of their relationship to the testator, again for millionaire decedents only. This table reveals that there is somewhat more generation-skipping than is indicated in the above analysis because the remaindermen may be more than one generation removed from the life tenants. This aspect is revealed by the basic Treasury tables, which are not reproduced here. They show, for example, that of all the trusts created by the millionaire decedents whose tax returns were filed in 1957, the surviving spouse was the sole life tenant in trusts holding property with a value of $102 million. The remaindermen by relationship to the testator, and the value of the trusts involved, were as follows:

Remaindermen	Amounts (In thousands of dollars)
Children only	52,427
Parents only	437
Brothers or sisters only	1,165
Grandchildren only	3,729
Other relatives only	6,696
Nonrelatives only	3,139
Charity only	6,495
Subject to power of appointment	5,910
Children and grandchildren	7,184
Children and other relatives	649
Children and charity	609
Brothers or sisters and others	1,740
Grandchildren and nonrelatives	2,368
Other relatives and nonrelatives	5,521
Other undescribed categories	4,236
Total	102,305

With respect to the same year, 1957, for the millionaires, the children were the sole life tenants in trust having a total corpus of $153 million. The remaindermen by relationship to the testator, and the value of the trusts involved, were as follows:

Remaindermen	Amounts (In thousands of dollars)
Children only	949
Brothers or sisters only	241
Grandchildren only	121,582
Great grandchildren only	864
Other relatives only	1,550
Nonrelatives only	1,867
Charity only	1,418
Subject to power of appointment	10,678
Spouse and nonrelatives	140
Children and nonrelatives	1,236
Grandchilden and great grandchildren	3,283
Grandchildren and other relatives	2,877
Grandchildren and nonrelatives	4,489
Grandchildren and charity	513
Other relatives and nonrelatives	485
Other undescribed categories	842
Total	153,014

The foregoing indicates some, but probably not a significant amount of, additional generation-skipping as the result of skipping a generation between the life tenants and the remaindermen.

Considered together, the additional generation-skipping revealed by Tables B-8 and B-9 and by the Treasury study is substantial but is not of such dimension as to affect significantly the revenue estimates described earlier. The revenue effects of taxing the termination of life estates would not be altered at all. Indeed, some other taxing device would have to be constructed to attack the skipping of generations that occurs through (1) transfers to trusts in which the first life beneficiary is more than one generation removed from the testator and (2) transfers of trust property, on termination, to remaindermen who are more than one generation removed from the last life tenant. Such a tax, to be uniform in application, should also be imposed upon outright bequests that skip more than one generation. To be sure, the trust, with its almost unlimited flexibility, facilitates the kind of additional generation-skipping described above.

Comments on Generation-Skipping

One may wonder why the wealthier citizens of the country do not take greater advantage of the tax savings to be derived from long-term trusts. The instability characteristic of our time, and perhaps the lack of family solidarity, may account for the failure of testators to look as far ahead as the tax advantages might dictate. The fact that estates today are composed largely of securities as distinguished from landed wealth may also be significant.

The data given above on 1957 and 1959 estate tax returns suggests that the normal family trust today involves a substantial amount of one-generation skipping but little beyond that. But the pattern shown in the 1957 and 1959 returns may not reflect the current practice. The dates of execution of the wills of the decedents whose returns were filed in 1957 and 1959 are not furnished. Presumably most of the millionaires' wills had been revised after the marital deduction was introduced in 1948.

Family trust dispositions may vary from one part of the country to another; and lawyers within the same community differ as to the amount of generation-skipping that is presently being generated through inter vivos and testamentary trusts. Discussions that the author has held with lawyers in New York lead him to believe that there is currently a considerable amount of one-generation skipping, but relatively little beyond that. Indeed, several lawyers have noted recent instances in which clients left the bulk of their property outright to their children (who had already attained majority and were responsible persons). They did this because: (1) it is their children whom they wish primarily to benefit, not their grandchildren or great grandchildren; (2) each generation should bear the direct responsibility for the management of the family property—and with the responsibility of decision-making goes authority, including parental authority; and (3) the possibility that the property passing to subsequent generations upon the death of the children may bear a higher estate tax burden than if it had been placed in trust is largely irrelevant and may be offset by the use that the children will make of the entire property over a substantial period. However, some lawyers, both in New York and elsewhere, have indicated that in recent years a number of wealthy individuals have concluded that most of the advantages of complete ownership can be given to the beneficiary of a trust, and that the pattern may be changing in the direction of greater use of trusts to skip generations. It seems certain that the limited (nontaxable) power of appointment in the life tenant is in greater use now than the 1957 and 1959 data would indicate.

Whether a serious effort should be made to modify the present treatment, for example, by imposing a transfer tax on the termination of a life estate, depends upon one's view of the estate tax generally, and of the social utility of trusts. It also depends upon whether it is felt that the present amount of generation-skipping through trusts raises a substantial equity problem. The question is fundamentally one of equity since the revenue gained by the change would be relatively small.

The American Law Institute in 1963 undertook a comprehensive study of estate and gift taxation. The topics include generation-skipping through various forms of bequest and the legal problems that would be encountered in any change in the present law. This study should provide a basis for judgment as to the desirability of changing the present system.

Relationship of Tenants and Remaindermen to Grantor

Table B-8 sets forth data with respect to noncharitable trusts created at death by the millionaires in terms of the relationship, in principal categories only, of life tenants or tenants for a term of years to the grantor, by size of gross transfers at death. Table B-9 contains data with respect to noncharitable trusts created at death by millionaires in terms of the relationship, in principal categories only, of remaindermen to the grantor, by the size of gross transfers; the relationship categories include charity and trusts subject to power of appointment. There are two matters in connection with these tables or their underlying data that deserve comment.

First, an analysis was made of the amount of trust corpus subject to a power of appointment in the life tenant, but no attempt was made to classify the type of power as a general[5] or nongeneral[6] power.

[5] It must be remembered that a general power of appointment held by a surviving spouse in a marital deduction trust is not regarded as a power for purposes of this study, the transfer itself being regarded as not made in trust.

[6] A nongeneral power is any power of appointment under which the holder cannot appoint the property to himself, his creditors, his estate, or his estate's creditors. Limited, nontaxable powers of appointment of this kind are often used, for example, a power in the life tenant to appoint the property among his issue. And the economic restriction placed upon the life tenant who is entitled only to income from the trust property is often lightened by giving the life tenant the power,

Hence, it is not possible to determine from any of the data available how much trust corpus was subject to a nongeneral power of appointment that would not have required the inclusion of the trust corpus in the holder's estate. However, it is clear that the figures given set an outer limit for the amount of trust corpus subject to such nongeneral powers.

The amount of trust corpus subject to a power of appointment in the life tenant for the millionaires in 1957 was $19.5 million out of total trust corpus of $455.2 million, or 4 percent. For 1959 the equivalent figures are $30.0 million out of $448.0 million, or 7 percent (see Table B-9).

Second, there is an almost complete absence of a mandatory direction to the trustee to accumulate income. The only testamentary transfers under which trust income was directed to be accumulated in 1957 or 1959 consist of two trusts set up by 1959 millionaire decedents with a total combined corpus of $100,000 in which there was a mandatory direction to accumulate income for a term of years for the benefit of grandchildren. An examination of the data that was compiled for lifetime transfers reveals no lifetime transfer in which a mandatory direction to accumulate was present. Apparently in cases in which the grantor expected the income to be accumulated, the trustee was given the discretion either to accumulate or distribute income.

Powers of Trustee to Invade Corpus

Table B-10 reports for the three sample strata the power of the trustee to invade the corpus of noncharitable trusts created during life and at death. In this category the data were gathered only in connection with lifetime and testamentary transfers combined, as was noted above. The value of trust corpora subject to an unlimited power is somewhat lower than might have been expected: 13.7 percent of the total for the 1957 millionaire returns and 18.4 percent for the 1959 millionaire returns, for example. The popularity of the power limited by a standard is evidenced by the fact that 52.0 percent and 52.1 percent of trust corpora for 1957 and 1959 millionaire returns, respectively, were subject to such a power.

The propensity of each of the three estate size classifications to use trustee powers is remarkably similar. The data contained in the reca-

---

described in section 2041 (b) (2) of the Code, to appoint to himself or others annually the greater of $5,000 or 5 percent of the value of the trust corpus. This power must be noncumulative, that is, it must lapse annually, if the lapse is to avoid estate and gift tax consequences.

TABLE B-10. *Noncharitable Trusts Created During Life and at Death, by Power of Trustee to Invade Corpus, All Decedents, Summary by Sample Strata, 1957 and 1959*

(Dollar amounts in thousands)

Size of gross transfers	Total number of trusts	Total value of trusts	Unlimited power		Power limited by standard		No power	
			As a percentage of total number of trusts	As a percentage of total value of trusts	As a percentage of total number of trusts	As a percentage of total value of trusts	As a percentage of total number of trusts	As a percentage of total value of trusts
1957								
Small	66	$3,803	10.6	16.5	47.0	46.1	42.4	37.4
Medium	466	64,694	10.5	11.4	54.8	61.0	34.8	27.6
Large	1,532	500,291	12.7	13.7	52.9	52.0	34.3	34.3
1959								
Small	91	5,356	17.6	18.6	50.5	58.2	31.9	23.2
Medium	576	77,007	17.7	17.1	56.9	58.3	25.3	24.6
Large	1,932	498,522	16.9	18.4	51.7	52.1	31.4	29.5

Source: U. S. Treasury Department.

pitulation by sample strata show that the percentages are similar in both categories for both years.

Noncharitable Bequests by Marital Status

Table B-11 compares noncharitable bequests made in trust by millionaires with those not made in trust on the basis of the marital status of the decedent. Table B-12 shows the value of noncharitable bequests made by husbands, wives, widowers, and widows, and by the husbands and widowers combined and by the wives and widows combined. The figures show in the case of the millionaires that women tend to bequeath their property in trust to a greater extent than do men. Thus, in both years the percentage of the value of noncharitable bequests in trusts is higher for women than men and is higher for wives than husbands. However, for 1957 and for the two years combined, the millionaire widowers had a higher percentage of noncharitable bequests in trusts than did the millionaire widows.

TABLE B-11. *Noncharitable Bequests in Trust and Not in Trust, by Marital Status, Millionaires, 1957 and 1959*

(Dollar amounts in thousands)

Marital status	Total number of decedents	Noncharitable bequests other than in trust		Noncharitable bequests in trust	
		Number of decedents	Amount	Number of decedents	Amount
1957					
Husband	524	523	$550,445	308	$209,655
Wife	64	63	48,148	40	29,493
Widower	130	128	72,348	71	74,654
Widow	258	255	195,723	130	96,772
Single	104	100	67,185	42	27,285
Divorced or separated	39	37	25,957	16	17,388
1959					
Husband	523	522	597,116	313	194,823
Wife	77	76	52,802	45	33,601
Widower	155	147	98,175	80	57,046
Widow	259	254	176,289	146	116,336
Single	94	89	51,051	43	22,467
Divorced or separated	29	28	13,820	19	23,740

Source: U. S. Treasury Department.

TABLE B-12. *Value of Noncharitable Bequests in Trust as a Percentage of Value of All Noncharitable Bequests, Millionaires, 1957 and 1959*

Item	1957	1959
Husbands	27.6	24.6
Wives	38.0	38.9
Widowers	50.8	36.8
Widows	33.1	39.8
Men[a]	31.3	26.6
Women[b]	34.1	39.6

Source: U.S. Treasury Department.
[a] Total of husbands and widowers.
[b] Total of wives and widows.

APPENDIX C

Gifts During Life

C. LOWELL HARRISS

FEDERAL AND STATE tax laws generally impose less burden on non-charitable distributions of wealth made as gifts during life than on those that are bequests at death. Ordinarily the total tax is minimized when a substantial fraction—but not all—of the total of a married person's wealth above some "modest" amount—$200,000 or so—is transferred in the form of gifts during life.

Tax Advantages of Gifts

Gifts have a federal tax advantage for several reasons: (1) Gift tax rates are one-fourth less than those of the estate tax. (2) The gift tax itself is not a part of the base of the tax, as is the estate tax. Even if a gift is included in the estate because it was made in contemplation of death or to take effect at death, any gift tax paid is not itself taxed as part of the gross estate. (3) Property given during life is removed from brackets that would be subject to the highest estate tax rates applicable in the particular case. (4) A gift tax exemption and multiple exclusions are available without curtailing the specific exemption for the estate tax. (5) Gifts of property often remove later income yield from a higher to a lower personal income tax bracket. If the donor's charitable contributions in a particular year have not reached the maximum amount deductible, a gift of property to a charitable organization will reduce his income tax for that year.

State taxes as a rule are also lower on gifts than on bequests. In fact, only one-fourth of the states have gift taxes, and they are generally very much less than the tax that is applicable if the property is retained in the estate for transfer at death. The danger of multiple state taxation of the same property is reduced by a gift of assets that might otherwise fall under the death tax jurisdiction of more than one state. State personal income tax on the donee on income from the property later may be less than it would be on the donor.

Tax Disadvantages of Gifts

Nevertheless, gifts may have tax *disadvantages,* too, as compared with transfers at death. (1) A person of more than modest wealth who seeks to minimize total tax must retain enough wealth to make use of the estate tax exemption and to take advantage of the rates in what for him are the lower brackets of the estate tax. (2) The marital deduction for the estate tax is larger, the larger the estate. While this may not offer a way of reducing *total* tax, it does bear directly on the death tax. (3) The amount used to pay the gift tax is no longer available for earning income. (4) For purposes of computing a capital gain, the *donee* receives as his basis the basis in the hands of the donor; an *heir,* however, gets as his basis the value used for death tax purposes; if assets have appreciated, the stepping-up of the basis upon transfer at death will help reduce his income tax on capital gains realized subsequently. In computing loss, the donor's basis or the value at the time of gift, whichever is lower, will be used by the donee. Widely differing conditions face owners of property as they try to take account of the probable future taxes growing out of capital gains and losses on gifts as compared with bequests.

Uncertainties growing out of taxation alone, to say nothing of those from other sources, affect the apparent desirability of disposing of property before death. For example, an owner of property needs to take account of possible changes between the present and the time of death, whenever that date may be, in the value of assets, in tax rates, and in the provisions of the tax law. The importance attached to tax reduction (or tax minimization) naturally varies from person to person. The choices made depend on many factors, some of which are intensely personal. Sometimes practical difficulties—intra- and inter-family conflict, uncertainty, or change; business problems, existing or potential—restrict inter vivos transfers even when a person is legally free to dispose of property that, if held, will be included in his estate. Ignorance of tax law, as well as of other considerations, exerts an influence that is always difficult to evaluate, especially from the outside.

Nevertheless, estate, gift, income, and in some cases inheritance tax rates reach very high levels. One would expect taxes to exert a strong pressure for action to reduce, even though not necessarily to minimize, the total burden, assuming testators care at all about their heirs. The necessary action usually is to distribute before death a considerable portion of medium-sized estates and the bulk of very large holdings. No exact mathematical formula applies, even for tax minimization. Any generalization about the best proportion to give during life requires qualification just to take account of tax considerations alone. The principle, however, is clear and is illustrated in more detail later in this appendix.

Tax preference for inter vivos distribution over that at death has existed from the earliest days of death taxation, first by the states, then, beginning in 1916, by the federal government. Its practical importance grew with the rise in tax rates. Estate and income tax rates were increased greatly in 1932, the year that also brought the gift tax.[1] The estate-planning literature has not failed to point out the tax advantages of inter vivos giving. The evidence analyzed later, however, indicates that relatively little use has been made of lifetime giving even when it would have significantly reduced the tax on total transfers.

Would not anyone owning enough wealth to be subject to estate tax and dying as late as 1956 or 1958—as did most of those covered by this study—have learned of the tax differentials between gifts and bequests? There is no way to be sure. Most holders of substantial fortunes must have been alerted to the tax differentials. And probably many persons with smaller amounts would have been apprised of the alternatives. An unknown number, however, may have paid little attention to the problem. Perhaps many had not really seen the facts (for example, those whose net worth rose considerably with the postwar increase in prices of real estate and common stock).

Quality of Data on Gifts During Life

Among the figures obtained in the Treasury special study of estate tax returns filed in 1957 and 1959 are some on inter vivos gifts. Unfortunately the data are not fully satisfactory. Information on gifts during life is incomplete, and there is no firm basis for judging the extent of the inadequacy. For the most part, the data come from two sources. Donors of more than $3,000 a year to one person are "required" to file a gift tax return covering each year's gifts. The estate tax return calls for the reporting of gifts made during life.[2]

[1] A gift tax was imposed from 1924 to 1926.

[2] See Appendix A.

The data on gifts by persons leaving gross estates above $500,000, it appears, are more reliable than are those for smaller estates, in part because the audit of larger estates was more complete. Even for these large estates, however, there may be no compelling reason for revenue agents to make a serious effort to find unreported facts on outright gifts made more than three years before death. Under the law in effect since 1950, such gifts are not taxable as made in contemplation of death. However, an audit of estate tax returns may be a means of uncovering unpaid gift tax. Moreover, the agents have reason to look for gifts that might be considered as taking effect at death, such as those in some trusts; but these are a type more likely to be reported by the executor.

Several crude checks can be made on the adequacy of gift reporting. Gifts from June 1932 through 1958 (including charitable gifts) reported for gift tax purposes were about $23 billion gross; nearly $9 billion were taxable.[3] The amounts estimated from the special study samples for the two years combined (1957 and 1959) were $1 billion including charitable gifts, and $830 million for noncharitable gifts alone. The latter figures exclude gifts that were taxed as part of the estate since such gifts were included in the estate in the special study. Also excluded are gifts that were attributed to the spouse for gift tax purposes. The total amount shown as noncharitable gifts made by the decedents in the sample came to slightly over 9 percent of all gifts that were taxed in the twenty-six years. The $478 million of taxable gifts made in 1958—and some of the gifts made in 1957 and 1956—might reasonably be excluded from the cumulative total on the grounds that few people dying in 1956 or later would have made taxable gifts in these years that were not later included in the estate. If this is done, the coverage in the special tabulations rises to about 10 percent of the total of taxed gifts from 1932 to the approximate year of death of persons included in the special study.

The two years covered in the study are roughly two twenty-fifths of the period of the life of the gift tax, or 8 percent. The gifts reported total somewhat over 10 percent of those subject to gift tax in the appropriate period. Such coverage—10 percent of taxed gifts in 8 percent of the time—may suggest that under-reporting of gifts in the sample was not very extensive. This conclusion is reinforced slightly by the fact that gifts that were included in the estate for tax purposes are not

[3] U. S. Congress, Joint Economic Committee, *The Federal Revenue System: Facts and Problems* (1961), p. 253. Figures for four of the years have been estimated as the average, in each case, of the preceding and following year totals.

classed as gifts in these tabulations but are considered to be part of the estate. The more relevant basis of comparison, however, may well be total, rather than taxed, inter vivos gifts—the $23 billion mentioned above for the 1932-58 period. On this basis, less than 4 percent of the total was included—less than half of the percentage of the time period. Considerable under-reporting seems to be indicated by this measure, which is weak, however, in several respects.[4]

A more refined method yielding another indication of the total amount of (noncharitable) lifetime gifts made by the decedents and the tax incurred is to calculate the probability that a dollar reported among gifts in some prior year was given by a donor who died in a given year, such as 1957 or 1959.[5] If the age of the donor in the prior year is known, and if the mortality rates to which he is subject over the interval between the prior and given years is also known, it is a relatively simple task to compute his survival probability and his probability of dying. The product of these two probabilities is then the probability that a dollar given in some prior year was given by a donor who died in a particular year; and the expected value of gifts made in a prior year that may be attributed to decedents of a particular year is the product of this compound probability and the amount of gifts made in the prior year.

The results of such calculations depend very much on assumptions as to the age distribution of donors, its invariance, etc. Taking the average age of donors as sixty and using the U. S. Total Population (1949-51) Mortality Table,[6] for example, these calculations were made for 1957 and 1959 returns separately and together, and the results were compared with similar estimates for 1945, a year when the matching of gifts was not subject to as great suspicion of incompleteness. The results indicated that the undermatching of gifts was considerably more serious for the 1957 than for the 1959 returns, for some unexplained

[4] For example, it is not at all clear that the decedents of 1957 and 1959 represent about 8 percent of the gift tax-paying capacity measured by aggregate gifts reported in twenty-six years: (a) there is not a one-to-one correspondence between gift donors and those who will be subject to estate tax; (b) aggregate gifts in the twenty-six-year period include gifts made by generations other than that to which the 1957 and 1959 decedents belonged.

[5] This technique was first used by Gerard Brannon of the Office of Tax Analysis of the U. S. Treasury Department in a comment on an earlier version of this paper. It was subsequently modified by Dr. Seymour Fiekowsky.

[6] Actually the estate-tax population, being a select-risk group, would probably have lower mortality rates than does the population at large.

reason. Though this rather surprising outcome is very sensitive to the various assumptions made, our conclusion must still be that there is considerable under-reporting of gifts in the data as they stand. Most of the gifts not included in the tabulations were probably "small," however; in other words, it seems reasonable to conclude that large gifts were more likely to be covered than small ones.

Gift tax returns for 1958 showed exclusions and the specific exemption accounting for 56 percent of total gifts. Charitable gifts were nearly 13 percent of total gifts. Nontaxed but reported gifts (other than those to charity) were almost twice the total of taxed gifts. There is no basis for estimating the volume of gifts that may not be reported on gift tax returns, either because the law does not require it or for any other reason. Clearly large totals can escape the figures because there is no legal requirement to report gifts of less than $3,000 per donee per year.

For purposes of the first part of this appendix we have judged that the undermatching error is probably not significantly different for assessing the importance to millionaire estate taxpayers of transfers by gift and does not warrant separating the 1957 from the 1959 millionaire data. For all decedents, however, we have separated 1957 and 1959 returns here. The "millionaire" category will be considered first in some detail. The frequency of gift-making, the amounts transferred by gifts inter vivos, and other facets of the behavior pattern of transferors will be considered. The same questions will be examined for all decedents in more summary fashion.

Gifts by Millionaire Decedents

For the sake of simplicity, the term "noncharitable" will generally be omitted. All references to gifts will be limited to noncharitable gifts unless there is specific indication to the contrary. As regards gifts, the tax records for millionaire estates were doubtless more complete than for smaller estates because for the former the audit tends to be more thorough and record-keeping probably more generally accurate.

Frequency

Out of 2,256 decedents in the millionaire group in the returns for the two years studied, the records for 1,312 indicated gifts (including charitable) during life as shown in Table C-1.

The greater detail of Tables C-2 and C-3 reveals that, excluding charitable gifts, about 46 percent of the available tax returns for millionaires did *not* show gifts (48 percent for 1957 and 44 percent for 1959). Some decedents, of course, have made relatively small gifts for which no gift tax reporting was required. It is also conceivable that some persons with wealth of the size implied in these estates failed to report accurately. Some gift tax returns could not be located. Even after allowing for all reasonable possibilities, it is still surprising that 1,037 millionaires out of 2,256 dying in the middle or late 1950's had

TABLE C-1. *Gifts During Life and at Death, Millionaire Decedents,[a] 1957 and 1959 Returns Combined*

Size of gross transfers (In thousands of dollars)	Number of decedents	Transfers (in millions of dollars)				Number of decedents making gifts
		Total amount of gross transfers	At death	During life		
				Charitable	Non-charitable	
Under 900	99	64	62	b	2	29
900– 1,000	137	132	131	b	1	36
1,000– 1,250	523	587	569	2	16	253
1,250– 1,500	381	520	495	2	23	211
1,500– 1,750	236	383	358	3	20	142
1,750– 2,000	181	340	316	1	21	125
2,000– 3,000	317	778	721	7	46	211
3,000– 5,000	215	819	743	6	63	164
5,000–10,000	115	762	681	14	60	91
10,000 or more	52	1,112	931	78	83	50
Total[c]	2,256	5,495	5,007	111	336	1,312

Source: U. S. Treasury Department.
[a] Unlike the other tables in this appendix, this table includes charitable gifts.
[b] Less than $500,000.
[c] Details may not add to totals due to rounding.

apparently made little attempt to distribute more than small amounts of wealth before death (excluding charitable contributions).

In millionaire estates of all size classes there were decedents who had made no gifts. Out of 52 making gross transfers of $10 million or more, 4 reported no gifts. Clearly, however, the wealthiest decedents made relatively more frequent use of gifts than did other millionaires. The same conclusion can be drawn concerning the $5 million to $10 million group; 91 out of 115 (79 percent) showed gifts. Excluding the few cases at the bottom of the size distribution, the relative frequency in the use of gifts increased steadily (with one exception) with the amount of gross transfers.[7]

The average amount given varied widely from one size class to another, but of course it tended also to increase with the size of gross transfers. The average amount of gift tax paid was only a few thousand dollars except for the very highest groups. As a percentage of even the small total of gifts, gift tax paid was small except perhaps for the top group. In contrast, estate tax in all size classes was one-fourth or more of the noncharitable bequests.

TABLE C-2. ***Gross Transfers at Death and During Life, Millionaire Decedents, 1957 and 1959 Returns Combined***

(Dollar amounts in thousands)

Size of gross transfers	Number of decedents	Amount of gross transfers	Number of decedents making noncharitable gifts during life	Noncharitable gifts	Gift tax paid	Noncharitable bequests	Taxes paid by estate	Average[a] noncharitable gifts	Average[a] gift tax paid
Under $900	99	$64,224	28	$2,364	$54	$47,651	$12,475	$84	b
900– 1,000	137	131,741	34	1,075	—	93,011	28,437	32	—
1,000– 1,250	523	586,797	228	15,685	496	401,216	134,041	69	$2
1,250– 1,500	381	519,533	196	22,560	1,124	343,083	116,978	115	6
1,500– 1,750	236	382,687	130	20,483	1,434	237,811	86,513	158	11
1,750– 2,000	181	339,574	117	20,951	1,574	208,943	81,876	179	13
2,000– 3,000	317	777,779	195	46,246	3,762	434,304	195,031	237	19
3,000– 5,000	215	819,025	153	63,386	6,600	434,298	225,288	414	43
5,000–10,000	115	761,824	90	59,775	6,960	338,184	227,999	664	77
10,000 or more	52	1,111,654	48	83,060	19,058	314,716	342,102	1,730	397
Total	2,256	5,494,838	1,219	335,585	41,062	2,852,319	1,450,740	275	34

Source: U. S. Treasury Department.
[a] For those estates reporting gifts. Dashes indicate no entry.
[b] $1.9 thousand.

Comparing the 1957 with the 1959 group for transfers over $1 million (the data are not reproduced here), one finds in the later year higher percentages making gifts in all size classes but one, where the percentages are the same. The differences are small, and the factors that bear on any interpretation are so mixed that any conclusion must

[7] Only 315 millionaires showed charitable gifts during life. This figure cannot be accurate. Those who have accumulated such large estates must have had substantial incomes—in a class with those taxpayers who very regularly report charitable gifts on their income tax returns. (Since tax-exempt bonds were rarely as much as 20 percent of even large estates, tax-exempt interest during life would not generally have been great enough to account for the difference.) The nonreporting for gift or estate tax purposes of charitable gifts during life apparently involves no penalties; hence omission is understandable.

TABLE C-3. *Gross Transfers at Death and During Life, Millionaire Decedents, 1957 and 1959 Returns Combined, Percentages*

Size of gross transfers (In thousands of dollars)	Number of decedents in class as percentage of all millionaire decedents	Amount of gross transfers in class as percentage of total gross transfers	Noncharitable lifetime gifts		Gift tax paid as a percentage of noncharitable gifts	Estate tax paid as a percentage of noncharitable bequests
			Estates reporting, as a percentage of total in class	As a percentage of total gross transfers		
Under 900	4.4	1.2	28.3	3.7	2.3	26.7
900– 1,000	6.1	2.4	24.8	0.8	—	30.6
1,000– 1,250	23.2	10.7	43.6	2.7	3.2	33.4
1,250– 1,500	16.9	9.5	51.4	4.3	5.0	34.1
1,500– 1,750	10.5	7.0	55.1	5.4	7.0	36.4
1,750– 2,000	8.0	6.2	64.6	6.2	7.5	39.2
2,000– 3,000	14.1	14.2	61.5	5.9	8.1	44.9
3,000– 5,000	9.5	14.9	71.2	7.7	10.4	51.9
5,000–10,000	5.1	13.9	78.3	7.8	11.6	67.4
10,000 or more	2.3	20.2	92.3	7.5	22.9	108.7
Total	100.0	100.0	54.0	6.1	12.2	50.5

Source: U. S. Treasury Department.

be highly tentative. Nevertheless, it appears that this evidence is not inconsistent with the hypothesis that, as time passes, relatively greater use will be made of avoidance opportunities.[8]

Amounts

Gifts are valued for gift tax purposes as of the time of gift. These values may differ substantially, or only a little, from the value of the same property at death. In the years before the deaths represented here, there was a general rise in common stock and real estate prices. (*Statistics of Income*[9] shows that for 1959 these two types of property

[8] An alternative hypothesis, that gifts are analogous to consumption expenditures (not transfer tax minimization devices), might also be supported by the evidence of more widespread gift-making in the later returns, since these reflect the behavior of people who had eight to ten years in which to take advantage of the effective reduction of gift tax rates resulting from the introduction of the marital deduction in 1948 whereas the earlier sample had only six to eight years in which to do so. Still another factor to be borne in mind is the possibly greater degree of under-reporting in the 1957 returns than in the 1959 sample that was pointed out earlier.

[9] U. S. Treasury Department, Bureau of Internal Revenue.

accounted for about two-thirds of gross estates and of reported gifts.) On the average, therefore, the values at the time of gift were probably somewhat lower than the worth of the same property at the dates of death.

The millionaires reported total noncharitable gifts, other than gifts taxed in the estate, of $336 million; their gross transfers before estate tax totaled $5.5 billion (Table C-2). The gifts, therefore, were about 6 percent of total transfers of $5.5 billion (including tax, gifts, and all charitable transfers). It is not possible from the data to determine noncharitable gifts as a percentage of transfers for only those estates reporting such gifts. Gifts plus gift tax were $377 million, less than 7 percent of the total transferred during life and at death. Even recognizing that the data on reported gifts are incomplete and that the values at the time of gift tended to be lower than at death, the amounts transferred during life seem small in the light of the potential tax advantages obtainable from more extensive use of gifts.

Comparison of Gift and Estate Tax Rates Applicable

The amount of gift tax paid by the millionaire decedents was $41 million, compared with their estate tax total of $1.4 billion.

For the whole millionaire group, the tax on gifts averaged about 12 percent of the amount given (excluding charitable gifts, it will be recalled), while the average rate on estates was around 50 percent (55 percent in 1957 and 47 percent in 1959) of total noncharitable bequests. (See Table C-4.) Averages, however, are of less interest than marginal rates in the interpretation of materials such as we have here. Marginal rates will have differed more than average rates.

The group with over $10 million had average net estates of over $12 million, excluding charitable bequests. The heirs of these decedents received a total of about $315 million; the estate tax paid was about $342 million, an average rate of over 50 percent of the total net estate. The marginal tax rate in most cases must have been at or near 77 percent, which is the rate the law imposes on taxable estates in excess of $10 million, and some state death tax would often have been added. The marginal gift tax rate would have been much lower, although above the average of 23 percent of noncharitable gifts for decedents in this highest gross transfer class. The average gifts made by these decedents came to over $1.7 million. The tax rate on gifts from $1.5 to $2.0 million is 33¾ percent; since the gift tax itself is not part of the tax base, a marginal gift tax rate of 33¾ percent would correspond to an estate tax rate of about 25 percent (on a larger base because it includes tax), whereas the marginal estate tax rate applicable

TABLE C-4. *Taxes as a Percentage of Gross Transfers, Gifts, and Bequests, Millionaire Decedents, 1957 and 1959 Returns Combined*

Size of gross transfers (In thousands of dollars)	Gift tax as a percentage of			Estate tax as a percentage of	
	Total noncharitable gross transfers	Total noncharitable gifts	Estate tax	Total noncharitable gross transfers	Total noncharitable bequests
Under 900	[a]	2.3	0.1	26.1	26.7
900– 1,000	—	—	—	30.2	30.6
1,000– 1,250	0.1	3.2	0.4	32.1	33.4
1,250– 1,500	0.3	5.0	1.0	32.0	34.1
1,500– 1,750	0.6	7.0	1.7	33.5	36.4
1,750– 2,000	0.7	7.5	1.9	35.6	39.2
2,000– 3,000	0.8	8.1	1.9	40.6	44.9
3,000– 5,000	1.3	10.4	2.9	45.3	51.9
5,000–10,000	1.7	11.6	3.1	57.3	67.4
10,000 or more	4.8	22.9	5.6	86.0	108.7
Total	1.3	12.2	2.9	45.2	50.5

Source: U. S. Treasury Department.
[a] 0.03 percent.

was actually around 77 percent. At $3 million the gift tax rate is 42 percent.[10]

Marginal death tax rates of over 35 percent would have applied on most millionaire estates. More than half of the decedents in the $1 million to $1.25 million group reported no gifts; for them the marginal rate on small gifts would probably have been zero, or 2¼ percent, compared with an estate tax rate of at least 35 percent in most cases (on a base that also included the tax).

In short, *differences* in the marginal rates applicable—those that were effective or those that were available—must certainly have been large for almost all millionaires.

Charitable Gifts Compared with Charitable Bequests

The under-reporting of charitable gifts (as indicated in note 7 to this appendix) was apparently large. Yet comparisons with bequests are still of some interest. Charitable gifts during life of $111 million reported by the millionaires compare with $704 million charitable be-

[10] No allowance is made here for complications growing out of differing opportunities to make use of the marital deduction during life and at death.

quests. Purely tax considerations would at times indicate that contributions during life are more economical than philanthropic bequests of equal amount. Gifts to charity during life frequently have a tax advantage (in the form of a reduction in income tax) not enjoyed when the property is held until death and then bequeathed to charity. The marital deduction, however, exerts a somewhat offsetting effect because amounts in the estate destined for charitable uses are included in the total used in computing the 50 percent limitation on the amount allowed as a marital deduction. Nontax factors too may well have been of deciding importance. Whatever the reasons, these millionaires chose to wait until death to make substantial gifts of capital to charitable organizations.

Gifts Taxed in the Estate

Inter vivos gifts that were taxed in the estate (as made in contemplation of death, etc.) are not shown directly in the special study. (*Statistics of Income* no longer segregates these items.) However, the study does show the amount of the credit that the estate received for gift tax. Such credit was allowed when the gift was taxed in the estate, and in 195 millionaire estates (in the two years) amounted to a total of $9.5 million. This total is about one-fourth of the reported $41 million gift tax paid on gifts of $336 million that were not included in the estate.

Would the relationship of tax to gifts have been generally the same for gifts included in the estate as for the $336 million not included? If the relationship had been the same, the inter vivos gifts included in the estate would have been nearly $80 million (not including gift tax)—or about 3 percent of gross transfers at death. The use of average relationships is not necessarily appropriate, however. Moreover, the cumulative feature of the gift tax would lead one to expect that those gifts made shortly before death would be subject to higher gift tax rates than the average on gifts over the lifetime. It is difficult to find any basis for estimating the size of the adjustment factor. Although the actual amount of gifts taxed in the estate was probably less than $80 million, one cannot be certain whether the amount estimated on the basis of average relationships errs in being above or below the true amount.

The 1957 data on gift tax credit differ from those for 1959 by a large percentage, doubtless in part a reflection of the apparent difference between the completeness of matching for the two years noted earlier. The credit for gift tax in 1959 was $8 million, but it was only $1.6 million in 1957. The number of returns claiming credit differed,

TABLE C-5. *Noncharitable Gifts in Trust, Millionaire Decedents, 1957 and 1959 Returns Combined*

Size of gross transfers (In thousands of dollars)	*Number of noncharitable gifts in trust*	*Amount as a percentage of*	
		Total gross transfers	*Total noncharitable gifts*
Under 900	1	[a]	2.4
900– 1,000	4	0.1	16.9
1,000– 1,250	33	0.3	12.8
1,250– 1,500	38	0.7	15.1
1,500– 1,750	27	1.0	17.8
1,750– 2,000	35	1.2	20.1
2,000– 3,000	56	1.3	22.6
3,000– 5,000	44	1.7	22.6
5,000–10,000	40	3.6	46.3
10,000 or more	23	2.7	35.6
Total	301	1.7	28.5

Source: U. S. Treasury Department.
[a] 0.09 percent.

too, though not so markedly (7 percent of all millionaire estates in the earlier year, 10 percent in the later). The absolute amounts are too small, however, to provide a basis for saying that the actions of the two groups of decedents indicate any trend.

Use of Trusts in Lifetime Giving

The millionaire group, according to the figures, did not make extensive use of trusts in lifetime giving, as Table C-5 indicates. Less than one-third, $96 million, of the total of reported noncharitable lifetime gifts were in trust (Table C-6). Fewer than one out of four decedents making lifetime gifts (301 of 1,219) used trusts. For the $5 million to $10 million group, however, the use of trusts was more frequent than for the average—about 44 percent. Around the $1,000,000 level of gross transfers (the two groups from $900,000 to $1,250,000) trusts were used in 14 percent of the cases in which gifts were made. In only one of the twenty-eight estates with gross transfers under $900,000 that made noncharitable gifts was a trust used in giving.

The numbers are small. They do indicate that decedents disposing of large amounts of property used trusts in lifetime giving relatively more frequently than did millionaires as a group. But what is more striking, they indicate that only 13 percent of millionaires made lifetime gifts in trust. Only nine individuals made noncharitable gifts *exclusively* in trust.

Over $71 million of the $96 million in gifts to (noncharitable) trusts during life was for one generation only, as defined by the Trea-

TABLE C-6. *Noncharitable Gifts in Trust and Not in Trust, Millionaire Decedents, 1957 and 1959 Returns Combined*

(Dollar amounts in thousands)

Size of gross transfers	Number of decedents with noncharitable gifts	Total amount of noncharitable gifts	Noncharitable gifts in trust		Noncharitable gifts not in trust		Gifts in trust as a percentage of total	
			Number of decedents	Amount	Number of decedents	Amount	Number	Amount
Under $900	28	$2,364	1	$56	28	$2,308	3.6	2.4
900– 1,000	34	1,075	4	182	34	893	11.8	16.9
1,000– 1,250	228	15,685	33	2,013	228	13,672	14.5	12.8
1,250– 1,500	196	22,560	38	3,417	196	19,143	19.4	15.1
1,500– 1,750	130	20,483	27	3,653	130	16,830	20.8	17.8
1,750– 2,000	117	20,951	35	4,212	116	16,739	29.9	20.1
2,000– 3,000	195	46,246	56	10,440	192	35,806	28.7	22.6
3,000– 5,000	153	63,386	44	14,294	152	49,032	28.8	22.6
5,000–10,000	90	59,775	40	27,687	88	32,088	44 4	46.3
10,000 or more	48	83,060	23	29,599	46	53,461	47.9	35.6
Total	1,219	335,585	301	95,553	1,210	240,032	24.7	28.5

Source: U. S. Treasury Department.

sury for the purposes of this study (Table C-7).[11] Most of the gifts in trust—over $58 million—were for a donee other than the spouse.[12] There were few dispositions for "long" periods. Only $1.6 million went into trusts for two generations plus a term of years, or longer. Thus a group of over 2,200 millionaires disposing of almost $5.5 billion of property (before tax) made gifts during life of only 0.03 percent of this

[11] See also the discussion of trust duration in Appendix B.

[12] The estate tax marital deduction reduces what would otherwise be the appeal of gifts in trust for a spouse.

TABLE C-7. ***Noncharitable Trusts Created During Life, Millionaire Decedents, 1957 and 1959 Returns Combined***

(Dollar amounts in thousands)

Size of gross transfers	Number of decedents creating trusts during life	Number of trusts	Total value of trusts	Trusts for a term of years		One generation only, life tenant: Spouse		One generation only, life tenant: Other than spouse	
				Number	Amount	Number of trusts	Amount	Number of trusts	Amount
Under $900	1	1	$56	—	—	1	$56	—	—
900– 1,000	4	5	182	—	—	—	—	2	$32
1,000– 1,250	33	65	2,013	8	$137	6	413	33	880
1,250– 1,500	38	75	3,417	6	159	15	715	38	1,212
1,500– 1,750	27	67	3,653	5	313	8	383	43	2,091
1,750– 2,000	35	77	4,212	14	792	12	873	47	2,265
2,000– 3,000	56	140	10,440	13	1,251	30	1,899	76	5,459
3,000– 5,000	44	145	14,294	6	131	15	1,423	71	7,059
5,000–10,000	40	159	27,687	4	123	10	2,438	106	16,425
10,000 or more	23	277	29,599	3	173	16	5,182	248	22,608
Total	301	1,011	95,553	59	3,079	113	13,382	664	58,031

Size of gross transfers	One generation plus a term of years		Two generations only		Two generations plus a term of years		Three generations only	
	Number of trusts	Amount	Number of trusts	Amount	Number of trusts	Amount	Number of trusts	Amount
Under $900	—	—	—	—	—	—	—	—
900– 1,000	—	—	3	$150	—	—	—	—
1,000– 1,250	8	$184	4	144	5	$110	1	$145
1,250– 1,500	6	566	6	450	4	315	—	—
1,500– 1,750	6	621	3	183	2	62	—	—
1,750– 2,000	3	147	1	135	—	—	—	—
2,000– 3,000	6	552	10	625	5	654	—	—
3,000– 5,000	26	3,047	18	2,409	9	225	—	—
5,000–10,000	15	6,050	23	2,596	1	55	—	—
10,000 or more	1	502	9	1,134	—	—	—	—
Total	71	11,669	77	7,826	26	1,421	1	145

Source: U. S. Treasury Department.

amount in trusts to extend for more than two generations. By number, about two-thirds of the trusts were for one generation with a life tenant other than the spouse.

Decedents making gross transfers of $10 million or more reported gifts of $1.6 million in lifetime trusts that extended beyond one life. This amount was about 5 percent of the total of $30 million they gave in trust. The $1.6 million was an inconsequential portion of the $1.1 billion of which they disposed.

The larger part of the amount given in trusts that extended beyond one life was in trusts for one life plus a term of years, rather than for the longer periods. In short, lifetime gifts by millionaires through long-term trusts involved amounts that were not large enough in total to lead to any substantial amount of tax avoidance. However,

TABLE C-8. *Ratio of Gross Transfers at Death to Total Gross Transfers,*[a] *Millionaire Decedents, 1957 and 1959 Returns Combined*

Size of gross transfers (In thousands of dollars)	Number of decedents	Number of decedents by ratio of gross transfers at death to total gross transfers							
		Under 40%	40–50%	50–60%	60–70%	70–80%	80–90%	90–100%	100%
Under 900	99	1	—	—	1	2	12	13	70
900– 1,000	137	—	—	—	—	—	1	35	101
1,000– 1,250	523	1	1	—	—	5	33	213	270
1,250– 1,500	381	1	—	1	2	13	56	139	169
1,500– 1,750	236	—	2	3	6	17	26	88	94
1,750– 2,000	181	—	—	2	6	12	23	82	56
2,000– 3,000	317	2	2	2	7	20	49	129	106
3,000– 5,000	215	4	2	4	7	18	27	102	51
5,000–10,000	115	1	1	2	6	14	16	52	23
10,000 or more	52	2	1	3	6	4	14	20	2
Total	2,256	12	9	17	41	105	257	873	942

Source: U. S. Treasury Department.
[a] Includes charitable gifts and gift and estate taxes.

in specific cases the amounts may have been great enough to create more than minor inequalities among individuals.[13]

Transfers at Death as Related to Total Distribution: Other Evidence

Table C-8 contains additional evidence showing that millionaires in the great majority of cases made little use of inter vivos gifts of amounts large enough to have been reported. In 42 percent of the millionaire estates, gross transfers at death were 100 percent of total gross transfers. In these cases, in other words, no lifetime gifts at all were reported, and in almost as many cases gifts, including those to charity, were 10 percent or less of gross transfers.

Only twenty-one millionaire decedents out of 2,256 (1 percent) dis-

[13] See the discussion in Appendix B on testamentary trusts and the similar conclusion reached there.

posed of half or more of their wealth during life. Twelve showed gifts (*including* charitable) amounting to 60 percent or more of their gross transfers; nine reported gifts that represented 50 to 60 percent of total gross transfers.

In seventy-nine cases, or about 3.5 percent, 30 percent or more of the gross transfer was given during life; twelve of the top group ($10 million and over) were in this category. In only four out of ninety-nine cases did millionaire decedents who made gross transfers of less than $900,000 report disposing of over 20 percent during life.

There does appear to be a pattern of greater use of gifts by those with larger amounts of property, but the indications from these data are weak.

Influence of Age

A person 70 years old in 1956 was at least 45 when the gift tax went into effect in 1932. A person 80 years old in 1958 was at least 53 in 1932. More than two-thirds—68 percent—of the millionaires were 70 or over at death; 38 percent were 80 or more, and they would have been 53 or over in 1932. Over 8 percent of all decedents were 90 years old or more. In Table C-9, as in C-8, *charitable* bequests and gifts *are included.* A classification of decedents by age and size of gross transfer is not available, but average gross transfers at death and average size of gifts by those in each age group are shown. Property holdings were concentrated more heavily in the upper age groups. Most of the people, and more clearly those disposing of most of the property, were in their middle years or beyond when the gift tax went into effect. In some cases, therefore, there is the possibility of significant gifts before enactment of the gift tax.

In two age groups—70 to 80 and 80 to 90—the percentage of millionaires reporting gifts was above the average, though only slightly so —2 or 3 percentage points. Of course, these two age groups are near the average because they are responsible for 60 percent of all estates. Gifts by the two age groups—50 to 60 and 60 to 70—were 3 or 4 percentage points below the average. Fewer decedents under 50 years of age (only 45 percent) had made gifts, and the probability that they had disposed of much before 1932 is not high. For those over 90, the frequency of lifetime giving was 57 percent, just about the average for all millionaire decedents.

About 57 percent of the total of gifts plus gift tax were made by the 38 percent of decedents who were 80 years old or more. Gifts by

TABLE C-9. *Composition of Gross Transfers*[a] *by Age of Decedents, Millionaire Decedents, 1957 and 1959 Returns Combined*

(Dollar amounts in thousands)

Age of decedents	Number of decedents	Gross transfers: Tota amount[a]	Gross transfers at death[b]	Gifts plus gift tax: Number of decedents with gifts	Gifts plus gift tax: Total gifts plus gift tax[c]	Average size of total gross transfers	Average size of gross transfers at death	Average size of gifts plus gift tax
Under 30	1	$1,118	$1,118	—	—	$1,118	$1,118	—
30 and under 40	6	31,596	30,827	3	$769	5,266	5,138	$256
40 and under 50	49	76,816	74,238	22	2,578	1,568	1,515	117
50 and under 60	213	365,793	347,746	114	18,047	1,717	1,633	158
60 and under 70	444	999,743	933,724	245	66,019	2,252	2,103	269
70 and under 80	664	1,487,864	1,366,395	399	121,469	2,241	2,058	304
80 and under 90	673	2,006,836	1,783,741	415	223,095	2,982	2,650	538
90 and over	188	491,909	436,947	107	54,962	2,617	2,324	514
Not stated	18	33,163	32,114	7	1,049	1,842	1,784	150
Total	2,256	5,494,838	5,006,850	1,312	487,988	2,436	2,219	372

Source: U. S. Treasury Department.
[a] Includes charitable bequests and gifts and gift and estate taxes.
[b] Includes charitable bequests and estate tax.
[c] Includes charitable gifts.

decedents under 70 involved dollar amounts that were considerably smaller as a percentage of the decedents' gross transfers than the average. While approximately the same number of decedents were in the two age groups 70 to 80 and 80 to 90, the total dollar amount involved in gifts of the 80 to 90 year old decedents was almost double that in the 70 to 80 year old group. Only seven millionaires were under 40; their gifts, which totaled $800,000, were less than 3 percent of their gross transfers of $33 million.

Number of Years in Which Gifts Were Reported

Most of the millionaire decedents were "older" people, having been beyond "middle age" for fifteen years or more at the time of death. Many presumably would have accumulated property some years before death. They would ordinarily have had an opportunity after accumulating wealth to dispose of it by gift, and perhaps rather systematically, as is suggested by estate-planning literature, in order to avoid some tax. Table C-10 (which also includes charitable gifts) shows the frequency of gift-making as reported. Only sixty-nine millionaires had a record of making gifts in fifteen or more years. The

TABLE C-10. *Number Making Gifts During Life, by Size of Gross Transfers and by Number of Years in Which Gifts Were Made, Millionaire Decedents, 1957 and 1959 Returns Combined*[a]

Size of gross transfers (In thousands of dollars)	Total number of decedents	Number of decedents who made no gift	Number of decedents who made gifts[b] by number of years in which gifts were made											
			Total	1 yr.	2 yrs.	3 yrs.	4 yrs.	5 yrs.	6 yrs.	7 yrs.	8 yrs.	9 yrs.	10 to 14 yrs.	15 yrs. or more
Under 900	99	70	29	15	5	1	1	3	—	—	2	—	1	1
900– 1,000	137	101	36	23	6	1	2	—	2	—	1	—	—	—
1,000– 1,250	523	270	253	80	58	40	25	16	15	7	1	2	9	—
1,250– 1,500	381	170	211	47	49	21	30	16	10	9	11	7	7	4
1,500– 1,750	236	94	142	28	23	24	13	10	13	7	5	4	9	6
1,750– 2,000	181	56	125	18	21	14	19	11	14	6	6	3	9	4
2,000– 3,000	317	106	211	30	36	30	16	19	11	11	8	14	28	8
3,000– 5,000	215	51	164	23	20	23	7	12	10	8	11	7	25	18
5,000–10,000	115	24	91	7	11	6	4	9	8	2	6	4	23	11
10,000 or more	52	2	50	2	1	4	1	2	3	2	4	3	11	17
Total	2,256	944	1,312	273	230	164	118	98	86	52	55	44	122	69

Source: U. S. Treasury Department.
[a] Charitable gifts are included.
[b] Includes 93 decedents who made only charitable gifts.

years were not necessarily consecutive. This group contained a disproportionate number of those making gross transfers of $10 million or more (33 percent, compared with only 2 percent of all millionaires).

Nearly twice as many (122) made gifts in ten or more years but not over fourteen years. Yet 273 millionaires had made gifts in one year only. And even some decedents in the $10 million and over group had not made (or at least had not reported) frequent gifts; two such wealthy decedents had made gifts in only one year and one in only two years. Two decedents with gross transfers of over $10 million reported *no* gifts during life, charitable or noncharitable. Among those who made gifts, there were thirty-six decedents making gross transfers of over $5 million who did not make lifetime gifts *in more than four years,* and there were twenty-six who reported no gifts at all.

Fewer than 30 percent of all millionaire decedents reported gifts in more than three years. Assuming that a record of gifts in three years or less fails to establish a "pattern" of distribution through gifts (especially for decedents who were aged 70 or older at death), the figures show little in the way of systematic inter vivos giving. At this point, however, the deficiencies of the data may be relatively more significant than in some other cases. Gifts totaling less than the amount of the annual exclusion for each donor do not have to be reported. Conceivably, therefore, these data may significantly understate the extent of "pattern" or annual distribution of amounts which, though small individually, could have added to a substantial total for all donors. These figures do not show whether or not the frequency of giving was associated with relatively large totals of gifts per donor.

All Decedents

Approximately 100,000 decedents for whom returns were filed in the two years made gross transfers estimated at $21 million. The figures for 1959 are about 10 percent higher than those for 1957, and the two years are generally separated throughout this part of the analysis for the reasons indicated above. Decedents with gross estates of less than $1,000,000 were divided into two groups. Those with gross estates of less than $300,000 are termed "small," and those with gross estates of $300,000 to $1,000,000, "medium." In 1957, 398 small and 876 medium estate tax returns were matched with previous gift tax returns; in 1959, the numbers were 471 and 968 (Table C-11). All comparisons here are in terms of these actual sample sizes, not of the "blown-up"

TABLE C-11. ***Gross Transfers at Death and During Life, All Decedents, 1957 and 1959***

(Dollar amounts in thousands)

Estate size	*Number of decedents*	*Total amount of gross transfers*	*Number of decedents making non-charitable transfers during life*	*Non-charitable gifts*	*Gift tax paid*	*Non-charitable bequests*	*Taxes paid by estate*
1957							
Small	398	$46,333	40	$1,147	$3	$41,388	$2,255
Medium	876	403,544	263	15,311	517	297,411	70,545
Large	1,119	2,787,869	583	154,652	19,999	1,415,053	775,149
1959							
Small	471	$56,318	48	$1,509	$9	$50,331	$3,084
Medium	968	461,536	299	21,579	884	341,359	78,363
Large	1,137	2,706,969	636	180,933	21,063	1,437,266	675,591

Source: U. S. Treasury Department.

figures used in the special study tables, in order to facilitate comparisons with the millionaire returns.[14]

General Magnitudes

For the small estates examined, noncharitable lifetime gifts had been made in 10.0 percent of the cases, amounting to 2.5 percent of total gross transfers including charitable transfers and estate and gift taxes in 1957 and 10.2 percent and 2.7 percent in number and amount, respectively, in 1959. Of the medium estates sampled, 30.0 percent made such gifts in 1957 and 30.9 percent in 1959, amounting to 3.8 percent and 4.7 percent, respectively, of total gross transfers in this sample strata. Both the frequency and the importance of gifts in the small and medium groups were much less than for the millionaires, 52.1 percent of whom made gifts in 1957 and 55.9 percent in 1959, amounting to 5.5 percent and 6.7 percent of their gross transfers, respectively.

Gift tax paid by small and medium estates in both years was al-

[14] See the discussion of the sampling problem in Appendix A above.

most negligible, amounting to less than 1 percent of the estate tax paid. Even for millionaires, gift taxes paid for the two years combined amounted to less than 3 percent of estate tax. Unless under-reporting of gifts on estate tax returns is very extensive, the noncharitable bequests of the 869 decedents in the small estate category included considerable property that could have been transferred by gift at far less

TABLE C-12. *Gross Transfers During Life and at Death, Percentages, All Decedents, 1957 and 1959*

(Dollar amounts in thousands)

Estate size	Number of decedents	Amount of gross transfers	Noncharitable lifetime gifts		Taxes	
			Number of estates reporting	As a percentage of gross transfers	Gift tax paid as a percentage of noncharitable gifts	Estate tax paid as a percentage of noncharitable bequests
1957						
Small	398	$46,333	10.0	2.5	0.3	5.4
Medium	876	403,544	30.0	3.8	3.4	23.7
Large	1,119	2,787,869	52.1	5.5	12.9	54.8
1959						
Small	471	$56,318	10.2	2.7	0.6	6.1
Medium	968	461,536	30.9	4.7	4.1	23.0
Large	1,137	2,706,969	55.9	6.7	11.6	47.0

Source: U. S. Treasury Department.

tax cost. Frequently there would have been no tax at all. Average estate tax paid by this group in the two years combined was over 5 percent of average gross transfers. In numerous cases the marginal rate was at least 28 percent ($60,000 to $100,000), and in many cases it must have been 30 percent ($100,000 to $250,000) of taxable estates.[15]

For the 1,844 estates in the "medium" group—gross estate at least $300,000 but under $1,000,000—estate taxes in 1957 and 1959 com-

[15] Because the special study tables do not classify returns by size of net taxable estate, no precise count can be made. *Statistics of Income, 1959,* p. 58, shows 3,253 estates in the $200,000-$300,000 net-estate-before-specific-exemption class and 3,677 in the $150,000 to $200,000 class.

bined were, on the *average,* 23 percent of bequests and 17 percent of gross transfers (including charitable and gifts). Gift taxes, however, averaged less than 4 percent of noncharitable gifts reported. The marginal gift tax rate would rarely have been much over 21 percent (taxable gifts from $60,000 to $100,000). Marginal estate tax rates would generally have been around 32 percent to 35 percent (taxable estates from $250,000 to $750,000), but in several cases the applicable marginal rate was probably 37 percent. Obviously the tax paid on these estates could have been reduced substantially by greater use of gifts.

Decedents with smaller holdings made relatively less use of gifts than did those with larger holdings (Table C-12). The number using gifts rises as the amount of wealth increases.

Gifts Taxed in the Estate

The amount of credit for gift tax cannot be used to form confident judgments about the amount of taxed gifts that were also included in the estate. The taxed gifts that were also taxed in estates consisted chiefly of property appearing in the estates of millionaires, whose gift tax credit was nearly $10 million, as was pointed out above. The number of estates affected was apparently small, though possibly several times the 200 or so millionaire estates receiving such credit.[16] Some gifts not subject to gift tax may have been included in estates.

Use of Trusts in Lifetime Giving

Table C-13 indicates that little use was made of inter vivos gifts in trust by the small and medium-sized estates. Only 2.5 percent and 4.2 percent of those decedents in the sample of small estates making noncharitable gifts made gifts in trust, in 1957 and 1959, respectively, and the gifts in trust amounted to only 2.2 percent and 4.4 percent of total gifts. For medium estates in both years, particularly 1959, the figures were larger for both frequency and amount, but by far the greatest use of trusts in lifetime giving was by the millionaire decedents.

Of the gifts that were made in trust, almost all were for one gener-

[16] Returns filed in 1959 in the special study show an estimated $9.8 million credit for gift tax when the figures are blown up to obtain estimates comparable to the millionaire data, whereas *Statistics of Income* shows $7.2 million. The discrepancy may well result from sampling error and differences due to audit. State death tax paid is shown as $227 million in the special study; the credit for state death tax shown in *Statistics of Income* was $131 million. The two figures are not necessarily inconsistent, since state death tax often exceeds the credit.

TABLE C-13. *Noncharitable Gifts in Trust and Not in Trust, All Decedents, 1957 and 1959*

(Dollar amounts in thousands)

Estate size	Number of decedents with non-charitable gifts	Total amount of non-charitable gifts	Noncharitable gifts in trust		Noncharitable gifts not in trust		Gifts in trust as a percentage of all gifts	
			Number of decedents	Amount	Number of decedents	Amount	Number	Amount
1957								
Small	40	$1,147	1	$25	40	$1,123	2.5	2.2
Medium	263	15,311	13	687	262	14,623	4.9	4.5
Large	583	154,652	132	45,044	577	109,608	22.6	29.1
1959								
Small	48	1,509	2	67	48	1,442	4.2	4.4
Medium	299	21,579	33	2,261	298	19,319	11.0	10.5
Large	636	180,933	169	50,509	633	130,424	26.6	27.9
1957 and 1959								
Small	88	2,656	3	92	88	2,565	3.4	3.5
Medium	562	36,890	46	2,948	560	33,942	8.2	8.0
Large	1,219	335,585	301	95,553	1,210	240,032	24.7	28.5

Source: U. S. Treasury Department.

ation only, mainly with a life tenant other than the spouse, as is indicated in Table C-14. There was almost no use of trusts for two generations plus a term of years or for longer; the twenty-seven cases among the large estates involved total dollar amounts of only $1.6 million, while only two such instances (totaling only $59 thousand in 1959) appeared among the medium and none among the small estates.

Transfers at Death as Related to Total Dispositions

Approximately 86 percent of the decedents examined made all of their reported transfers (including charitable transfers and estate tax) at death—90 percent of those with small estates, nearly 70 percent of those in the medium group, and 40 percent of the millionaires (Table C-15). A very few, mainly in the millionaire group, disposed of 40 percent or more of their gross transfers during life. More than 90 percent of all decedents in the sample made gifts of 10 percent or less of their

TABLE C-14. *Noncharitable Trusts Created During Life, by Type of Trust, All Decedents, 1957 and 1959*

(Dollar amounts in thousands)

Estate size	Number of decedents creating trusts during life	Number of trusts	Total value of trusts	Trusts for a term of years		One generation only: Life tenant: spouse		One generation only: Other than spouse	
				Number	Amount	Number	Amount	Number	Amount
1957									
Small	1	1	$25	—	—	—	—	1	$25
Medium	13	20	687	—	—	3	$69	12	476
Large	132	413	45,044	10	$534	57	10,495	272	25,790
1959									
Small	2	2	67	—	—	1	10	1	57
Medium	33	62	2,261	2	22	20	707	32	723
Large	162	598	50,509	49	2,545	56	2,887	392	32,241

Estate size	One generation plus a term of years		Two generations only		Two generations plus a term of years		Three generations only	
	Number	Amount	Number	Amount	Number	Amount	Number	Amount
1957								
Small	—	—	—	—	—	—	—	—
Medium	2	$110	3	$32	—	—	—	—
Large	18	3,852	36	3,300	20	$1,073	—	—
1959								
Small	—	—	—	—	—	—	—	—
Medium	6	740	—	—	1	6	1	$53
Large	53	7,817	41	4,526	6	348	1	145

Source: U. S. Treasury Department.

total gross transfers. Only about 5 percent gave away (including charitable gifts) 20 percent or more of their property before death.

Of the decedents for whom gifts (including charitable) were reported, the amount given plus gift tax came to less than 10 percent of gross transfers for 30.4 percent of the small estates, 57.9 percent of the medium estates, and 66.4 percent of the large estates (1957 and 1959

TABLE C-15. ***Ratios of Gross Transfers at Death to Total Gross Transfers, All Decedents, 1957 and 1959***

Estate size	Number of dece- dents	Number of decedents by ratios of gross transfers at death to total gross transfers							
		Under 40%	40–50%	50–60%	60–70%	70–80%	80–90%	90–100%	100%
1957									
Small	398	1	—	1	6	14	7	13	356
Medium	876	—	1	6	9	17	70	168	605
Large	1,119	4	3	9	13	58	113	427	492
1959									
Small	471	—	1	4	2	10	19	15	420
Medium	968	2	1	4	15	28	93	169	656
Large	1,137	8	6	8	28	47	144	446	450
1957 and 1959									
Small	869	1	1	5	8	24	26	28	776
Medium	1,844	2	2	10	24	45	163	337	1,261
Large	2,256	12	9	17	41	105	257	873	942

Source: U. S. Treasury Department.

returns combined).[17] A smaller though still substantial proportion reported gifts plus gift tax of from 10 percent to 20 percent of gross transfers. Obviously these decedents who did utilize gifts failed by far to make reasonably full use of opportunities to minimize tax by this means.

Number of Years in Which Gifts Were Reported

The majority of the decedents reporting gifts (including charitable) did so for gifts in one year only in all estate classes (Table C-16). Out of all the decedents sampled—most of whom at death were over 70 years old, and many over 80—only seventy-one reported making gifts in fifteen years or more, and sixty-nine of these were millionaires. Only 122 of the 2,256 millionaires gave in ten to fourteen years, as did eighteen of the 1,844 medium estates. No small estate in the sample reported gifts in more than five years. Systematic giving year after year of $3,000 or more per donee was apparently infrequent.

[17] The figures on which this paragraph is based are from the Treasury Department special study.

TABLE C-16. *Number of Decedents Making Gifts by Number of Years in Which Gifts Were Made,*[a] *All Decedents, 1957 and 1959*

Estate size	Total number of decedents	Number who made gifts	Decedents who made gifts[b] by number of years in which gifts were made										
			1	2	3	4	5	6	7	8	9	10–14	15 or more
1957													
Small	398	41	32	7	—	1	1	—	—	—	—	—	—
Medium	876	270	125	60	36	15	6	8	4	6	1	9	1
Large	1,119	626	153	112	82	51	47	35	21	23	15	61	26
1959													
Small	471	51	33	10	6	1	1	—	—	—	—	—	—
Medium	968	313	104	70	44	29	16	12	11	9	6	9	1
Large	1,137	686	120	118	82	67	51	51	31	32	39	61	43
1957 and 1959													
Small	869	92	65	17	6	2	2	—	—	—	—	—	—
Medium	1,844	583	229	130	80	44	22	20	15	15	7	18	2
Large	2,256	1,312	273	230	164	118	98	86	52	55	54	122	69

Source: U. S. Treasury Department.
[a] Charitable gifts are included.
[b] Includes a few decedents who made *only* charitable gifts.

Tentative Conclusions

One must be cautious in accepting the above conclusions because of uncertainty about the adequacy of the data. The figures leave little doubt that owners of property could reduce the total tax on the transfer of their wealth, and by substantial amounts, by making larger gifts during life. Much of the $2.9 billion estate tax paid in these two years could have been avoided under existing law; the present estate tax is thus, to a surprising extent, a form of "voluntary taxation."

The Treasury is "protected" in a sense by whatever forces, presumably mainly nontax, induce owners of large, medium, and smaller holdings of property to retain their wealth until death. There has been an upward trend in gifts in recent years; the total reported for 1960 was double that of 1950.[18] The rise in gifts, however, has been

[18] U. S. Congress, Joint Economic Committee, *The Federal Tax System: Facts and Problems* (1964), p. 286.

somewhat slower than the rise in taxable estates. Apparently, therefore, the relative gap is about as large as in the past.

Gift tax data from *Statistics of Income* show that considerable use is made of exclusions from year to year. For 1958, for example, exclusions reported were $540 million out of $1,870 million total gifts (including charitable). There is no basis for judging how much more was given in smaller amounts that donors did not report. As has already been noted, over a period of years, a person may dispose of a total of wealth which is large but which incurs no gift tax and will not be included in the estate. Executors may feel little reason to report these gifts which the law specifically exempts from tax. The total amounts involved are not great as a percentage of large estates. For the much greater number of medium and small estates, however, the gifts can be very large in relation to the total transferred.

APPENDIX D

Estate and Gift Tax Base by Brackets

C. LOWELL HARRISS

THE ESTATE AND GIFT taxes receive little attention in discussions of revision of the federal tax system. The group on whom these levies bear heavily is so small that it can have little influence in getting a reduction in rates. There is little or no evidence that its members are trying. Furthermore, there is scarcely any objection raised to the occasional suggestion that greater reliance be placed on this revenue source. These suggestions may stem from a desire for more progression in the tax system (or some related objective) or for the added revenue that would result. The revenue objective, however, is being realized, in part at least, without a change in the law. From 1955 to 1965 the yield of estate and gift taxes almost tripled to $2.7 billion a year. This is probably well over one-third as much as the yield of the entire portion of the personal income tax rate structure over 20 percent prior to the Revenue Act of 1964.[1]

The rates, though starting at 3 percent, rise to 25 percent at $50,000 of taxable estate, 35 percent at $500,000, 70 percent at $6 million, and 77 percent over $10 million. The scope for rate increases in order to increase revenue is limited and probably confined to the lower ranges. However, perhaps the objective might be to reduce total estate tax burdens or to rearrange rates for some purpose. Income and excise tax changes (or proposals) offer precedents for estate (and gift) tax revision for other purposes than an increase in revenue. In any consideration of change, one benefits from knowing about the "location" of the actual and potential tax base.

[1] See note 1, p. 1 above.

Data from the Special Study

From time to time data on the gift and estate tax bases have appeared in *Statistics of Income.*[2] The figures, however, have not been suitable for estimating the *potential* base of *gifts plus transfers at death* because only exceptional gifts are included in the estate tax figures. This gap in our knowledge can now be closed partially by using data from the special study.[3] As was explained in Appendix A above, the study attempted to combine (a) gifts during life with (b) transfers at death for decedents whose estate tax returns were filed in 1957 and 1959. Both taxable and nontaxable returns are covered. Even though the data on gifts are incomplete, the figures tell more than does any other source about the wealth transferred by decedents as gifts and bequests plus the amounts used to pay gift and estate tax. This appendix draws on the material in a form somewhat different from the most familiar one. The data are then compared with those from *Statistics of Income.*

The special study uses the concept "gross transfer," which is (a) the decedent's wealth at death (b) *minus* his debts and the expenses of administering the estate (c) *plus* those of his lifetime gifts that were reported on gift or estate tax returns and the gift tax itself.

The study tables show the amount of gross transfers by size, that is, by *class,* of gross transfer on the basis generally used for data on size distributions of income or wealth. In 1959, for example, decedents whose gross transfers were from $200,000 to $300,000 made transfers by gift and bequest and paid tax that totaled an estimated $1.4 billion.[4] For those with gross transfers under $100,000, the figure was $1.7 billion; for those transferring $10 million or more, the total was $510 million. In other words, the tables tell how much the decedents in each group passed to others, including the tax collector, except for gifts not reported.[5]

[2] Issued annually by the U. S. Internal Revenue Service.

[3] U. S. Treasury Department.

[4] Throughout this chapter reference is made to the blown-up estimated figures computed by the Internal Revenue Service on the basis of the samples drawn as is explained in Appendix A above.

[5] Gifts (or the portions thereof) that are nontaxable because of the exclusion are included if reported. We have no knowledge of the volume of gifts not reported because of the exclusion. Assume two gifts, one for $2,999 and one for $3,001. The first need not be reported. The second should be. In the tables here it counts for its full amount even though at most only $1 would be taxable under present law (unless it was made in contemplation of death, etc.).

TABLE D-1. *Gross Transfers by Amount in Each Bracket, 1957 and 1959*

Gross transfer brackets (In thousands of dollars)	Decedents		Amount of gross transfers (In millions of dollars)		Percent of total amount	
	Number[a]	Percent, cumulative	In bracket	Cumulative	In bracket	Cumulative
			1957			
Over 10,000	26	[b]	341	341	3.5	3.5
5,000–10,000	64	0.2	225	566	2.3	5.8
3,000– 5,000	105	0.4	265	831	2.7	8.5
2,000– 3,000	155	0.8	266	1,097	2.7	11.2
1,750– 2,000	78	0.9	98	1,195	1.0	12.2
1,500– 1,750	118	1.2	121	1,316	1.2	13.4
1,250– 1,500	197	1.6	158	1,474	1.6	15.0
1,000– 1,250	284	2.2	220	1,694	2.2	17.2
900– 1,000	208	2.7	112	1,806	1.1	18.3
800– 900	189	3.1	131	1,937	1.3	19.6
700– 800	[c]	[c]	161	2,098	1.6	21.2
600– 700	[c]	[c]	204	2,302	2.1	23.3
500– 600	677	6.4	257	2,559	2.6	25.9
400– 500	1,071	8.7	341	2,900	3.5	29.4
300– 400	1,943	12.9	491	3,391	5.0	34.4
200– 300	4,791	23.2	749	4,140	7.6	42.0
100– 200	15,686	57.1	1,627	5,767	16.5	58.5
0– 100	19,896	100.0	4,112	9,879	41.6	100.0
Total[d]	46,333		9,879			
			1959			
Over 10,000	26	[e]	250	250	2.2	2.2
5,000–10,000	51	0.1	222	472	2.0	4.2
3,000– 5,000	110	0.3	243	715	2.2	6.4
2,000– 3,000	162	0.6	260	975	2.3	8.7
1,750– 2,000	103	0.8	100	1,075	0.9	9.6
1,500– 1,750	124	1.1	128	1,203	1.1	10.7
1,250– 1,500	202	1.4	169	1,372	1.5	12.2
1,000– 1,250	318	2.0	231	1,603	2.1	14.3
900– 1,000	214	2.4	119	1,722	1.1	15.4
800– 900	275	2.9	142	1,864	1.3	16.7
700– 800	379	3.6	177	2,041	1.6	18.3
600– 700	535	4.6	221	2,262	2.0	20.3
500– 600	629	5.7	277	2,539	2.5	22.8
400– 500	1,265	8.1	372	2,911	3.3	26.1
300– 400	2,444	12.5	534	3,445	4.8	30.9
200– 300	5,874	23.3	920	4,365	8.2	39.1
100– 200	18,395	57.1	1,971	6,336	17.6	56.7
0– 100	23,398	100.0	4,859	11,195	43.4	100.1
Total[d]	54,504		11,195			

Source: U. S. Treasury Department.

[a] The column on the left must be interpreted as meaning amount of total gross transfers of each taxpayer when used with the first two columns, showing number and percentage distribution of taxpayers, respectively. It must be interpreted as size of bracket when used with the remaining columns.

[b] 0.06.

[c] Sampling variability deemed so large as to make estimates based on sample unreliable.

[d] Details may not add to totals due to rounding.

[e] 0.05.

Another question is also of interest. How much of what might be considered the total potential tax base was below $100,000, how much above $10 million, etc.? That is, how much revenue would be obtained by a specified set of bracket rates? Table D-1, which shows for the two years 1957 and 1959 the amount of gross transfer in each bracket, answers these questions.[6] The figures include amounts given or bequeathed to charity and also the much larger amounts paid as tax. Amounts free of tax because of the specific exemption and the marital deduction are also included. Although details for the two years differ somewhat, the general outlines are similar.

Over 41 percent of the (reported) property transferred by the estate tax returnees in each of the two years was in the bracket under $100,000. Another 17 or 18 percent was in the next bracket, $100,000 to $200,000. With another 8 percent falling in the third bracket, $200,000 to $300,000, two-thirds of the gross transfer total is in the brackets $0 to $300,000 (in 1959, 69 percent). Well over half of the total gross transfers fell in the brackets $0 to $200,000. In contrast, in 1957 only 3.5 percent of total gross transfers were in the top bracket, $10 million and over (2.2 percent in 1959), and only 6 percent in the brackets above $5 million (4 percent in 1959).

In absolute terms the gross transfers falling in the brackets above $5 million totaled $566 million in 1957 and $472 million in 1959. The amount in the top bracket, $10 million and over, is only about one-twentieth of that in the brackets below $300,000.

More than half of the potential tax base under an integrated gift and estate tax with no exemption or gift tax exclusion would have been under $200,000 in these years; only slightly more than one-tenth would have been above a level ten times as high, $2 million. The

[6] These distribution-by-bracket figures were obtained as follows: Consider the *bracket* $5 million to $10 million. There were twenty-six estates in the gross transfer *class* over $10 million. Each of these estates contributed $5 million to the $5-million-wide *bracket* $5 million to $10 million, or a total of 26 x $5 million, that is, $130 million. There were sixty-four estates in the gross transfer *class* $5 million to $10 million, with total gross transfers of $415 million. How much did these estates contribute to the *bracket* $5 million to $10 million? We know how much they contributed to the brackets below $5 million—64 x $5 million, or $320 million. The remainder of the gross transfer total in the $5 million-$10 million *class,* $95 million, must have fallen in the $5 million-$10 million *bracket.* Estates with gross transfers in *classes* below $5 million of course contributed nothing to the $5 million-$10 million *bracket.* Hence the total gross transfers lying in the $5 million-$10 million *bracket* must be $130 million + $95 million, or $225 million.

amount in brackets above $1 million was about the same as the potential base from $100,000 to $200,000 (ignoring exemptions).

It is not possible from the data available to determine how much each *bracket* was reduced by charitable contributions and bequests, exemptions, the marital deductions, and exclusions. Nor is it possible to find the amount and the relative importance of gifts during life, or the amount taxed, in each bracket. Some owners of large amounts of wealth made large gifts to heirs or contributed substantial amounts to charities. Others with equal wealth did little or nothing of this sort. The available data do not distinguish the property involved in such transfers in a way that is related to brackets.

Data from *Statistics of Income*

The tax returns filed in 1959 and covered in the special study tabulation for that year are more or less the same as those for which figures are presented in *Statistics of Income, 1958,* Fiduciary, Gift, and Estate Tax Returns, Filed During Calendar Year 1959.[7] The differences seem to be slight.[8] The special study figures, however, reflect in some cases the effects of audit so that one would expect the amounts taxed, and the tax, to be higher than is shown on tax returns.

Tables D-2, D-3, and D-4 are based on *Statistics of Income.* They show for taxable, nontaxable, and all returns, respectively, the amount of gross estate by bracket. The estate concept underlying these figures differs in several ways from the gross transfer concept used in Table D-1. The major differences are that most gifts during life, gift tax, and charitable contributions during life are not included among assets of the estate. On the other hand, debts and other obligations and costs of administering the estate are included, not deducted as for the special tabulation. The bracket sizes also differ somewhat.

For *taxable returns* filed in 1959 (Table D-2) the distribution of gross estate by bracket is much the same as the distribution for *all* returns of gross transfers by bracket (Table D-1) except that somewhat more appears in the highest brackets (relatively or proportionately) and somewhat less in the lower brackets—2.5 percent vs. 2.2 percent in

[7] Nonresident aliens are excluded in both cases.

[8] Precise comparisons are possible in only a few cases because concepts differ. However, *Statistics of Income* shows 55,685 returns, while the special study covers 54,504; charitable bequests in the two totaled $669 million and $595 million, and tax before credits, $1.3 billion and $1.5 billion, respectively. See Appendix A above for further comparisons and an explanation of the differences.

TABLE D-4. *Gross Estates by Amount in Each Bracket: All Estates, Taxable Estates, and Nontaxable Estates,* Total, Taxable, and Nontaxable Returns *Filed in 1959*

Gross estate brackets (In thousands of dollars)	Decedents		Amount of gross estates (In millions of dollars)		Percent of total amount	
	Number[a]	Percent,[a] cumulative	In bracket	Cumulative	In bracket	Cumulative
Over 20,000	7	[b]	54	54	0.5	0.5
10,000–20,000	21	[c]	153	207	1.3	1.8
5,000–10,000	57	0.2	238	445	2.0	3.8
3,000– 5,000	101	0.3	255	700	2.2	6.0
2,000– 3,000	184	0.7	268	968	2.3	8.3
1,000– 2,000	771	2.0	652	1,620	5.6	13.9
500– 1,000	2,242	6.1	980	2,600	8.4	22.3
300– 500	3,646	12.6	972	3,572	8.3	30.6
200– 300	5,676	22.8	941	4,513	8.1	38.7
150– 200	6,403	34.3	778	5,291	6.7	45.4
120– 150	7,116	47.1	672	5,963	5.8	51.2
100– 120	7,176	60.0	592	6,555	5.1	56.3
90– 100	4,545	68.1	356	6,911	3.1	59.4
80– 90	5,269	77.6	405	7,316	3.5	62.9
70– 80	6,301	88.9	463	7,779	4.0	66.9
60– 70	6,158	100.0	527	8,306	4.5	71.4
0– 60	12	100.0	3,341	11,647	28.7	100.1
Total[d]	55,685		11,647			

Source: U. S. Internal Revenue Service, *Statistics of Income, 1958*

[a] The column on the left must be interpreted as meaning amount of gross estate of each taxpayer when used with the first two columns, showing number and percentage distribution of taxpayers, respectively. It must be interpreted as size of bracket when used with remaining columns.

[b] 0.01.

[c] 0.05.

[d] Details may not add to totals due to rounding.

specific exemption but *after* the marital deduction. Almost one-third—33.2 percent—was under $60,000, and almost one-half—49.0 percent—was under $100,000. One-tenth—$700 million—was over $1 million. The last percentage point of the rate scale, the difference between 76 percent and 77 percent on amounts over $10 million, yielded $390,000. The rates over 70 percent produced about $4.6 million in revenue.[9]

[9] Computed by applying 5 percent to the tax base in the $7 million to $10 million bracket and 7 percent to the tax base in the bracket over $10 million. While the estimate is rough, the error can hardly be large. No allowance is made, of course, for any revenue loss that may have been due to use of tax avoidance measures that would not have been used if the bracket rates had been lower by the number of percentage points at issue.

TABLE D-5. *Taxable Estates: Net Estate by Amount in Each Bracket,*[a] *Returns Filed in 1959*

Net estate brackets (In thousands of dollars)	Decedents		Amount of net estate		Percent of total amount	
	Number	Percent,[b] cumulative	In bracket	Cumulative	In bracket	Cumulative
			(In millions of dollars)			
Over 20,000	1	[c]	8	8	0.1	0.1
10,000–20,000	7	[d]	31	39	0.4	0.5
7,000–10,000	10	[e]	37	76	0.5	1.0
5,000– 7,000	18	[f]	50	126	0.7	1.7
4,000– 5,000	20	0.1	44	170	0.6	2.3
3,000– 4,000	33	0.2	71	241	1.0	3.3
2,000– 3,000	112	0.5	140	381	2.0	5.3
1,000– 2,000	441	1.7	349	730	5.0	10.3
900– 1,000	124	2.0	70	800	1.0	11.3
800– 900	168	2.4	85	885	1.2	12.5
700– 800	199	2.9	102	987	1.5	14.0
600– 700	304	3.7	127	1,114	1.8	15.8
500– 600	461	4.9	166	1,280	2.4	18.2
400– 500	775	6.9	224	1,504	3.2	21.4
300– 400	1,404	10.6	327	1,831	4.7	26.1
200– 300	3,253	19.0	540	2,371	7.8	33.9
150– 200	3,677	28.6	447	2,818	6.4	40.3
100– 150	8,555	50.8	731	3,549	10.5	50.8
80– 100	7,180	69.4	458	4,007	6.6	57.4
60– 80	11,772	100.0	642	4,649	9.2	66.6
0– 60	1	100.0	2,311	6,960	33.2	99.8
Total[g]	38,515		6,960			

Source: U. S. Internal Revenue Service, *Statistics of Income, 1958.*

[a] Net estate is amount after all deductions except the $60,000 specific exemption. The $2.3 billion deducted on account of the exemption resulted in a tax base of $4.7 billion.

[b] The column on the left must be interpreted as meaning amount of net estate of each taxpayer when used with the first two columns, showing number and percentage distribution of taxpayers, respectively. It must be interpreted as size of bracket when used with remaining columns.

[c] 0.003.

[d] 0.02.

[e] 0.05.

[f] 0.09.

[g] Details may not add to totals due to rounding.

One contrast may be of interest. The *gross* estate in the over $10 million bracket of taxable gross estates was $207 million (Table D-2). But the *net* estate in the over $10 million bracket of net estates was $39 million (Table D-5). The difference is large but easily explained. Charitable bequests and the marital deduction from these gross estates came to more than $225 million; of the twenty-eight estates with gross amounts over $10 million, only eight had net amounts above this level.

Conclusion

It is clear, of course, that the overwhelming mass of what might be considered the potential tax base is in the "lower wealth" range. Approximately one-third of the value of gross transfers (special study) in the under-$100,000 bracket was made by persons whose total gross transfers came to less than $100,000. The gift and estate tax exemptions themselves total $90,000. With only a little use of the marital deduction, gift tax exclusions, or contributions, no tax at all would need to be paid on transfers of $100,000 or less. Yet some tax was paid.

Persons making larger gross transfers—$200,000 or even more—are also able to cut into the amount taxable below $100,000 much more than they have. Nevertheless, the base in this range is substantial—probably fifteen to twenty times the amount over $1 million.

The 642 net estates over $1 million were not much reduced by the personal exemption—a total of about $39 million. They had $642 million taxed below $1 million and about $690 million over that amount. For these largest estates the rates applicable to the first million applied to almost as much tax base as did the rates above. The 201 net estates with $2 million or more contained approximately $370 million which was taxed in brackets over $2 million and $400 million below. The eighty-nine estates over $3 million had $240 million taxed over $3 million and $270 million below.

Each percentage point applied on the nearly $4 billion that was taxed under $1 million yielded almost as much as 6 percentage points on all above $1 million. Each percentage point under $1 million brought revenue equal to 11 percentage points on everything over $2 million.

Finally, to put the calculations in this brief study in perspective, it should be noted that all these figures relate solely to the small portion of the population liable to file estate tax returns (or, in some tables, to pay estate tax). Estimates for 1953, for example, show that less than 2 percent of the adult population had over $60,000 in assets; yet they held about 30 percent of the total assets and equities of the personal sector in that year.[10] The decedents for whom no estate tax returns were filed in the years of our study presumably transferred more than twice as much wealth as those covered, but the average amount would have been only a small fraction of the average of even the lower brackets shown here.

[10] Robert J. Lampman, *The Share of Top Wealth-Holders in National Wealth, 1922-56* (Princeton University Press—National Bureau of Economic Research, 1962), pp. 18, 23.

APPENDIX E

Comparison of Data from Treasury Department Special Studies

SEYMOUR FIEKOWSKY

THERE ARE INNUMERABLE and ultimately insoluble problems involved in comparing the three special studies of 1945, 1951, and 1957 and 1959 estate and gift tax data. The two most difficult problems arise from differences in criteria for selecting sample cases, and the probable differences in value of "estate and gift dollars." In the 1945 and 1951 studies certain amounts of "net estate before exemption" were adopted as selection criteria; and in the 1957 and 1959 study, amounts of gross estate were used. Comparisons between the 1945 and 1951 tabulations, aside from differences arising from a $500,000 minimum net estate in 1945 and $300,000 minimum in 1951, are difficult because the marital deduction was operative in 1951 but not in 1945. Although the number is not known, many estates were excluded from the 1951 study that were of the same size as some actually selected in 1945 (with net estates greater than $500,000) because the decedent made use of the marital deduction and therefore had less than the 1951 minimum $300,000 net estate. This results in an inherent dissimilarity in the sex-marital distributions of study returns, particularly in the lower ranges of the wealth-size distributions in the two years.

The 1957 and 1959 study, on the other hand, by using gross estate selection criteria, is less restrictive than either of the two predecessor studies in including wealth transferors of any given amount in the sample. In addition to the problem arising from the marital deduction, which was effective in 1951, both the 1945 and 1951 studies also include disproportionately fewer decedents making contributions and owing debts than does the study for 1957 and 1959. Since indebtedness is generally negatively related to age, in any particular stratum of wealth transferors, the 1945 and 1951 studies include fewer "young" decedents. Finally, although little can be said constructively about the measurement of dollar values of wealth transferred, it is believed by many that the period 1945-59 was one of depreciation, that is, that asset prices rose more rapidly than their "real" value.

One way to deal with the divergencies in sample coverage among these three studies would be to concentrate attention on those upper strata of the 1945 and 1951 studies that minimize exclusions likely to distort comparisons with the 1957 and 1959 study. From an examination of the gross transfer distributions of the three studies it was determined that above $700,000 the three studies were roughly comparable. But, in comparing 1945 with 1951 above this level, it is clear that the 1951 data under-represented husbands and wives; among the 1951 decedents with $800,000 or more gross transfers, however, the marital status distribution seems comparable with 1945. It was decided, then, to compare 1945 decedents with $700,000 or more gross transfers with 1951 decedents for whom $800,000 or more gross transfers had been identified.

Selection of a suitable segment of the 1957 and 1959 decedents for making comparisons is complicated by the random sample selection of cases with less than $1,000,000 gross estate. Since both the 1945 and 1951 studies, and the 1957 and 1959 stratum over $1,000,000, used all available returns, they cannot, to be statistically correct, be compared directly with data subject to an additional degree of sampling variability. Whatever sampling errors there are in the selected cases with less than $1,000,000 gross estate in 1957 and 1959, when the sample data are projected by some multiplier to represent all the returns in the strata from which they were selected, these errors are also magnified. Furthermore, since many of the published 1957 and 1959 tabulations of interest do not classify the data by size of gross transfer, it was decided to use the entire "millionaire" stratum for comparisons with 1945 and 1951.

Finally, a comparison of 1957 and 1959 returns disclosed that, for unknown reasons, 1957 data significantly under-represent donors among the decedents of that year. It therefore appeared necessary to restrict attention to the 1959 returns.

In an extremely crude fashion, the choice of study strata for comparison may provide some "correction" for changing dollar values in the eyes of those who consider this important. The minimum gross transfer included for 1951 is 14 percent above that for 1945; and, although there are 33 gross transfers of less than $800,000 and 114 cases altogether under $1,000,000 included in the 1,137 cases of 1959 millionaires, most exceed this level, which is about 20 percent above the 1951 minimum. Indeed the average of gross transfers of returns included in the 1951 study is 2 percent above 1945, and the average 1959 gross transfer is 9 percent above 1951. Whether these differences in dollar level are to be interpreted as "adjustments" for changes in dollar values over the period, or "real" differences to be accounted for in evaluating observed differences among the three studies, is a matter that must be left to the reader to decide. The author would prefer to interpret these as "real" differences.

Finally, it should be noted that the 1959 cases used in the comparison still include cases of very great indebtedness and philanthropic contributions that have no counterparts in either the 1945 or the 1951 cases. It is unlikely that disproportionate numbers of heavily indebted decedents in the 1959 sample can have palpable effects on comparisons of transfers, since all transfers are net of debt and administrative expenses in any event; but the probably greater number of generous philanthropic donors among the 1959 sample obviously tends to overstate charitable contributions relative to the earlier samples.

Table E-1 shows those inter-study comparisons of gifts and bequests that may be drawn for all three studies; it also shows how well matched the selected strata are with respect to marital-status distribution. Perhaps the most notable differences revealed are as follows:

1. Proportions of decedents with matched prior gift tax returns diminish from study to study. From 77 percent of 1945 decedents making gifts before death, the proportion drops to 71 percent in 1951, and to 60 percent in 1959. In part, this steep decline is attributable to the large volume of pre-1932 gifts matched to the 1945 cases: 29 percent of the 1945 decedents appear to have made gifts before the advent of the 1932 gift tax, and the value of these gifts account for nearly 45 percent of *all* gifts and gift tax paid by these returnees. And it is also possible that a relative understatement of 1959 returnees' gifts for administrative reasons has contributed to an excessive indicated decline in the propensity to make gifts. Nevertheless, the propensity to make reportable gifts has obviously been declining from the era represented by the 1945 returnees to that of the 1959 cases.

2. The amount transferred by gift and tax has declined even more precipitously than has the proportion of gift-makers. From 22 percent of gross transfers by gift and tax in 1945, the proportion transferred in this mode declined to 15 percent in 1951 and to less than 10 percent in 1959.

TABLE E-1. *Comparative Gifts and Bequests, 1945, 1951, and 1959 Special Treasury Studies*

Item	Number			Percent		
	1945[a]	1951[b]	1959[c]	1945[a]	1951[b]	1959[c]
Total number of decedents	548	631	1,137	100.0	100.0	100.0
With gifts	420	446	686	76.6	70.6	60.4
Before June 1932	159	75	—	29.0	11.9	—
After June 1932	398	438	686	72.6	69.5	60.4
With transfers in trust	401	467	690	73.2	74.0	60.7
With charitable transfers	243	311	535	44.3	49.3	47.1
Marital status						
Husband	244	309	523	44.5	49.0	46.0
Widower	78	76	155	14.2	12.0	13.6
Wife	38	48	77	6.9	7.6	6.8
Widow	118	116	259	21.5	18.4	22.8
Other	70	82	123	12.8	13.0	10.8
	(Millions of dollars)			(Percentage of gross transfers)		
Gross transfers[d]	1,175	1,377	2,707	100.0	100.0	100.0
During life	257	205	256	21.9	14.9	9.5
At death	919	1,172	2,451	78.2	85.1	90.5
Average per return	2.144	2.182	2.381	—	—	—
Tax paid[d]	350	362	697	29.8	26.3	25.7
Estate	339	n.a.	652	28.9	n.a.	24.1
Gift	11	n.a.	45	0.9	n.a.	1.7
Transfers after tax[d]	825	1,015	2,010	70.2	73.7	74.3
Charitable	99	161	392	8.4	11.7	14.5
Noncharitable	726	854	1,618	61.8	62.0	59.8
In trust	331	378	499	28.2	27.5	18.4
Not in trust	395	476	1,120	33.6	34.6	41.4
To spouse	100	197	485	8.5	14.3	17.9
To others	295	279	635	25.1	20.3	23.5

n.a. Not available.
[a] Includes decedents with gross transfers exceeding $700,000.
[b] Includes decedents with gross transfers exceeding $800,000.
[c] Includes decedents with *gross estates* exceeding $1,000,000.
[d] Details may not add to totals due to rounding.

3. The propensity to make transfers in trust (lifetime and at death) appears to be declining. Although the proportion of transferors using trusts remained steady at about 74 percent in 1945 and 1951, by 1959 it had slipped to 61 percent. Certainly some of this apparent decline is attributable to undermatching of gifts in 1959. But even allowing for this, a significant decline in propensity to make trusts is clearly indicated. (Could this be the result of the marital deduction? See below.)

4. Matching this decline in propensity to transfer in trust is a less marked decline in intensity of trust transference. From $825,000 per trust transferor in 1945, the amount per transferor declined to $810,000 in 1951, and to $725,000 in 1959, notwithstanding the aforementioned increase in average size of gross transfers.

5. The propensity to make reportable contributions (lifetime and at death) may be said to have increased slightly. In 1945 only 44 percent of the sample had reported contributions; in 1951 this rose to 49 percent; in 1959 the proportion had slipped somewhat to 47 percent (no doubt due to undermatching of gifts).

6. The intensity of contributions increased markedly. Of identified contributors, those in 1945 transferred an average of $409,000, those in 1951, $518,000, and those in 1959, $733,000. Even allowing for the larger wealth amounts in 1951 and 1959, this indicates an increase in generosity among those who are philanthropically inclined, a group still less than a majority of all those included in the elite samples. Another way this effect is described in the accompanying table is by the share of gross transfers, after gift and estate tax, that is passed as contributions and as transfers to persons. In 1945, 12 percent of this net disposable property was given and bequeathed to philanthropic organizations; in 1951 the percentage rose to 16; and in 1959 it reached 20 percent. And this phenomenon occurred in the face of declining tax burdens due to the marital deduction.

7. Mirroring the decline in transfers by trust, outright transfers to individuals increased markedly, but at a rate somewhat lower than that of contributions. Although total transfers to individuals dropped from 88 percent of net disposable property in 1945 to about 80 percent in 1959, the decline in trust transfers enabled outright transfers to individuals to rise from about 48 percent of disposable property in 1945 and 1951 to 56 percent in 1959. Virtually all of this increase in outright transfers to individuals seems to be accounted for by bequests to spouses. In 1945 bequests to surviving spouses averaged $354,000 per married decedent in the sample; in 1951 the average rose to $552,000, and in 1959, reached $808,000. That the 1945-59 increase in outright

transfers is attributable to interspousal transfers may be seen in the distribution of transfers to persons in trust and outright. In both 1945 and 1951, about the same proportion of transfers to individuals were outright (54-56 percent), but in 1959, the proportion leaped to 69 percent. Thus in 1951, before testators had had enough time to adjust fully to the testamentary possibilities opened up by the marital deduction, bequests to spouses apparently were increased at the expense of other heirs; in 1959 there was a general reduction in trust transfers, making possible greatly increased outright transfers to spouses.

A final set of comparisons between the 1951 and 1959 returns is presented; the necessary data for 1945 are not available. In Table E-2, comparisons of testamentary trust transfers by decedents with *gross transfers* of $1,000,000 or more are presented. This choice of strata in the two years was dictated by the available tabulations.

The table contains percentage distributions of tenancy and remainder interests in testamentary trusts by class of beneficiary. Due to the aggregative character of trust data, it was necessary to allocate arbitrarily

TABLE E-2. *Life Tenancies, and Tenancies for a Term of Years and Remainder Interests in Property Bequeathed in Trust by Decedents, 1951 and 1959, with Gross Transfers of $1,000,000 or More, by Beneficiary Class*

Tenants or remaindermen	Percent of trust property: In which tenancy bequeathed		Percent of trust property: In which remainder interest bequeathed		Percent of share allocated[b]: In tenancies		Percent of share allocated[b]: In remainder interests	
	1951	1959	1951	1959	1951	1959	1951	1959
Parents	0.1	0.4	[a]	0.1	55.0	21.9	100.0	100.0
Siblings	6.1	6.5	1.4	0.7	41.9	22.2	7.9	28.8
Spouse	22.7	24.2	0.2	0.3	21.6	21.7	57.3	2.6
Children	42.0	44.1	24.5	16.0	20.2	21.1	9.7	16.0
Grandchildren	12.6	8.5	36.0	42.4	37.1	44.2	7.9	11.6
Great grandchildren	0.3	0.2	6.7	7.9	100.0	81.9	23.1	21.0
Other relatives	13.4	8.5	19.7	14.7	21.7	28.7	93.1	14.6
Others	2.8	7.6	11.5	17.9	55.5	49.1	1.3	24.9
Total	100.0	100.0	100.0	100.0	25.5	26.2	25.5	16.0
Amount (in thousands of dollars)	268,453	443,481	268,453	443,481				

Source: U. S. Treasury Department.

[a] Less than 0.05 percent.

[b] Whenever tenancies or remainder interests were shared by two or more of the beneficiary classes shown, each class was allocated a fractional share.

the value of trust corpora to both tenants and remaindermen when the tabulated beneficiary class included more than one of the eight classes listed in Table E-2. For example, if spouse and children were indicated as tenants of a $100,000 trust, interest in $50,000 was assigned to the class "spouse" and $50,000 to the class "children." Implicit in this allocation is the assumption that tenants concurrently enjoy the income from trust property in equal shares. Similarly remainder interests shared by more than one beneficiary class were assumed to be equally shared by all classes named as remaindermen. The extent to which these allocations of interest enter the shares of particular beneficiary classes is shown in the table. It is shown, for example, that "parents," who enjoyed rights of tenancy in 0.4 percent of all trust bequests in 1959, were allocated 22 percent of their share, the remaining 78 percent being trusts in which they were sole tenants.

Perhaps the most striking characteristic of the 1951 and 1959 distributions of both tenancies and remainder interests is their similarity. We have seen previously that a much smaller fraction of 1959 transfers than of 1951 transfers was made in trust and that spouses received substantially larger outright bequests in 1959. Yet in both years spouses had tenancies in 23 to 24 percent of all testamentary trust property, and the same proportion of their shares was arbitrarily allocated (22 percent). Of course, in 1959 the absolute share of spouses in trust property was smaller per person. It would appear that a certain effect of the marital deduction has been to reduce the inheritances of nonspouse heirs, particularly in trust property. And the distribution of remainder interest among the eight classes of beneficiaries has not changed dramatically. Only the relative shares of decedents' children and grandchildren seem affected by the shift in pattern of testamentary dispositions. Although the combined share of children and grandchildren in remainder interests is the same in both years (about 60 percent of the total), in 1959 the children's share had dropped by 8 percentage points while the grandchildren's share had increased by 6 points. One may speculate that, prior to the marital deduction, a large remainder interest in trusts designed to maintain surviving spouses devolved upon children. With the increase in outright transfers to spouses, this motivation for trust establishment has weakened (and thus trust creation waned), leaving tax-minimization motives more dominant among the transferors using trusts. Thus relatively more of a relatively shrunken total of trust property skips an additional generation.

Tables E-3 through E-10 give summary data by gross transfer classes of information tabulated from the 1945, 1951, and 1957 and 1959 studies.

TABLE E-3. *Disposition of Gross Transfers by Size of Gross Transfers, 1945 Returns*

Size of gross transfers (In thousands of dollars)	Number of decedents	Gross transfers (dollar amounts in millions): Total amount	Charitable transfers: Number of decedents	Charitable transfers: Amount	Noncharitable transfers: Total amount	Noncharitable transfers, In trust: Number of decedents	Noncharitable transfers, In trust: Amount	Noncharitable transfers, Other than in trust: Number of decedents	Noncharitable transfers, Other than in trust: Amount	Gross federal estate and gift taxes
500– 600	95	$53	25	[a]	$39	54	$16	94	$23	$13
600– 700	110	71	35	$ 1	53	69	19	109	34	18
700– 800	83	62	25	[a]	46	45	16	82	30	16
800– 900	69	58	22	1	43	41	15	68	28	15
900– 1,000	43	41	19	1	30	32	12	43	18	10
1,000– 1,250	87	98	35	4	71	65	31	85	40	24
1,250– 1,500	51	69	18	2	50	38	24	50	25	18
1,500– 1,750	41	66	13	3	47	33	18	41	29	17
1,750– 2,000	28	53	13	2	38	20	14	28	24	12
2,000– 3,000	63	152	38	14	98	56	54	63	44	39
3,000– 5,000	49	186	32	15	116	41	49	49	66	55
5,000–10,000	23	166	19	18	86	20	38	23	49	61
10,000 and over	11	224	9	37	103	10	60	11	42	84
Total[b]	753	1,299	303	100	818	524	366	746	452	381

Source: U. S. Treasury Department.
[a] Less than $500,000.
[b] Details may not add to totals due to rounding.

TABLE E-4. *Composition of Gross Transfers by Size of Gross Transfers, 1945 Returns*

Size of gross transfers (In thousands of dollars)	Number of dece-dents	Gross transfers (dollar amounts in millions)							
				Gifts between June 7, 1932 and Dec. 31, 1944				Gifts prior to June 7, 1932	
		Total amount	Transfers at death	Number of dece-dents	Total gifts plus gift tax	Total gifts	Gift tax	Number of dece-dents	Total gifts
500– 600	95	$53	$50	30	$2	$2	[a]	1	[a]
600– 700	110	71	66	64	5	5	[a]	5	[a]
700– 800	83	62	57	51	5	5	[a]	1	[a]
800– 900	69	58	52	41	5	5	[a]	8	$1
900– 1,000	43	41	37	32	4	4	[a]	7	[a]
1,000– 1,250	87	98	85	62	11	10	[a]	19	3
1,250– 1,500	51	69	57	38	9	9	[a]	15	3
1,500– 1,750	41	66	53	29	9	8	$1	16	5
1,750– 2,000	28	53	38	24	9	9	1	14	6
2,000– 3,000	63	152	121	52	17	16	1	29	14
3,000– 5,000	49	186	148	38	22	20	2	25	16
5,000–10,000	23	166	132	22	21	19	2	15	12
10,000 and over	11	224	140	9	30	27	3	10	54
Total[b]	753	1,299	1,035	492	150	140	11	165	114

Source: U. S. Treasury Department.
[a] Less than $500,000.
[b] Details may not add to totals due to rounding.

TABLE E-5. *Composition of Gross Transfers by Size of Gross Transfers, 1951 Returns*

Size of gross transfers (In thousands of dollars)	Number of decedents	Gross transfers (dollar amounts in millions)							
				Gifts between June 7, 1932 and Dec. 31, 1950				Gifts prior to June 7, 1932	
		Total amount	Transfers at death	Number of decedents	Total gifts plus gift tax	Total gifts	Gift tax	Number of decedents	Total gifts
300– 400	321	$113	$110	78	$2	$2	[a]	5	[a]
400– 500	284	127	120	127	6	6	[a]	8	[a]
500– 600	231	126	118	117	8	7	[a]	6	$1
600– 700	204	132	125	97	6	6	[a]	11	1
700– 800	141	104	97	76	7	7	[a]	5	1
800– 900	91	77	71	48	6	5	[a]	6	[a]
900– 1,000	79	75	71	41	4	4	[a]	2	[a]
1,000– 1,250	121	134	118	87	13	12	$1	13	4
1,250– 1,500	83	115	107	52	7	7	[a]	8	1
1,500– 1,750	65	106	93	47	11	10	1	9	1
1,750– 2,000	40	74	67	28	7	6	1	3	[a]
2,000– 3,000	68	162	140	59	19	17	2	11	3
3,000– 5,000	31	118	118	25	11	10	1	6	6
5,000–10,000	39	260	212	37	36	32	3	11	12
10,000 and over	14	256	192	14	58	52	6	6	6
Total[b]	1,812	1,979	1,743	933	200	184	16	110	36

Source: U. S. Treasury Department.
[a] Less than $500,000.
[b] Details may not add to totals due to rounding.

TABLE E-6. *Disposition of Gross Transfers by Size of Gross Transfers, 1951 Returns*

Size of gross transfers (In thousands of dollars)	Number of decedents	Gross transfers (dollar amounts in millions)								
		Total amount	Charitable transfers		Noncharitable transfers					Gross federal estate and gift taxes
						In trust		Other than in trust		
			Number of decedents	Amount	Total amount	Number of decedents	Amount	Number of decedents	Amount	
300– 400	321	$113	77	[a]	$88	139	$25	312	$63	$24
400– 500	284	127	78	$1	98	152	34	279	64	28
500– 600	231	126	72	1	98	123	34	226	64	27
600– 700	204	132	60	3	103	131	35	204	68	26
700– 800	141	104	54	3	80	92	30	140	50	21
800– 900	91	77	36	2	59	61	23	89	36	16
900– 1,000	79	75	29	2	58	55	18	79	40	15
1,000– 1,250	121	134	42	4	103	87	40	120	63	28
1,250– 1,500	83	115	41	6	82	65	36	82	46	26
1,500– 1,750	65	106	29	4	77	50	33	64	43	25
1,750– 2,000	40	74	19	4	52	32	26	39	26	18
2,000– 3,000	68	162	45	9	113	47	45	67	68	40
3,000– 5,000	31	118	21	8	75	27	38	31	36	36
5,000–10,000	39	260	35	51	130	29	57	39	73	79
10,000 and over	14	256	14	71	106	14	62	14	44	79
Total[b]	1,812	1,979	625	170	1,321	1,104	536	1,785	785	488

Source: U. S. Treasury Department.

[a] Less than $500,000.

[b] Details may not add to totals due to rounding.

TABLE E-7. *Composition of Gross Transfers by Size of Gross Transfers, 1957 Returns*

Size of gross transfers (In thousands of dollars)	Number of decedents	Gross transfers (dollar amounts in millions)					
		Total amount	Transfers at death	Lifetime transfers			
				Number of decedents	Total gifts plus gift tax	Total gifts	Gift tax
Under 100	19,896	$1,468	$1,454	[a]	[a]	[a]	[b]
100– 200	15,686	2,120	2,050	2,318	$70	$70	[b]
200– 300	4,791	1,112	1,091	[a]	[a]	[a]	[b]
300– 400	1,943	673	649	513	24	24	[b]
400– 500	1,071	475	456	352	19	19	[b]
500– 600	677	369	357	231	11	11	[b]
600– 700	432	280	262	189	17	16	[b]
700– 800	[a]	[a]	[a]	135	13	13	[b]
800– 900	189	159	151	94	7	6	$1
900– 1,000	208	197	187	128	9	9	[b]
1,000– 1,250	284	318	303	147	15	14	1
1,250– 1,500	197	268	253	112	15	15	1
1,500– 1,750	118	191	178	65	13	12	1
1,750– 2,000	78	147	138	52	9	8	1
2,000– 3,000	155	381	356	101	24	22	2
3,000– 5,000	105	400	370	72	30	27	3
5,000–10,000	64	415	373	48	42	38	4
10,000 and over	26	601	509	24	93	83	10
Total[c]	46,333	9,879	9,432	6,348	447	424	23

Source: U. S. Treasury Department.
[a] Sampling variability is in excess of 50 percent.
[b] Less than $500,000.
[c] Details may not add to totals due to rounding.

TABLE E-8. *Disposition of Gross Transfers by Size of Gross Transfers, 1957 Returns*

Size of gross transfers (In thousands of dollars)	Number of decedents	Gross transfers (dollar amounts in millions): Total amount	Charitable transfers: Number of decedents	Charitable transfers: Amount	Noncharitable transfers: Total amount	In trust: Number of decedents	In trust: Amount	Other than in trust: Number of decedents	Other than in trust: Amount	Gross federa estate and gift taxes
Under 100	19,896	$1,468	2,412	$44	$1,410	[a]	[a]	19,395	$1,325	$14
100– 200	15,686	2,120	2,412	78	1,933	3,021	$217	15,486	1,715	109
200– 300	4,791	1,112	[a]	[a]	960	[a]	[a]	4,779	857	114
300– 400	1,943	673	370	26	547	583	88	1,919	460	99
400– 500	1,071	475	297	31	364	463	80	1,071	283	80
500– 600	677	369	154	13	284	257	55	677	229	71
600– 700	432	280	170	13	214	189	51	432	163	53
700– 800	[a]	[a]	94	15	[a]	140	41	[a]	[a]	[a]
800– 900	189	159	[a]	[a]	115	95	28	188	87	36
900– 1,000	208	197	85	11	144	102	38	208	106	42
1,000– 1,250	284	318	111	20	226	162	64	281	162	72
1,250– 1,500	197	268	94	20	186	105	47	195	139	61
1,500– 1,750	118	191	57	19	129	62	31	115	98	44
1,750– 2,000	78	147	42	13	96	49	35	78	61	38
2,000– 3,000	155	381	84	41	238	95	80	155	158	102
3,000– 5,000	105	400	59	35	247	66	78	104	169	118
5,000–10,000	64	415	45	79	209	49	89	63	120	127
10,000 and over	26	601	22	192	191	19	64	26	127	218
Total[b]	46,333	9,879	7,406	697	7,730	8,046	1,274	45,585	6,456	1,452

Source: U. S. Treasury Department.

[a] Sampling variability is in excess of 50 percent.

[b] Details may not add to totals due to rounding.

TABLE E-9. *Composition of Gross Transfers by Size of Gross Transfers, 1959 Returns*

Size of gross transfers (In thousands of dollars)	Number of decedents	Gross transfers (dollar amounts in millions)					
				Lifetime transfers			
		Total amount	Transfers at death	Number of decedents	Total gifts plus gift tax	Total gifts	Gift tax
Under 100	23,398	$1,749	$1,736	[a]	[a]	[a]	[b]
100– 200	18,395	2,540	2,465	2,330	$74	$74	[b]
200– 300	5,874	1,412	1,363	[a]	[a]	[a]	[a]
300– 400	2,444	828	792	849	36	[a]	$1
400– 500	1,265	566	545	420	21	21	[b]
500– 600	629	341	323	260	18	18	1
600– 700	535	345	322	281	23	23	1
700– 800	379	284	272	148	12	11	[b]
800– 900	275	231	212	163	19	18	1
900– 1,000	214	202	193	90	8	8	[b]
1,000– 1,250	318	355	335	179	19	18	2
1,250– 1,500	202	278	256	117	22	20	1
1,500– 1,750	124	201	185	83	16	15	1
1,750– 2,000	103	193	178	73	15	14	1
2,000– 3,000	162	397	365	110	32	30	2
3,000– 5,000	110	419	373	92	46	42	4
5,000–10,000	51	347	309	43	39	35	3
10,000 and over	26	510	423	26	88	78	9
Total[c]	54,504	11,197	10,647	7,732	550	522	27

Source: U. S. Treasury Department.
[a] Sampling variability is in excess of 50 percent.
[b] Less than $500,000.
[c] Details may not add to totals due to rounding.

TABLE E-10. *Disposition of Gross Transfers by Size of Gross Transfers, 1959 Returns*

Size of gross transfers (In thousands of dollars)	Number of decedents	Gross transfers (dollar amounts in millions)									Gross federal estate and gift taxes
		Total amount	Charitable transfers		Noncharitable transfers						
					Total amount	In trust		Other than in trust			
			Number of decedents	Amount		Number of decedents	Amount	Number of decedents	Amount		
Under 100	23,398	$1,749	2,721	$21	$1,712	2,823	$126	23,297	$1,585		16
100– 200	18,395	2,540	2,229	73	2,314	3,338	226	18,092	2,088		152
200– 300	5,874	1,412	[a]	[a]	1,229	1,630	205	5,761	1,024		156
300– 400	2,444	828	659	53	663	754	105	2,419	557		112
400– 500	1,265	566	365	25	446	549	96	1,259	350		95
500– 600	629	341	184	17	260	258	52	623	208		64
600– 700	535	345	172	20	263	253	56	529	207		62
700– 800	379	284	128	5	222	211	57	373	165		56
800– 900	275	231	134	12	177	171	44	275	132		42
900– 1,000	214	202	82	13	151	117	39	213	112		39
1,000– 1,250	318	355	96	18	255	179	66	315	188		82
1,250– 1,500	202	278	76	15	201	123	59	199	142		62
1,500– 1,750	124	201	57	18	137	77	41	123	96		46
1,750– 2,000	103	193	49	13	134	71	42	103	92		46
2,000– 3,000	162	397	97	58	243	103	82	160	161		96
3,000– 5,000	110	419	77	55	251	77	89	109	162		114
5,000–10,000	51	347	35	50	189	34	57	51	132		108
10,000 and over	26	510	25	161	207	24	63	26	144		143
Total[b]	54,504	11,197	8,245	653	9,053	10,792	1,507	53,927	7,546		1,491

Source: U. S. Treasury Department.
[a] Sampling variability is in excess of 50 percent.
[b] Details may not add to totals due to rounding.

APPENDIX F

The Effect on Saving of the United States Estate and Gift Tax

SEYMOUR FIEKOWSKY

IN DISCUSSING THE effect of death taxation on saving-investment rates, it is wise to distinguish clearly the affected taxpayer group. In both the United States and Great Britain, estate taxpayers comprise no more than 5 to 6 percent of the adult population, the highest stratum of wealth-owners. At any one time in the United States about 30 percent of these estate taxpayers are women. Virtually all of these women have wealth which they inherited or received by gift in the first instance; indeed, three-fourths of women estate taxpayers are widows, and the remaining fourth undoubtedly inherited wealth from, or were given it by, relatives. Or they gained it by managing community property with their husbands.

Characteristics of Male Estate Taxpayers

The male 70 percent of the estate taxpayer group is harder to characterize. Studies of the relationship between the wealth of British death taxpayers and the wealth of their predecessors have been made by Wedgwood[1] (1924 decedents) and Harbury[2] (1956-57 decedents). These clearly show that a disproportionately large fraction (75-80 percent) of the top male death taxpayers (the highest 5 percent) had fathers who were, in their generation, in the death taxpayers group. But these studies also show virtually no correlation between the *amount* of

[1] Josiah Wedgwood, *The Economics of Inheritance* (London: Routledge, 1929, and Penguin Books, 1939), pp. 145-67.

[2] C. D. Harbury, "Inheritance and the Distribution of Personal Wealth in Britain," *Economic Journal* (Dec. 1962), pp. 845-68.

these elite death taxpayers' sons' estates and the *amount* of their fathers' estates. Presumably, in the more dynamic United States economy, there is no closer association between probable inherited wealth and size of estate. Sons of wealthy fathers are undoubtedly more likely to achieve wealth, but the size of the sons' estates cannot be readily predicted from the size of their fathers'. Thus a rough characterization of male estate tax wealth is that it is largely "self-made," due allowance being made for the advantages in education and business opportunity accruing to sons of wealthy parents.

In the United States, the wealth held by male estate taxpayers (and potential taxpayers in the living population) alone accounts for nearly one-fourth of all private wealth. And if the wealth of their widows and other female dependents is added to their own, the total share of private wealth they account for exceeds one-third. Thus the estate taxpayers are significant suppliers of asset-holding services in the United States. But, more particularly, unlike the remaining 95 percent of the population, whose estates at death are below $60,000 (gross), these wealth-holders have a persistent affinity for assets. Their estates do not "peak" at some age between 50 and 60 and then decline. Rather, their estates continue to grow even beyond the age of 80! Clearly these economically significant asset-holders do not, as a group, accumulate in order to even out their lifetime income streams. They intentionally accumulate estates which they fully expect to retain until death.

But their behavior, as evidenced by studies of the inter vivos transfers they make, as well as by studies of estate distributions over 40 years, also plainly indicates that, except for the concern they show for the welfare of their widows and minor dependents, these remarkable wealth-holders do not characteristically dispose of their estates in ways that maximize the net transfers to their successors. Despite the great gains to beneficiaries if wealth were transferred by gift rather than by bequest, reportable gifts are neither so numerous nor so extravagantly large as to justify an inference that they were made in order to minimize the transfer tax. Nor does the asset composition of the estate of these taxpayers betray any great concern for the eventual impact of the estate tax. Cash holdings with which to meet tax liabilities have never increased in line with rising tax rates; and aggregate cash and insurance policy proceeds decline as a proportion of total estate as size of estate increases, while tax liabilities progressively rise.

From the point of view of male estate taxpayers, then, the *prospect* of death taxes has had a negligible effect upon accumulation incentives. Since the taxpayers with whom we are here concerned are aged and very wealthy, it is safe to assume that their after-tax estates under recent tax structures appear to them ample to discharge whatever obligations they feel they have to their dependents. On the other hand, men in lower wealth strata, whose estates are intended more exclusively to provide support for surviving dependents, might be induced by death taxes to accumulate larger estates. Heirs of the very wealthy, then, bear the brunt of death taxation in the form of diminished net inheritances.

It is convenient to classify heirs of the very wealthy into two groups: those who, like their predecessors, are so "gifted" and psychologically motivated that they accumulate massive amounts of wealth; and all others, like widows and nonacquisitive offspring of wealthy decedents, who are essentially passive heirs to wealth. If the British experience referred to above is generalized upon, it may be said that the tax-reduced inheritances of the former class of heirs will neither frustrate these heirs in their pursuit of wealth nor significantly affect the size of their asset holdings. If untaxed inheritances are viewed as purchases of assets at zero price, a death tax payable on estates may be considered to be the "price" heirs pay to purchase estates intact. Considering their high propensity to amass wealth, these sons (who are like their fathers) may even be expected to sacrifice consumption (by borrowing against the future income of estate property) in order to maintain the estates intact, particularly when the estates are comprised largely of business assets or controlling interests in corporations.

If the inheritances of this group are reduced by the amount of death tax, however, and the nature of the estate assets is such as not to induce these heirs to try to keep the estates intact, the lifetime resources of these individuals are thereby reduced by the amount of the tax. In this event, there is no *a priori* reason to expect that they will consume either more or less than they might have with undiminished inheritance; they are as likely as not to use their increased resources to sustain their unending pursuit of wealth. But the value of assets in their final balance sheet totals depends far less on the amount they may have inherited (and the size of the tax bite) than on the astuteness with which they manage their asset portfolios during the remainder of their lives. It must always be remembered that neither inherited nor self-produced wealth has attached to it guaranteed price tags. Over the remaining lifetimes of heirs certain asset prices will rise, and others will fall; even in periods of generally increasing or decreasing prices, particular prices may vary differentially.

It is thus no more possible at the death of an ultra-wealthy son of an ultra-wealthy father to isolate in his final net worth account the effect of death tax paid by liquidating some assets from the father's estate than it is to isolate the effect of a mid-career investment loss of equivalent size. It is the peculiar talent of these persons to "create" asset values, more frequently than not by the "destruction" of asset values held by less talented wealth-owners. Thus the analogy between the consumption-saving decision process by which ordinary citizens accumulate property and the enterprise process by which great wealth accumulators amass theirs breaks down. If the lifetime financial statements of very large wealth-holders could be assembled, the impact of a death tax on their inheritances would appear as a subset of random events affecting the aggregate amount of asset-holding that they have been able to perform. If this subset is small relative to the entire set of impinging events, its effect on the aggregate of lifetime asset-holding will be negligible. In terms of measuring saving-consumption allocations by the parties of interest, the result will be nil.

This argument may also be stated in another way. If the accumulators of wealth under consideration here hold wealth not in order to consume it ultimately but rather for the prestige, social status, and generalized "power" wealth confers upon them, consumption-savings decisions will have little ultimate effect on the size of their wealth-holdings at any point of time, or on the aggregate of dollar-years of asset-holdings they have performed during their lifetimes. People who *achieve* great wealth do not normally "save" that wealth out of previously "earned" income; they "save" from the capital gains earned through their successful investment decisions. The *ex post* "savings" of this group are poorly, if at all, correlated with their *ex ante* "savings."

Passive Heirs

Turning to the second, passive group of heirs to estate tax wealth, we find the effect of inheritance diminution by death taxation easier to identify. By definition, these heirs—widows and nonacquisitive successors to wealth—rely heavily on the inheritances they receive from their husbands (fathers) for support of their living standards for the remainder of their lives. Death taxation, as we have already deduced from the postulated characteristics of the original wealth accumulators, reduces their net inheritances. The inheritance reduced by death tax means for these heirs a diminished net worth and a correspondingly diminished income flow therefrom. For them, wealth is potential consumption, for themselves and for others who may survive them. Depending on how they weight their own as against their successors' enjoyment of the pleasures that may be purchased by the income flow from, and liquidation of, the inherited wealth, they run down their inherited net worth more or less rapidly. If their utility function is more inelastic with respect to personal consumption, they will "dissave" more than they would have if their inheritance had not been diminished by the tax. But if their utility function is more inelastic with respect to the consumption of their successors, they will "dissave" less, particularly as they contemplate the likelihood of the death tax bite when they pass on. In both cases personal consumption by heirs is diminished by the tax, but less in the former case than the latter. In both cases, the asset-holding service performed for the remainder of the heirs' life is less than it would have been had there been no death tax. And less service is performed in the former than in the latter case. (This may be called the "Ricardo effect"; a death tax reduces capital stocks by more than an equivalent annual tax.)

But the rate of "dissaving" of these passive heirs is not simply a function of the rate at which they consume out of capital; it is also a function of the ineptness with which their wealth is managed. Heirs to a successful family enterprise might become impoverished by mismanagement almost as quickly without the interposed weight of a death tax as with it. Indeed, it is reasonable to suggest that a side effect of death taxation that operates to offset the negative effect of such taxes on the asset-holding capacity of these passive heirs is to alert testators to the need to assure continued good management of their property if the beneficiaries are to be protected from their own ineptitude. The sale of closely held businesses to larger corporations and decisions to place property in trust for heirs, for example, may be more readily taken by testators who doubt the capacities of their successors, using the impending death tax to mask the implied slur on the successors' acumen.

The foregoing analysis of the impact of death taxation on social saving-investment rates indicates that, like any tax, a death tax reduces savings and that the magnitude of the effect depends on the relative importance of passive heirs in the aggregate of private wealth ownership. The *prospect* of such taxes either has no effect, as on the elite wealth accumulators, or, for the more modestly endowed masses of wealth-holders whose estates are devoted entirely to supporting dependent successors, it may induce additional saving. Heirs to the elite fortunes, therefore, may be said to bear the full weight of death taxation, while heirs of the less affluent testators may bear somewhat less than the full weight. In any event, the lifetime "savings" achieved by heirs who are themselves potential members of the elite estate taxpayers' stratum are not greatly affected by variations in the amount of their net inheritances. Only the savings of passive heirs will certainly be diminished over their lifetimes by net reductions in their inheritances.

The Estate Tax and Passive Heirs

In order to assess the probable magnitude of the aggregate impact of death taxation in an economy such as the United States, let us return our attention to the passive heirs. These have been characterized as individuals whose welfare is a function of their own personal consumption and, possibly, that of particular successors. If the utility functions of these individuals include only their lifetime consumption, their estates would have an expected value of zero at death; if their utility functions include consumption by their successors, their estates would have some positive expected value that equilibrates the marginal utility of their own with their successors' consumption. In the latter case, if inter vivos transfers either are not taxed, or are taxed at preferentially lower rates than are testamentary transfers, the expected value of their estates would be lower. For such individuals, an estate tax is preferable to any inheritance tax of equal yield that discriminates against classes of heirs, either through progressive rate schedules or consanguinity scales for exemptions and/or rates. This is because an estate tax permits them to choose a pattern of estate distribution undistorted by differential rates of tax.

For example, if we postulate that these persons make all their provision for successors through bequests, and we further assume that *all* members of society have these utility functions, the aggregate of all estates at death would be an index of the numbers of persons concerned about their successors and the intensity of their concern. Imposition of death taxes in such a society would obviously induce a substitution of personal consumption for successors' consumption by these testators. Thus there would be a relative decline in aggregate estates proportional to the elasticity of substitution between personal consumption and bequests.

Note that this relative decline in estates is *not* the proportion by which the estate tax reduces aggregate private wealth-holding nor the proportion by which the rate of saving is reduced in the economy. Even those persons who plan to leave no estates perform some saving and asset-holding during their lifetimes in order to shift portions of their uneven income stream; and those who do plan to leave estates similarly redistribute income over their lifetimes. Thus a proportionate decline in estates is a much smaller proportionate decline in the stock of private wealth. If, for example, half the private stock of wealth is used as a reserve fund to provide retirement income and similar redistributions through the lifetime of individuals, and the other half is held as a reserve fund created by individuals for each other's support, a death tax will fall only on the second half; if the tax induces a 50 percent reduction in estates, the total private stock will be reduced by a maximum of 25 percent, or less if the reserve fund expands to accommodate higher lifetime consumption by frustrated testators. Whatever the magnitude of the reduction in estate wealth, in the after-tax equilibrium the effects of the reduction in private wealth are dispersed among all members of society. The current "generation" of testators is the prior "generation" of heirs. In the extreme, if all bequests were prohibited, although there would no longer be transfers between generations, the private stock of capital would not be eradicated.

If individuals were all engaged in maximizing lifetime utility functions cast in terms of consumption quantities, a stationary state would probably be the result. Economic growth in such an economy is accelerated by appeals to the current "generation" to provide more for the future, for only in this way may all enjoy the fruits of a large stock of wealth, part of which at least is passed by bequest. A death tax counters this appeal and thereby retards growth in the stock of wealth to the detriment of all. (This may be called the "Taussig effect": inhibiting the accumulation of private fortunes by limiting the right of bequest produces evil social consequences.)

The Estate Tax and U. S. Economic Growth

Is the fifty-year record of the estate tax in the United States, thirty of which have included reasonably severe rate schedules, consistent with the view that economic growth has been inhibited by the tax? The answer must be an unqualified no for the following reasons:

1. Those individuals who have been subject to the estate tax apparently did not have utility functions in which real consumption quantities were significant variables. For example, any index of goods and services prices suitable for this select group would surely show that in the thirties the value of money rose somewhat and has steadily

declined since then. Moreover, beginning in the thirties, personal income taxes applicable to this group rose sharply, diminishing the real consumption value of income flows from wealth and hence the real consumption value of the wealth itself. The steep rise in income taxation was more than matched by a corresponding increase in the severity of estate tax rates and gift tax. Yet despite all these discouragements to wealth-holders of the stationary state type, the total stock of private wealth has grown, and the share of this increasing stock held by, say, the upper 5 percent of the wealth-holders is slowly returning to its predepression levels. This is happening despite the continuation of an unprecedentedly high rate of growth in ownership of such assets as insurance and annuity reserves and consumer durables—assets that have not usually attracted estate taxpayer classes.

2. There is no indication that estate accumulators have become discouraged by the high rates of the death tax. If current "generation" accumulators had been discouraged by the tax legislation of the thirties and early forties, the following should have resulted:

a. The distribution of estate taxpayer estates would have become more equal, that is, a greater concentration of estates near the exemption level would have occurred as the larger estates failed to grow, and the smaller estates (truly held for consumption purposes) increased slightly. This has not happened.

b. The proportion of widows among estate taxpayers would have risen as active accumulators (husbands, widowers, and single men) moved to thwart the Internal Revenue Service, since widows would report estates inherited from the prior generation of unthwarted accumulators. This has not happened.

c. A marked effort to minimize transfer tax liabilities by making gifts and creating generation-skipping trusts would have been manifest. It was not.

On the whole, then, although it may not be an overstatement to say that consumption of market goods and services looms large in the welfare functions of 90 percent of the citizens of the United States, the 10 percent in whose welfare functions asset ownership is the major variable (deflated only by some index of status and power value of wealth dollars) have been deterred neither by the income tax nor by the estate tax—not by the income tax, because capital gains are not taxed until death, and then not separately; not by the estate tax, because these individuals know that they could not take their wealth with them even if estates were not taxed.

The conclusion to which the above chain of reasoning inexorably leads is that the aggregate reduction in saving resulting from imposition of an estate tax in an economy whose growth is sparked by Schumpeterian innovators is likely to be small, far smaller than the reduction that would occur if an annual tax with an equal yield were assessed.

APPENDIX G

Information on Certain Estates

CARL S. SHOUP

ALTHOUGH ALL ESTATE TAX returns must of course remain unidentified (except to appropriate officials of the Treasury Department), it is possible to compile data, from *Statistics of Income,*[1] on a few unidentified estates that are not aggregated with data for other estates. These individual cases are useful in illustrating certain extreme tendencies among estate taxpayers. Case No. 1 in Table G-1 illustrates, for a very large estate, and Cases Nos. 2, 5, and 6, for estates of from $3 million to $6 million, how the taxpayer can calculate within a narrow margin the amount of charitable bequest, together with (in Cases 1, 2, and 6) the marital deduction, that will insure nontaxability of the entire estate. Case 4 illustrates the other extreme: a taxpayer with $32 million gross estate who made a $50 thousand charitable bequest and paid a net estate tax of $16 million. Case 3 simply illustrates how great a lapse of time can occur between death and filing. (The $40,000 exemption did not apply after 1942.)

[1] U. S. Treasury Department, Internal Revenue Service.

TABLE G-1. *Information on Certain Estates, Returns Filed in 1959 or 1961*

(Dollar items in thousands)

Item	Taxpayer No.					
	1[a]	2[a]	3[b]	4[b]	5[c]	6[c]
Gross estate, total	22,510	3,360	52	31,676	4,949	5,916
Real estate		5	50	59	107	95
Federal bonds				2,002		88
State and municipal bonds		15		26,784	405	996
Other bonds				454		
Corporate stock	22,259	3,210			3,865	4,215
Cash	55	80		2,245	508	175
Mortgages and notes	37	1	1			182
Life insurance	85	27				143
Annuities						4
Other property	74	22	1	132	64	18
Deductions, total	22,453	3,301		3,918	4,910	5,906
Funeral and administrative expenses	1,347	112	1	2,966	332	116
Debts and mortgages	1,022	139		902	19	20
Net losses during administration						
Marital deduction	10,070	1,555				2,890
Charitable bequests, total	10,014	1,495		50	4,559	2,880
Educational, scientific, or literary institutions, total	10,014	1,495			4,522	2,880
Publicly owned		1,495				1,440
Privately owned	10,014				4,522	1,440
Religious						
Other charitable				50	37	
Other deductions						
Disallowed deductions						
Allowable deductions	22,453	3,301	1	3,918	4,910	5,906
Net estate before exemption	57	59	51	27,758	39	10
Exemption	60	60	40	60	60	60
Taxable estate			11	27,698		
Gross estate tax before credits			[i]	19,716		
Tax credits, total				4,038		
State death taxes				3,908		
Federal gift taxes						
Prior transfers						
Foreign death taxes				130		
Net estate tax	0	0	[i]	15,678	0	0
Information items						
Jointly owned property	34					
Powers of appointment					25	
Life insurance not includible in estate						
Transfers during decedent's life						
Sex, age, marital status			Husband, 60 to 70[d]	Woman, 80 or over[e]	Man, 50 under 60[f]	Man, 60 under 70[g]
Date-of-death value, or alternate value?			DDV[h]	DDV[h]		

[a] U. S. Internal Revenue Service, *Statistics of Income, 1960*, Fiduciary, Gift, and Estate Tax Returns Filed during Calendar Year 1961, pp. 47–50.
[b] *Statistics of Income, 1958*, Fiduciary, Gift, and Estate Tax Returns Filed during Calendar Year 1959, p. 58.
[c] *Ibid.*, p. 60. [d] *Ibid.*, p. 62.
[e] Classed in "other decedents" (that is, other than married, divorced, unmarried), *Ibid.*, p. 68.
[f] *Ibid.*, p. 69. [g] *Ibid.*, p. 70. [h] *Ibid.*, p. 71. [i] Less than $500.

APPENDIX H

Selected Readings in Death Duties and Gift Taxes[1]

Advisory Commission on Intergovernmental Relations. *Coordination of State and Federal Inheritance, Estate, and Gift Taxes.* Washington: The Commission, 1961.

Barna, Tibor. "The Burden of Death Duties in Terms of an Annual Tax," *Review of Economic Studies,* November 1941.

Bittker, Boris I. "Recommendations for Revision of Federal Estate and Gift Taxes," in U. S. Congress, Joint Committee on the Economic Report, *Federal Tax Policy for Economic Growth and Stability.* Papers Submitted by Panelists. Washington: Government Printing Office, 1955.

Büchner, Richard. "Erbschaft- und Schenkungsteuern," *Handbuch der Finanzwissenschaft,* Zweiter Band, pp. 539-56. Wilhelm Gerloff and Fritz Neumark, editors. Tübingen: J. C. B. Mohr, 1956.

Cartter, A. M. "A New Method of Relating British Capital Ownership and Estate Duty Liability to Income Groups," *Economica,* August 1953.

Casner, A. James. *Estate Planning.* Boston: Little, Brown, 1961.

________. "Property Disposition under the Federal Estate and Gift Taxes," in U. S. Congress, Joint Committee on the Economic Report, *Federal Tax Policy for Economic Growth and Stability.* Papers Submitted by Panelists. Washington: Government Printing Office, 1955.

Chirelstein, Marvin A., Langdon Day, and Elisabeth A. Owens. *Taxation in the United States,* World Tax Series, Harvard Law School, International Program in Taxation. Chicago: Commerce Clearing House, 1963, pp. 182-269.

Craven, George. *The Gift Tax* (revised to November 1960). New York: Practising Law Institute, 1960.

Crum, William Leonard. *The Distribution of Wealth: A Factual Survey Based upon Federal Estate-Tax Returns.* Harvard University, Graduate School of Business Administration, Business Research Studies, No. 13. Cambridge, October 1935.

[1] With a few exceptions, this list is restricted to publications of approximately the past ten years.

Ecker-Racz, L. L. "Federal-State Death Tax Relations in the United States," *Canadian Tax Journal,* May-June 1961.

Eisenstein, Louis. "The Rise and Decline of the Estate Tax," in U. S. Congress, Joint Committee on the Economic Report, *Federal Tax Policy for Economic Growth and Stability.* Papers Submitted by Panelists. Washington: Government Printing Office, 1955.

Fiekowsky, Seymour. "On the Economic Effects of Death Taxation in the United States." Unpublished doctoral thesis, Harvard University, 1956.

________. "On the Significance of Successors' Welfare as a Motivation for the Accumulation of Wealth," *Proceedings, Western Economic Association,* 1956, pp. 42-48.

Fijalkowski-Bereday, G. Z. "The Equalizing Effects of the Death Duties," *Oxford Economic Papers,* N.S. II, 1950, 176-97.

Fortuna, Vasco N. P. "The Sociometric Theory and the Estate Duty," *Public Finance,* No. 3, 1951.

Groves, Harold M. "Selecting a Suitable Form of Death Levy," *Revue de Science et de Législation Financières,* April-June 1952, pp. 267-96.

________, and Wallace I. Edwards. "A New Model for an Integrated Transfer Tax," *National Tax Journal,* December 1953.

Hall, J. K. "Incidence of Death Duties," *American Economic Review,* March 1940.

Harbury, C. D. "Inheritance and the Distribution of Personal Wealth in Britain," *Economic Journal,* December 1962.

Harriss, C. Lowell. "Economic Effects of Estate and Gift Taxation," in U. S. Congress, Joint Committee on the Economic Report, *Federal Tax Policy for Economic Growth and Stability.* Papers Submitted by Panelists. Washington: Government Printing Office, 1955.

________. "Estate Taxes and the Family-Owned Business," *California Law Review,* March 1950.

________. "Federal Estate Taxes and Philanthropic Bequests," *Journal of Political Economy,* August 1949.

________. "Federal Estate Tax Administration," *Taxes—The Tax Magazine,* April 1950.

________. *Gift Taxation in the United States.* Washington: American Council on Public Affairs, 1940.

________. "Liquidity of Estates and Death Tax Liability," *Political Science Quarterly,* December 1949.

________. "Proposals to Exempt Life Insurance Used to Pay Estate Tax," *Tax Law Review,* January 1950.

________. "Quelques conséquences économiques de l'impôt fédéral sur les successions aux Etats-Unis," *Revue de Science et de Législation Financières,* XLII, no. 2.

________. "Sources of Injustice in Death Taxation," *National Tax Journal,* December 1954.

_______. "Stock Prices, Death Tax Revenues, and Tax Equity," *Journal of Finance,* September 1950.

_______. "Wealth Estimates as Affected by Audit of Estate Tax Returns," *National Tax Journal,* December 1949.

Hoover, G. E. "The Economic Effects of Inheritance Taxes," *American Economic Review,* March 1927.

Horne, R. Cozens-Hardy. "Modern Methods of Minimising Taxation: IV—Discretionary Settlements," *British Tax Review,* September 1957.

Institut International de Finances Publiques. *Impôts sur la fortune y inclus droits de succession. Debt Management.* Congrès de Zurich, Septembre 1960, XVIe session.

Iowa Law Review. Symposium on State Inheritance and Estate Taxation. March 1941.

Johnson, Alvin H. "Public Capitalization of the Inheritance Tax," *Journal of Political Economy,* XXII (1914), 160-80.

Kaldor, Nicholas. "The Income Burden of Capital Taxes," *Review of Economic Studies,* Vol. IX, no. 2 (Summer 1942). Reprinted in R. A. Musgrave and C. S. Shoup, eds., *Readings in the Economics of Taxation.* Homewood, Ill.: Irwin, 1959.

Kisker, Dr. Klaus Peter. "Die Erbschaftsteuer als Mittel der Vermögensredistribution." *Volkswirtschaftliche Schriften,* Heft 79, Herausgegeben von Dr. J. Broermann, Berlin. Berlin: Duncker and Humblot, 1964.

Lampman, Robert J. *The Share of Top Wealth-Holders in National Wealth, 1922-56.* Princeton: Princeton University Press, 1962.

Lewis, James B. *The Estate Tax* (revised to August 1960). New York: Practising Law Institute, 1962.

Loundes, Charles L. B., and Robert Kramer. *Federal Estate and Gift Taxes.* 2nd ed. St. Paul: West Publishing, 1962.

Meade, James E. *Efficiency, Equality and the Ownership of Property,* London: George Allen and Unwin, 1964.

Midland Bank Review. "Sixty Years of Death Duties," August 1954, London.

Murray, Alan P. *The Federal Tax System: Facts and Problems, 1964,* Materials Assembled by the Committee Staff for the U. S. Congress, Joint Economic Committee. Chap. 10: "Federal Estate and Gift Taxation." Washington: Government Printing Office, 1964.

Pechman, Joseph A. "Analysis of Matched Estate and Gift Tax Returns," *National Tax Journal,* June 1950.

Pigou, A. C. *A Study in Public Finance.* Chap. XIII, "Death Duties and Taxes on Investment Income." 3rd ed. London: Macmillan, 1949.

Prest, A. R. *Public Finance.* London: Weidenfeld and Nicolson, 1960, pp. 86-88, 284-87.

Revell, J. R. S. "Settled Property and Death Duties," *British Tax Review,* May-June 1961.

Rhodes, E. C. "The Distribution of Incomes and the Burden of Estate Duties in the United Kingdom," *Economica,* August 1951.

Rignano, E. *The Social Significance of the Inheritance Tax.* New York: Knopf, 1924.

Rudick, Harry J. "What Alternative to the Estate and Gift Taxes?," *California Law Review,* March 1950.

Scott, H. C. "Some Administrative Aspects of the Rignano Scheme of Inheritance Taxation" [with discussion], *Journal of the Royal Statistical Society,* March 1926.

Shoup, Carl S., and associates. *Report on Japanese Taxation by the Shoup Mission.* Vol. II, Chap. 8, "Taxes on Gifts and Bequests." Tokyo: General Headquarters, Supreme Commander for the Allied Powers, September 1949.

———, Roy Blough, and Mabel Newcomer. *Facing the Tax Problem.* New York: Twentieth Century Fund, 1937, pp. 311-17, 415-16, 500-502.

———, Robert P. Fox, and Bernard L. Shimberg. "Alternative Methods of Comparing Death Tax Due under American and British Laws," *Bulletin of the National Tax Association,* October 1938 and November 1938.

Shultz, William J. *The Taxation of Inheritance.* Boston: Houghton Mifflin, 1926.

Somers, Harold M. "Estate Taxes and Business Mergers," *Journal of Finance,* May 1958.

Stern, Philip M. *The Great Treasury Raid.* New York: Random House, 1962.

Surrey, Stanley S. "An Introduction to Revision of the Federal Estate and Gift Taxes," *California Law Review,* March 1950.

Trachtman, Joseph. *Estate Planning* (revised to May 1961). New York: Practising Law Institute, 1961.

Treanor, Glen R., and Roy G. Blakey. *Inheritance Taxes.* Minneapolis: League of Minnesota Municipalities, Publication 47, 1935.

U. S. Treasury Department, Advisory Committee, and Office of Tax Legislative Counsel (with the cooperation of the Division of Tax Research and Bureau of Internal Revenue), *Federal Estate and Gift Taxes: A Proposal for Integration and for Correlation with the Income Tax.* Washington: Government Printing Office, 1947.

———. *A Guide to Federal Estate and Gift Taxation* (as of January 1, 1963). Washington: Government Printing Office, 1963.

———. *Statistics of Income, 1960.* Fiduciary, Gift, and Estate Tax Returns Filed During Calendar Year 1961. Washington: Government Printing Office, 1963. (See also similar issues for earlier years.)

Vickrey, William S. *Agenda for Progressive Taxation.* New York: Ronald Press, 1947, Chaps. 7-10, Appendix IV.

———. "The Rationalization of Succession Taxation," *Econometrica,* Vol. XII, 1944, pp. 215-37.

Warren, William C., and Stanley S. Surrey. *Federal Estate and Gift Taxation: Cases and Materials.* New York: The Foundation Press, 1961. *1965 Supplement* by William C. Warren.

Wheatcroft, G. S. A. "The Anti-Avoidance Provisions of the Law of Estate Duty in the United Kingdom," *National Tax Journal,* March 1957.

________, and associates. "Comparison of Death Duties and Gift Taxes in Australia, Canada, United Kingdom, and United States." Mimeo. [Distributed at the Brookings conference.]

Wicksell, Knut. "Om arvsskatten" (on the inheritance tax), *Ekonomiks Tidskrift,* 1901, pp. 75-119.

Williams, Alan. *Public Finance and Budgetary Policy.* New York: Praeger, 1963, Chap. 5: "Taxes on Personal Wealth."

deWind, Adrian W. "The Approaching Crisis in Federal Estate and Gift Taxation," *California Law Review,* March 1950.

Index